Maureen Duffy was born in 1933 a[...]
King's College, London. Author o[...]
novels and non-fiction, she is a co[...]
Writers' Action Group.

Maureen Duffy lives in London.

Also by Maureen Duffy

THAT'S HOW IT WAS
THE SINGLE EYE
THE MICROCOSM
THE PARADOX PLAYERS
LYRICS FOR THE DOG HOUR (poetry)
WOUNDS
RITES
LOVE CHILD
THE VENUS TOUCH
I WANT TO GO TO MOSCOW
A NIGHTINGALE IN BLOOMSBURY SQUARE
CAPITAL
EVESONG (poetry)
THE PASSIONATE SHEPHERDESS
HOUSESPY
MEMORIALS OF THE QUICK AND THE DEAD (poetry)
INHERIT THE EARTH
GORSAGA
LONDONERS: AN ELEGY
MEN AND BEASTS
CHANGE

THE EROTIC
WORLD OF FAERY

Maureen Duffy

CARDINAL

A CARDINAL BOOK

First published in the United States of America by Avon Books,
a division of The Hearst Corporation 1980

First published in Great Britain by Hodder and Stoughton Ltd 1972

Published by Sphere Books in Cardinal 1989

Copyright © Maureen Duffy 1972

Reproduced, printed and bound in Great Britain by
The Guernsey Press Co. Ltd, Guernsey, Channel Islands.

ISBN 0 7474 0545 X

Sphere Books Ltd
A Division of
Macdonald and Co. (Publishers) Ltd,
27 Wrights Lane, London W8 5TZ
A member of Maxwell Pergamon Publishing Corporation plc

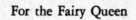

For the Fairy Queen

Preface

A book this length which treats of a subject this size must necessarily be superficial. Each chapter could have been a book in itself and even then there would have been much left out. I have not tried to proceed in strict chronological order but by themes which presented themselves only roughly by centuries. This means that Perrault will be found with Grimm and company among the "fairy stories," not at the beginning of the eighteenth century.

What I have done is to provide an introduction, suggestions for further work and, I hope, to open up a subject to public speculation which whether in the hands of folklorists or literary critics has remained closed for too long.

This is an unashamedly popularizing effort and therefore it is full of assertions and simplifications. No doubt I have made mistakes of detail but I do not think they affect the truth of the main argument. I would rather make those mistakes than say nothing. I am aware too that there will be great resistance to many of my suggestions, for I am concerned with unconscious processes which themselves provoke repression and resistance in all of us.

No writer in this field can be unaware of a tremendous debt to the work of K. M. Briggs and I should like to acknowledge my own while firmly pointing out that Dr. Briggs is in no way responsible for the use to which I have put her researches in English folklore, or for the conclusions, which are entirely mine. I did not, alas, have the benefit of her excellent *Dictionary of British Folklore* which was published after the major part of the book had been written.

My gratitude to the special folklore collection at Kensington and Chelsea Central Library is enormous, as is my debt to Robert Cook, who transcribed a very difficult manuscript. I should also like to thank Jane Osborn for many helpful editorial suggestions.

London 1971

Contents

The Erotic World of Faery

CHAPTER I

St. Augustine and the Satyr

O Faunus, lover of fleeing nymphs, go gently over my lands and smiling fields.

Horace

Satyrs are they who are called Pans in Greek and Incubi in Latin. And they are called Incubi from their practice of overlaying that is debauching. For they often lust lecherously after women, and copulate with them.

Blessed Isidore

The Background to Fayrie

The fairies are as immortal as the human beings who created them. They have been known to all times and all races as far as we have records. In the second half of the twentieth century they have held up the building of roads in Ireland that threatened their dwelling places; their dwarf figures look back at us in statuette from Egyptian tombs and now with the first rockets we have sent them ahead of us, much as they journeyed to settle the New World with the Pilgrim Fathers, exploding like a sun-burst peapod through space, colonizing and proliferating in all their recognizable manifestations: little green men; tall wan but very beautiful humanoids; hags and vamps; bodiless powers; all monstrous children of the serpent; red and blue devils; lost civilizations; the dead and all the legions of the supernatural.

However, unless one has a lifetime to spare, and the terrifying nineteenth-century industry and energy of a James George Fraser whose *The Golden Bough* is a kind of *Great Eastern* or Menai bridge to anthropology, some small area has to be chalked out of a seemingly limitless field of speculation. The fairies for this book then will be those of the last fifteen hundred years in the British Isles.

This raises immediately the justifiable question that could well have been the rejoinder to Barrie's, "Do you believe in fairies?" What is a fairy? My first answer is: anything of an extra-human nature not within the Christian fold, with the exception of the diabolics who were taken over by the Church much as human children were thought to be spirited away to fairyland; or as a thirteenth-century Latin poem has it:

> ... Ghosts and Fauns,
> Nymphs and Sirens, Hamadryads,
> Satyrs and ye Household Gods[1]

under which dignified classical pseudonyms we recognize brownies, fairies, elves, pucks and all the rout of British enchantment.

The Church and the Fairies

Until the edict of Constantine in A.D. 331 ordering the destruction of all heathen temples, religious toleration had been the norm rather than the exception in human practice. Neither the Egyptians, Persians, Romans nor Greeks tried to force the worship of their pantheons on subject peoples nor uniformly on their own people. Eagerly they saw correspondences between their own and other mythologies and adopted other rites to fill a spiritual gap. Late Rome enjoyed the presence of Isis of Egypt and Mithras of Persia as well as Jesus of Judea. The goddess of love was equally recognizable as Venus, Aphrodite or Astarte. Diodorus Siculus describing a huge stone circle in the middle of Britain which may well have been Stonehenge calls it the Britons' Temple of Apollo.[2] Myths flowed freely from end to end of the known world, carried by merchants,

---

[1] *Carmina Burana*, XXX

> ... Larve, Fauni, Manes,
> Nymphe, Sirene, Hamadriades,
> Satyri, Incubi, Penates

The translation is by Helen Waddell in her *The Wandering Scholars*. (Details of works cited are given in "Books Cited and Consulted," p. 367.)

[2] Diodorus Siculus, Book II, Chap. III. A historian contemporary with Julius Caesar. Compare too Plutarch *De Defectu Oraculorum* XVIII in his account of Britain, mid first century A.D. "Moreover, there is there, they said, an island in which Cronus is imprisoned, with Briareus keeping guard over him as he sleeps; for as they put it, sleep is the bond forged for Cronus. They add that around him are many deities, his henchmen and attendants." This is a possible early reference to an end of Arthur type story of the Isle of Avalon. See Sir John Rhys's introductions to Malory's *Le Morte D'Arthur*.

immigrants, slaves, soldiers and whole nations on the move. They circulated in more sophisticated artistic forms, literary and visual, among the educated, and as songs, recitations and icons among the illiterate. Any study of Romano-British inscriptions alone would convince of the variety of myths currently available in even a small island on the fringe of the empire. Though the various religions no doubt competed among themselves for the overt allegiance of their disciples they were not exclusive. A grave stele might bear the names of both classical and eastern or Celtic divinities.

Historicity, which is to religion what naturalism is to art, demanded another response. The Christian god with the jealousy of his Jewish origin pushed to the extreme (no longer "Thou shalt have no other gods *before* me" but "There is no other god") logically required the suppression of all other mythologies like a cuckoo in the mythopoeic nest. The Christ was an almost contemporary with a documented biography unlike the hero founders of other religions. Ravenously Christianity craved mankind's undivided emotional attention.[3]

It may be objected against the general religious tolerance of the Roman empire that the early Christians were martyred for their beliefs. Their own technical inability to recognize the validity of other religious experience put them in this position. In permitting all kinds of worship while insisting on allegiance to the divine emperor, the father of all and therefore authority incarnate, the Roman empire tacitly recognized that all gods and theogonies were manifestations of the human psyche as well as anticipating modern ideas on the paternalism of society. The refusal to render unto Caesar constituted a family rebellion which would undoubtedly bring the sword and divide son against father, brother against brother. Identified finally with the emperor, Christianity became as autocratic as the traditional Victorian father.

Yet in place of infinite variety of symbol and story it offered a very narrow range of possible emotional and artistic experience. There were the facts set for ever by an

[3] For the exclusiveness of Christianity see M. I. Finley, *Aspects of Antiquity*, pp. 178, 208–10.

approved text, incapable of variation or development except in the lives of the saints whose adventures for the most part followed an all too familiar pattern. Where Apuleius could invent the charming and necessary tale of Cupid and Psyche as late as the middle of the second century A.D.,[4] "O latest born and loveliest vision far," the Christian raconteur was driven to St. Lawrence's griddle or St. Catherine's wheel. Any attempt to fantasize on the life of Christ might well lead to the stake.

The Christian Church is usually given the credit for being the only institution to survive when barbaric hordes overwhelmed the Roman empire producing what is known as the Dark Ages, but this is a conclusion based on the Church's own naturally rather biased post hoc propter hoc appraisal backed up by the doctrine of the survival of the fittest. Had classical Greek civilization survived the onslaught of Persians, Romans and internecine conflict we might be more inclined to think that social institutions follow biological principles. We don't know what we may have lost through the triumph of the Christian Church any more than we know what English literature may regret in the death of John Keats at twenty-five. It may be that the artistic paucity of the centuries from A.D. 300 to 1000 is as much the result of extreme theoconcentricity as of constant warfare.

It's difficult for us now to realize quite how all-pervading the Church was. As patron, educator, bureaucrat, landlord, statesman, the cleric was as omnipresent as the god he represented. Complete monopoly of all that we would call white-collar jobs, and so of the whole skill and practice of writing, ensured a control of men's minds hardly conceivable today.

Such power brings its own terrors. Men were ever ready to slip into paganism or heresy. Anything could distract them. A lost battle might suggest that God was not all-powerful and they might try the enemy's gods or revive

---

[4] Apuleius's *The Golden Ass* contains the first account we have of this story (thought to have provided among other things Shakespeare with Bottom). It could be argued that he is retelling a current myth but he is generally reckoned to have invented it. Smith, *A Classical Dictionary*: "the fruit of Apuleius's own imagination or researches." See also Rose, *A Handbook of Greek Mythology*, p. 287.

memories of their own earlier divinities. As late as the eleventh century Bishop Wulfstan, thundering at the English for their lack of spirit against the Danes, accused them of moral backsliding and heathen worship in the familiar tones of reactionary homily.[5]

The pagan literature that survived was itself felt to be dangerous.[6] Here the Church was in great difficulty, for a language can only be taught and learnt by reading it and the literature of Latin, the international medium, was, apart from the theological writings of the Fathers, pre-Christian and almost intolerably seductive. "The songs of the poets are the food of demons," says Jerome, "the pagan learning, the pomps of rhetoric; their suavity is a delight to all men . . . The very priests of God are reading comedies, singing the love songs of the Bucolics, turning over Virgil: and that which was a necessity in boyhood, they make the guilty pleasure of their maturity."[7]

It was not just that men might be tempted to worship Jupiter and Bacchus instead of the Trinity. The stories themselves were distracting from thoughts of God and the very literary beauties of style and image seduced the mind from contemplating his beauty. God was seen as not only jealous but vain. Man was to be wholly withdrawn from the real world and set on God. "The whole sensible appearance of things is the lotus flower," says Paulinus of Nola. Not only pagan idols, poetry and fiction but finally the real world was to be rejected.

One qualification must be made here, however. The attitude outlined above was very peculiarly that of the Western Roman Church. Neither the Celtic nor the Greek branch was as antagonistic towards existing pagan writings and both indeed preserved and fostered their native literatures. In the case of the Celtic Church this was extremely important for the preservation and development of the fairies and the psychic and artistic health of the Middle

---

[5] His sermon (1014) includes a list of the chief evils the people were said to have fallen into which range from simple wickedness unspecified through murder, adultery, fratricide, incest, selling one's children into slavery, violating priests and fornication (various).

[6] See the opening chapter of *The Wandering Scholars* by Helen Waddell for a fuller illustration of this point.

[7] Ibid.

Ages. The Greek contribution is better known and doesn't concern our enquiry. It's interesting to speculate what would have happened had it been the Celtic and not the Roman brand of Christianity that came to dominate the Western world.

The Church and Sex

The Anglo-Saxons and the Celts were polygamous. So Caesar says of the Britons;[8] the English were clearly so since the synod of 786 decreed monogamy and there's no need to decree something which is already the accepted norm.[9] A reading of Irish and Welsh early literature soon reinforces Caesar's conclusion. Even farther it reflects the same sexual freedom that we are used to in the mythologies of Greece and Rome and not only freedom but positive enjoyment.

Against this must be set the attitude introduced by the Christian Church. "Lawful intercourse should be for the procreation of offspring, and not for mere pleasure,"[10] wrote Pope Gregory to St. Augustine in 601 when Augustine had asked for direction on certain problems arising from his new mission to the English. "It is not fitting that a man who has approached his wife should enter church before he has washed nor is he to enter at once though washed . . . for when a man's mind is attracted to those pleasures by lawless desire, he should not regard himself as fitted to join in Christian worship until these heated desires cool in the mind, and he has ceased to labor under wrongful passions." He then goes on to answer Augustine's next question about the sexual dreams and nocturnal emisions of priests and laymen: ". . . although the body cannot experience pleasure without the mind, yet the mind, in contending against the desires of the body, is to some extent unwillingly chained to them, having to oppose them

---

[8] *De Bello Gallico.*

[9] "We command, then, in order to avoid fornication, that every layman shall have one legitimate wife and every woman one legitimate husband in order that they may have and beget legitimate heirs according to God's law."

[10] Bede, *A History of the English Church and People*, Chap. 27.

for conscience sake, and strongly regretting its bondage to bodily desires."

All sexual desire is wrong; "the mere act of union becomes something that the pair have cause to regret."[11] The ideal is the life of the ascetic with all thoughts set on God. It is useless for the latter day Roman Church to suggest through some of its apologists[12] that marriage has always been looked on favourably by the Church; the facts are accessible and quite other.[13]

Such sublimation was very hard to impose. To see the conflict at its sharpest in one man any page from the Confessions[14] of the earlier St. Augustine will do. So hard was it that celibacy wasn't totally imposed on even the secular clergy until 1079.

In contrast was the Church's attitude to war. Bede says that the pagan priests were forbidden to carry arms or to ride a stallion. To us this would seem more in keeping with what were supposedly Christ's teachings but then one thinks of Bishop Odo of Bayeux going into battle with a mace because of the rule against priests shedding blood. Warfare for the right cause was glorious and approved by God, unlike sex; a situation still reflected in American attitudes to the depiction of violence and sex in art and the mass media. This bias is also noticeable in the preserved literature of the Dark Ages[15] unlike that of the Classical period before it. It is usually explained by saying that these were barbarians who were at the Iron Age stage of warrior culture and fighting was their chief interest.[16] That may be so but it was an interest encouraged by the Church, whereas the production of works of art on the other ab-

[11] Ibid.

[12] For example Denis de Rougement in Passion and Society where Romantic love is set up as the great new evil and deception in contrast to the Church's sanctioned marriage. But more on this later.

[13] See G. Rattray Taylor, Sex in History.

[14] A very great bildungstroman anticipating Portrait of the Artist as a Young Man by about fifteen hundred years. Joyce must have had it deeply in mind.

[15] I have used the Shorter Oxford English Dictionary definition 2, "the earlier period to 1100."

[16] Homer and company are said to have written of a Bronze Age warrior culture yet there is no lack of erotic interest in the Iliad and Odyssey. It was after all the ostensible cause of the Trojan War.

sorbing human theme was unthinkable. Since the Church had the monopoly of the copying and preservation of texts any seemingly erotic works that might have been produced would have undoubtedly been censored if only by neglect.[17] And the same Iron Age warrior culture pertained in Ireland where although there is a lot of fighting there is also a lot of sex (Finn and Diarmatt) and preservation of pagan myth.

Here the difference between Celtic and Anglo-Saxon literatures is particularly remarkable; compare for example *Cuchulain* and *Beowulf*. Yet there is continual mention in Anglo-Saxon texts of songs, minstrels and well-known stories. St. Dunstan is said to have enjoyed ballads; Caedmon crept away from the feast because when his turn came to sing he couldn't. It seems incredible that these warriors and their women sat about drinking and listening to the kind of recitations that wouldn't have seemed out of place in a Band of Hope meeting while the wicked Celts with the same social system were singing stories of love as well as fighting that were to form the basis of Romantic literature for hundreds of years. The stories of the *Mabinogion*, which were written down by Welsh monks, show great sexual freedom, particularly among women, who often make the initial advances.

The censoring influence of the Roman Church is to be seen in the different attitude to women in Anglo-Saxon and Celtic writing. Bede's history is full of abbesses, virgins, widows and retired matrons ruling large, often mixed, convents with great efficiency and imposing authority. Put together they make a formidable band of holy amazons.[18] Most of them were aristocratic ladies. Those who stayed in the world make equally efficient queens, like Alfred's daughter Æthelfled who won back five cities from the Danes. Anglo-Saxon women also had an equivalent of the married women's property act,[19] weren't forced to marry

[17] There are at least three fragments of poetry that hint that the Anglo-Saxons were not as immune to love as might be thought: the so-called *Husband's Message*, *Wife's Lament* and *Wulf and Eadwacer*, which suggests a married woman and her lover.

[18] In section E of the index alone there are: Eappa, Ebba, Edith, Ethelberga, Etheldreda, Ethelhilda and Earcongota.

[19] Dorothy Whitelock, *The Beginnings of English Society*, Chap. VII.

against their will and were "bought" from their fathers with a brideprice, instead of buying their husbands with a dowry. All this implies considerable freedom and status, as was the case among Celtic women, yet Anglo-Saxon literature with the exception of *Judith*, a poem on the Old Testament slayer of Holofernes,[20] has almost nothing to say of them.

Eve was the betrayer and tempter of Adam. She had taken the apple first. By St. Paul's command she was to be subject to her husband. Symbolically she represented the flesh while Adam represented the spirit. The flesh was temptation incarnate and as such to be avoided, desexed or abhorred as far as possible. "A certain nun, fair after the putridity of the flesh,"[21] Gregory the Great says, summing up all the attitudes. "The sirens have the faces of women because nothing so estranges men from God as the love of women."[22]

The Uses of Mythology

This then was the attitude of the early Church: monotheistic and monogamizing among a people used to polytheism and polygamy; seeking to control men's thoughts and desires and direct them all into the one Godward channel. Both religion and art provide ways, often intimately connected, since each tends to use the forms and products of the other, of dealing with, by expressing, man's conscious and unconscious preoccupations. Together they create a mythology which enables him to experience vicariously states and desires which he cannot live out himself. Through a myth in its however crude artistic expression he may sleep with his mother as Oedipus, be the subject of homosexual rape with Ganymede, murder an unwanted spouse with Clytemnestra or be the desired of all the world like Helen.

By controlling all the arts and attempting to seal off all other mythologies the Church deprived her members of

[20] Possibly written for that same Æthelflæd who reminds one of that earlier Celtic warrior queen Boudicca, model for Britannia.

[21] Helen Waddell, op. cit.

[22] Helen Waddell, op. cit.

any expression for most of their unconscious fantasies and at the same time narrowed the range of their conscious life by her sexual prohibitions.

She did of course offer a mythology of her own but unlike the mythologies of other religions it was superficially asexual. The god persons had no erotic adventures in their devotees' stead. Not even the saints, the equivalent of heroes like Hercules and Theseus, were allowed to express desire except for God and death.

God himself as father and son provided an object of sublimated homosexual identification for men and a limited heterosexual possibility for women.[23] "Then He took the soul into His divine arms, and placing His fatherly hand on her bosom, He looked into her face and kissed her well," which written in the thirteenth century, reminds us of Charles Wesley's:

> Jesu, Lover of my soul,
> Let me to Thy Bosom fly,

with its offering of sublimated sex to the imaginatively deprived of the English industrial revolution nearly six hundred years later. At the same time the concentration on the details of the passion and the martyrdoms of the saints gave expression to sado-masochistic feelings, sometimes acted out in orgies of public flagellation.

Naturally the artists attempted as many variations as possible within the limited range, in the visual arts as well as in literature. Every child knows about the illuminated manuscripts, the fine metalwork, the robes, but it's hard not to imagine that in a society less devoted to the ideals of religious asceticism and war there might not have been at least as much artistic expression as among the Byzantines who were equally subject to attacks by the infidel Moors. The loss to the visual arts may be even greater than that to literature. There is constant reference to pagan idols "made by man's handiwork" in Bede and we know that there was an unexplained sculptural renaissance immediately after the conversion. It would seem most likely that this was a direct continuation of a pagan school which

[23] G. Rattray Taylor, op. cit., Book I, Chap. 11.

gradually died out. Meanwhile poets and prose writers rang the changes through Ancient and Modern:[24] Jesus the warrior, the lover of man's soul, the willing victim, the loving son; Mary the intercessor like a spiritual Godiva, the sorrowing mother and, by the fourteenth century, "mother of her father and her brother," reflecting one of the Church's deep obsessions: incest.[25]

Demons, Angels, Witches

Like extras hired to fill out the background there were, however, various lesser characters, some of them on loan from folklore or doubling up in both Christian and pagan systems, sanctioned by the Bible, particularly the Old Testament,[26] and therefore holding an often not very respectable but orthodox place in theology. As such they were well situated to siphon off some of the unsublimated eroticism which the Trinity didn't absorb.

Angels were of two sorts: fallen and unfallen. Such was the obsession with sexuality that the blessed, unfallen were thought to be completely sexless and so the painters and sculptors consistently presented them, unambiguously ambiguous as the Louvre Hermaphrodite, desirable to both men and women yet responding physically to neither except under a symbolic shield as in the case of St. Theresa's visiting cherub whose great golden spear penetrated to her entrails with a piercing sweetness that caused her to utter several moans.[27]

Fallen angels on the other hand were devils, demons or fairies. The *Malleus Maleficarum* which must be one of the

[24] See for example the work of Cynewulf (born *c.* 750), particularly *Christ*, and *The Dream of the Rood*, for early treatments, especially the development of the cult of the Virgin Mary.

[25] The laws of consanguinity mask a sharp concern with incest taboos. It was thought particularly dreadful for a man to marry his stepmother since man and wife were one flesh and he was therefore marrying his father; similarly with marrying his sister-in-law. Psychologically the Church had a point, for the desire to marry one's stepmother or brother's wife may mask a desire for father or brother.

[26] See Robert Hughes's *Heaven and Hell in Western Art* for the biblical facts appropriate to each species.

[27] *The Life of St. Theresa*, translated by J. M. Cohen, Chap. 29.

nastiest works of fiction ever published, a manual of witch-craft compiled by two German Dominican Inquisitors in 1486, in Part I, Question 3, Whether children can be generated by Incubi and Succubi,[28] is quite clear on this point. Its chief authority is St. Augustine's *De Civitate Dei*. Satyrs and fauns "which are commonly called Incubi" are the fallen angels now in devilish shape and "have appeared to wanton women and have sought and obtained coition with them." "Satyrs are they who are called Pans in Greek and Incubi in Latin . . . and the Gauls name them Dussii."[29] The Gauls are the Celts and these "dusii" are the same as the British hobgoblins. They are sometimes called "pilosi" or the hairy ones,[30] which helps us to identify them with our native species. Lady Wilde, with several other collectors, has the Irish belief that all fairies are fallen angels, the devils being the ones that fall into hell while the more gentle fairies fell on dry land or into the sea.[31]

The *Malleus* is quite positive that there are only devils. ". . . the Good People as old women call them though they are witches, or devils in their forms,"[32] and the actions attributed to them are those Shakespeare gives Puck in *A Midsummer Night's Dream*, "the shrewd and knavish sprite."

> That fright the maidens of the villagery;
> Skim milk, and sometimes labour in the quern
> And bootless make the breathless housewife churn;

[28] For those, among them myself, who find these two like stalactites and stalagmites, succubi are for men, incubi for women. The answer to Question 3 is that a devil disguised as a female succubus receives semen from its bedfellow, whips it smartly through the air, being careful not to let it cool or evaporate, while itself changing into a male incubus and then gets into bed with a woman. The problems of paternity during an incubus close season are obviously very complicated. Merlin himself was said to be son of an incubus.

[29] Isidore of Sevile. He speaks of fig fauns, 1 Jeremias 39, which are taken to be so called because they feed on figs but the fig is also a symbol for the vulva, cf. Ital. dialect. fica.

[30] Lewis Spence, *British Fairy Origins*, Chap. VI.

[31] Lady Wilde, *Ancient Legends of Ireland*, p. 89.

[32] Part II, Question 2, Chapter 8. Certain remedies . . .

And sometime make the drink to bear no barm;
Mislead night-wanderers, laughing at their harm.[33]

He also mentions shape-changing into a three-legged stool,
a horse or a crab apple, an activity well known to the
witch-hunters. Again and again in the witch trials people
were accused of being witches because they had trafficked
with the fairies. In the ecclesiastical mind all sprites were
devils and their chief work was to provide opportunities for
fantasies of illicit sex.

As with the angels there are two kinds of witch: spirits
and humans. Popular idiom has always kept the word
witch for the female of the species and there is a sense in
which it is right. The Church knew no such human distinction. Witches could be of either sex though they were more
often likely to be female because women "are feebler both
in mind and body," "more carnal than a man," "have weak
memories," "are of inordinate affections and passions,"
vain, liars and "more bitter than death." "To conclude. All
witchcraft comes from carnal lust, which is in women in-
satiable."[34]

Apart from a brief period of paranoia under the early
Commonwealth, England, though not Scotland, escaped
the worst of the witch scare which lasted for two centuries.
Professor Trevor-Roper attributes this largely to the rarity
of judicial torture in England.[35] Though this was an important factor, it is an effect not a cause. Why was torture
not invoked here as it was in other countries to provide
confessions and counter-accusations? Our legal system admitted torture as a possibility and there is no distinction to
be made between Catholic and Protestant since both tortured and burnt alike. The answer I think is to be found in
the greater imaginative permissiveness of English society
and literature during this period. It was accepted that the
country people believed in fairies and they were constantly

[33] Act II, Scene 1.
[34] *Malleus Maleficarum*, Part I, Question 6. Why superstition is
chiefly found in women.
[35] *The European Witch-Craze of the Sixteenth and Seventeenth
Centuries*, Chap. 4, p. 90.

used as subject-matter for plays and poetry.[36] You cannot burn people for doing something which is currently showing in a popular comedy at the playhouse. By avoiding the extremes of both Puritanism and Catholicism and by producing a lively imaginative literature the English provided an outlet for sexual fantasy and reduced sexual guilt. James VI of Scotland, our royal demonologist, who had thought himself much inconvenienced by witches while he was at home found his interest in them subsiding in the freer atmosphere of the English court. "Incubi infest cloisters:" the greater the sexual repression the more violent the reaction. Conversely, the greater the social permissiveness, the artistic development and freedom, the fewer the manifestations of paranoia in hunters and hunted. Renaissance Rome was free of serious witchcraft as were the other civilized Italian cities but in the desolate Alps and Apennines it was found to be raging.

This particular aspect of the fairy world has led us to jump three centuries and the Channel, and in the next chapter we must go back and trace the development of fairy beliefs in this country, but there are one or two points which the witch craze throws up in its grotesque unrelief that can be considered here. In the first place the Inquisitors found something to persecute; once set going the craze generated its own impetus. The "something" was not a cult or an organized religion but a mass of so-called "folk" beliefs providing an imaginative alternative to Christianity among largely illiterate people, and an unconscious desire for greater sexual freedom.

Rightly the Church saw these two things as heresy. The minds even of the uneducated were not wholly concentrated on God. The educated could find their outlets in the reading of a now respectable classical mythology and its embodiment alongside Christian motives in art. Titian's erotic "poesie" of naked Venuses and Dianas for Philip II of Spain were painted for a royal patron who inaugurated a reign of terror in Flanders for peasant women who hoped they had slept with devils. The bonds of the Church had already been loosened in the twelfth century, now secu-

---

[36] See K. M. Briggs's *The Anatomy of Puck* for the diversity of English literary treatment during this period.

larism, humanism, and classicism were further eroding them and the Church was also split into two warring factions for the allegiance of men's minds.[37] Yet both factions had the same ideal: the resubjugation of a man's whole personality, body, mind and spirit to the Christian god. It was a little late, the very ferocity of the campaign suggests this, but the rearguard action was hard fought. Among other things it succeeded in separating educated and uneducated more than ever before.[38] The witch-hunters successfully applied the principle Marx saw as basic to capitalism, of divide and rule, exploiting village and personal enmities, family tensions, class and cultural non-understanding.

Exhausted, the Western world limped thankfully towards the Enlightenment. The fairies continued to carry off children and lovers, scamper naked and hairy in milk-maids' dreams, ride through the night sky, bewitch cattle and places and appear to old women as cats and toads. They gave up that unfortunate practice, never much encouraged in England anyway, of stealing penises and causing impotence and, on the whole, took more pleasing shapes when carrying someone away for a playmate. Perhaps they found it worked better, or perhaps it was simply that they were no longer called devils.

[37] As the wars of religion flowed back and forth across Europe with regions being first Catholic now Protestant then Catholic again so the witchcraft persecutions followed, each side finding it where the other had been.

[38] The horror of an educated Renaissance nobleman on being told that his peasantry were engaging in obscene and evil behaviour on the scale suggested by the Inquisitors can well be imagined. Even if he was strong-minded enough to think them "poor doting women" they must in their barbarity have seemed another species.

CHAPTER II

The Coming of the Fairies

Then all these things considered, there can no man reasonably gainsay but there was a king of this land named Arthur. For in all places, Christian and heathen, he is reputed and taken for one of the nine worthy, and the first of the three Christian men. And also he is more spoken of beyond the sea, more books made of his noble acts than there be in England, as well in Dutch, Italian, Spanish, and Greek, as in French.

William Caxton, 1485

CHAPTER 4

The Language of the ...

> ...
> ...
>
> —William Shakespeare

We are glamoured[1] by evolutionism which we have caught from Christianity. Christ was the fulfilment of all the law and the prophets, of Jehovah's promises to his people and the world. He is the apex of all religious thought. Religious evolutionism teaches that a religion is higher or lower in so far as it approximates most nearly to Christianity or is furthest from it. Systematized sacerdotalist monotheism is homo sapiens; animism the barely differentiated amphibia who have just crept out of the primal psychic slime. The Christian apologist anthropologist in the comparative study of religion sees all B.C. mythologies as stumbling steps towards annus domini.

Although some Christians, under the influence of existentialism, have become willing to abandon this rather nineteenth-century handmaid, evolutionism has passed to the historians and folklorists where it is tenaciously beloved and the mother of much misunderstanding. It leads to the belief that things must always be derived from other things as man and monkey are derived from some primal apish common ancestor. But there are men and there are the poor monkeys who instead of ascending the evolutionary tree have gone out on a thin downward-pointing limb. In the same way the Hellenistic is seen as a decadence while the main stem marches on proudly through Republican Rome; that culture which apart from its own delicate merits gave us the Byzantine and restored Classical Greece to the Western world by way of Araby. When applied to fairy beliefs in Britain evolutionism produces the verdict that they are the debased remnants of paganism,[2] that

[1] *Glamour*—a corruption of grammar and meaning "delusive or alluring charm, magic spell, etc."

[2] See for example H. R. Trevor-Roper's comments in Chap. 3, op. cit. on the origins of demonology.

there were once coherent Celtic and Teutonic mythologies of which we can see the remains in a folklore, only explicable as vestiges and in terms of the hypothetical systems which preceded them.

Religion cannot exist without art. Without sculpture, text, exhortation, ritual, painting, music, it has no expression, no presence. It is artists who elaborate and clothe mythologies, even if the basis of them is said to be recorded fact. What we recognise as the Greek pantheon whose stories we know as well as yesterday's news was made by Homer and Polyclitus, Sophocles and the architect of the Parthenon. As soon as there is any story to be told, any emotional effect to be conveyed, art is at work shaping, making coherent, creating. And art doesn't systematically progress. A painting by Piero della Francesca, fifteenth century, is not necessarily more primitive than one by Picasso, twentieth century, indeed it may appear just the opposite.

The Christian Church realized very well the dependence of religion on art when it made art dependent on the Church. For the dependence is not mutual: art can exist with only a secular mythology; the lives of men and women not seen as part of a theogony can provide its raw material. It will still make a mythology for that is the way we externalize the emotional impulses and situations we may never live out, or even know that we want to live out, but it need not be, in the accepted sense, religious.

Seen from this point of view monotheism is the least satisfactory because the most limiting system. With the coming of Christianity art was monopolized by the Church. Yet Christian mythology was not enough. The limitations which caused scholars to yearn for the pagan writers and then to feel guilt for their imaginative defection also affected the laity so that the folk artists were driven to make for themselves an alternative to Christianity which would express those mainly erotic impulses forbidden by the Church. By folk artists I mean minstrels, tellers of tales, dancers, singers and musicians who produced ballads, fairy lore, happenings like the Mayday festivities, rudimentary drama of folk plays, dances and rituals. The Church inveighed against them, and tried to suppress them in various ways, yet again and again they broke ranks and penetrated the upper levels of sophisticated art to the delight and refreshment of artists and audience.

There is no need to posit Celtic or Teutonic pantheons from which our fairy beliefs are derived, for they are a spontaneous creation changing with the exigencies of each period and expressing psychological truths for the individuals or groups who employed them. There is little evidence that those pantheons existed before such systems were forced upon them, by Christian monks[3] writing up the legends many hundreds of years later from the work of poets and professional storytellers and by determined folklorists, nationalist and apologist.[4]

However, although fairy beliefs aren't debased religious systems certain elements traceable to an earlier period do reappear in them and these are worth noting. Even so we must be careful not to regard them necessarily in a parent-child light. Similar folk beliefs have been found and catalogued from all over the world which should surely deter us from building the kind of circumstantial cardhouses made by many folklorists in their pursuit of antecedents. If a story which appears in a twelfth-century romance is hinted at in a seventh-century manuscript it is a waste of good critical space to construct the hypothetical intermediary stages and then conclude that the romance has distorted the original.[5] Because Titian and Veronese show two quite different interpretations of the Venus and Adonis legend, Titian the eager goddess trying to hold back the foolish boy who would go hunting, Veronese the huntsman lying back happily in Venus's lap, it doesn't mean that one

[3] Influenced of course by the artist-created Roman and Greek pantheons. I use pantheon in the sense of a carefully worked out trades-unionist system of defined deities who always appear in the same roles, instead of a mixed bag of assorted gods and goddesses whose functions constantly overlap. The first I believe to be the result of a long process of poetic working up under official sanction as in Greece and Egypt.

[4] Most texts are as late, eleventh and twelfth century, as the earliest Arthurian romances. The fullest mythology, the Scandinavian, is the work of poets who had travelled all over the known world and must have known the work of other minstrels and classical legends from the courts they visited.

[5] *Arthurian Tradition and Chretien de Troyes* by R. S. Loomis is a typical offender, though otherwise containing a great deal of interesting material.

of them is wrong in so far as he has misinterpreted Ovid's original poem of a millennium and a half before. The pursuit of Arthur has bedevilled us for long enough.

There is a built-in psychological device which makes children ask of a storyteller: "Is it true?" By this they mean not emotionally true but historically accurate. If the answer is "no" they feel betrayed and cheated. This same device works in grown-up children to reinforce belief with the trappings of fact and is constantly at work where a story contains a supernatural element. It's responsible for, among other things, the detail of fairy lore, the social precision in Romance and the science in science fiction. Because of this we must doubly beware of trying to find noncontemporary, authoritative explanations for any artistic or mythological phenomena. We remake our mythology in every age out of our own needs. We may use ideas lying around loose from a previous system or systems as part of the fabric. The human situation doesn't radically alter[6] and therefore certain myths will be constantly reappearing. Oedipus, Hamlet, Colette's Chéri and Lawrence's Paul, immortal sons and lovers, may easily be imagined harping on the same theme in some corner of the Elysian fields that is for ever motherland.

Anglo-Saxon Attitudes

Anglo-Saxon literature is full of the miraculous, both religious and secular. The laws of nature are broken by all the saints or God on their behalf. There are divine lights to reveal lost bodies, choirs of angels, healings, portents; all the holy paraphernalia arguing that the Anglo-Saxons themselves were quite used to the concept of supernatural happenings.

Although there is no evidence for an early pagan pantheon there were obviously gods, some of whose names are preserved for us in the days of the week: Woden, Wagner's Wotan and the Scandinavian Odin, the father of the gods

---

[6] Not yet, but genetics, laboratory babies, sex selection and so on may change it in the future and we shall have to invent accordingly to keep emotional pace with ourselves.

and men, Thunor, Thor, the hero warrior, Tiw and Freyr about whom we know little except that Freyr appears as part of a fertility trinity[7] among the Vikings. Woden seems to have been the most popular to judge by his common use in place-names and a mention in a charm which escaped Church censorship.[8] Wayland, the smith of the gods, was often mentioned in order to praise a particularly good sword in the heroic tales. Under pressure of the Viking invasions these gods were sometimes revived for worship but often with the Scandinavian forms of their names.

More important is the evidence for a mother earth goddess.

> Hail to thee earth, mother of men
> Be fruitful in (the) god's embrace
> Filled with fruit for the use of men[9]

is part of a long ritual for restoring fertility to bewitched fields which combines Christian and pagan elements. Earlier the goddess seems to be addressed by name as Erce but scholars are divided on this. Bede mentions another goddess, Eastre, who he says provided the name for Easter. She would seem to have been connected with a Spring fertility festival. Tacitus had written of a travelling goddess called Nerthus and her attendant priest among the Angles. She was drawn on a ceremonial cart. "Then are days of rejoicing, and festive are the places which she honors with her coming and her stay. Men go not to battle, nor do they carry arms; all iron is locked away." The journey ends with a ritual washing in a lake, the drowning of the attendant slaves and the return to the sacred grove.[10]

[7] P. V. Glob, *The Bog People*, pp. 156ff., for a fascinating discussion of the fertility goddess.

[8] D. Whitelock, op. cit., Chap. I.

[9] Hal wes thu, folde, fira moder,
beo thu growende on godes foethne;
fodre gefylled firun to mythe.

There is no way of telling in Anglo-Saxon whether the god referred to is the Christian god or the kind of young lover god of the goddess of many mythologies. Perhaps this was as well for the reciter and copyist.

[10] Tacitus, *Germania*.

Certain things in this story are familiar in fairy lore; the festival itself reminds us of the Mayday rites, trees and groves are particularly inhabited by fairies and penalties fall on anyone cutting them down,[11] in some places blood sacrifices are made to the fairies, secrecy is always enjoined on anyone who has any traffic with them, and iron is particularly mentioned which was a counter-charm.

Tacitus's comment on iron could be taken to mean simple weapons but this clearly isn't so since he has already disposed of those. Iron is magic because it is the instrument of death and castration, the two forms of impotence, and it must be locked away during fertility festivals. In the British Isles the fairies were especially feared on Mayday and every effort was made to keep them away[12] for this was, and still is according to the figures for conception based on the last census, a time of high human potency which they mustn't be allowed to blight. Guilt was at this time transferred to the fairies who were usually the embodiment of sexual fantasies.

The goddess is particularly important. It could easily be thought from example after example of Anglo-Saxon literature that no such concept had entered our ancestor's heads, an extraordinary idea when we consider other mythologies. It was however a particularly disturbing concept for the Church to fit in. Among the Irish, Brigid, who fulfilled the same function, being also a goddess of childbirth as we know from her connection with fire, was adopted as a saint but the process of sophistication had already begun with her. Erce was still very close to the earth and intractable material for canonization. The best thing to do was to repress her, so much so that without the accident of this charm we shouldn't have known of her existence. This lack of a female element until late[13] in Christianity is something we shall have to consider again.

It reflects the Church's attitude to women and appears in another form in the Latin lives of the saints and kings. One of the most written of women in the whole period was Ælf-

---

[11] Spence, op. cit., Chap. XI.
[12] Spence, op. cit., Chap. XI.
[13] The feast of the Immaculate Conception raising Mary to the hierarchy wasn't instituted until 1140.

thryth, wife of King Edgar, whom she married in 965 though the actual written texts about her belong to the twelfth century.[14] She was said to be very beautiful, which beauty caused the death of her first husband. Her lasciviousness caused the death of an abbot and her ambition that of her son-in-law, King Edward the Martyr. It seems likely however that the real lady may have fallen foul of St. Dunstan who accused her of adultery.

Her brush with the abbot is a splendid story. Riding through a forest he was forced to "satisfy the needs of nature" and was surprised on looking round carefully "as he was a modest man and of great integrity" to see the queen under a tree preparing a magic potion ("transformed by her caprice and magic art into an equine animal . . . so that she might satisfy the unrestrainable excess of her burning lust running and leaping hither and thither with horses, and showing herself shamelessly to them, regardless of the fear of God and the honor of the royal dignity"[15]). Later she attempted to seduce the abbot to keep him quiet and when this failed had him ingeniously murdered by her waiting women.

The stories read like contemporary romances but the core of them must belong to just after Ælfthryth's death. Obviously she was deeply hated by the Church even though she was supposed to have died in a convent in grief and penitence. What comes through most clearly is that she was hated because she was beautiful, sexy, ambitious and a woman. The shape-changing into a horse we shall look at later. An earlier misogynist story is told by Asser, King Alfred's biographer, of Queen Eadburgh, wicked daughter of a wicked mother, another lascivious, ambitious murderer.[16] Yet these forceful ladies seem more like the fierce "divining matrons" of the Germani whom Plutarch had mentioned in his Life of Julius Caesar and the "mighty women" who are the witches of the Anglo-Saxons.

---

[14] For all this story I am indebted to C. E. Wright, *The Cultivation of Saga in Anglo-Saxon England*, pp. 146–71, which, although I don't accept its main premise, contains many interesting texts. Her name means elf-strength.

[15] The Celts had a goddess Epona, noted by Roman writers, who rode a horse. Perhaps some idea of her lingered in the hatred of Ælfthryth and the form she took.

[16] Wright, op. cit., pp. 93–95.

The Elves

Another charm which mentions gods and witches also mentions elves, an important word for English literature[17] and for any consideration of the fairies. The word fairy itself didn't come into general use until the thirteenth century by a return of the idea through Norman French possibly because of a verbal association with "ferly" which from "sudden" in Old English came to mean "a marvel." As late as 1200 elf[18] was the word to describe Argante, the queen of the beautiful ladies who carry off Arthur to be healed in the Isle of Avalon.

The elves of the charm are responsible for elf shot, little invisible arrows (though sometimes they were identified with real flint arrowheads which were thought lucky) which caused disease. There's some dispute about whether this charm is against a sudden stitch or piercing of the skin by elf shot but that needn't greatly worry us. It has a kind of refrain:

Out little spear if herein you be

and the suggestion, in the beginning of the poem, of witches riding and yelling which reminds us of the Valkyries.

It's difficult from this charm to gather any more about the elves. Something might be made of the "little spear" implying that they were small but equally an arrow could be described as literally a little spear. It occurs in a book of Anglo-Saxon remedies generally referred to as *Lacnunga*. Several of these are headed *Wip dweorh*, meaning "against the dwarf" and dwarf then as now implied a small being. The manuscript is eleventh century and this seems to be the earliest definite mention of little fairies. In the elf shot charm they weren't gods or witches which have separate mention although belonging to the same species.

[17] Among other things it provided a pseudonym for Shelley who signed critical pieces E.K.—Elfin Knight.

[18] The form is "aeluan." Alvisc = elvish = fairy. It's to be found in Layamon's *Brut*, the first English poem we have after the Norman conquest. Chaucer uses both elf and fairy interchangeably in the fourteenth century.

They are also, in a passage from the long epic, *Beowulf*, lumped together as the descendants of Cain, the official position given them by Christianity which reminds us of the Greek story of the Titans being sprung from the blood of Cronos, with ogres, evil spirits of the dead and giants,[19] all of whom are denizens of fairyland that we shall meet again. And this is all our knowledge of these, apparently the earliest mentioned fairies, except for one very important yet minute clue.

The exception to the Church's general misogyny was the religious: nun, abbess, warrior maiden for God symbolized by the Old Testament Judith, the virgin who, brought to the tent of Holofernes to satisfy his lust cuts off his head while he is in a drunken stupor.[20] The poem is reckoned to date from about 900 and, unusually, inclines to rhyme and a kind of ballad metre. In spite of its heavy biblical emphasis Judith herself is described in one place as an "elf-beautiful woman."[21] Elves were not then just the ugly brethren of ogres and giants; they might shine. It's clearly a popular term for beautiful and indicates that elves were both masculine and feminine. That it should be used in such a poem is important too, for it suggests both that it was so much in use that it had slipped in unnoticed and that there was a lot of popular material, songs and stories, that wasn't preserved for one reason or another. It also suggests exactly the kind of fairy that we shall soon meet in flocks in ballad and romance and go on meeting for hundreds of years.

Beowulf itself also mentions a kind of water sprite called a nicor that haunted lakes and rivers and was still about five hundred years later infesting Loch Lomond.[22] But *Beo*-

---

[19] eotenas and ylfe and orcneas
   swylce gigantes
                    Beowulf, line 110.

[20] This very bloodthirsty piece is always described by scholars as "extremely fine." The head needs two strokes to sever it while the villian lies only half dead and it is carried home "all gory" in the bag their food was brought in by Judith's serving maid, "a prudent woman," a scene only tolerable as played by Mae West and Beulah.

[21] Line 14, "ides elfscinn"—literally elf-shining.

[22] Layamon's *Brut*. Kindly water sprites are common in Wales, Scotland and Ireland, and unkindly ones in England like Peg Powler and Jenny Greenteeth, who are great drowners, and as mermaids. See K. M. Briggs, *The Fairies in Tradition and Literature*, Chap. IV. In *Beowulf* they are rather like smaller versions of the Loch Ness

wulf is chiefly important as a fairy source for the horrific mother and son couple that seem forerunners of Caliban and Sycorax in *The Tempest,* Grendel and his dam who is part wolf. Grendel is a man-eater like Polyphemus or the giant in Jack the Giant Killer. Together they make a couple of extremes: he a cannibal, she whose mother-love leads her to murder; the anti-madonna and child. There is no pity for them in the poem any more than Prospero pities Caliban and Sycorax and in ridding mankind of this horrific pair Beowulf is taking on the power of evil and paganism.

His final battle is with a dragon, a creature common to Christianity and folklore, appearing in English ballads and folk plays and known in China and ancient Greece. The explanation of dragons must wait for the next chapter however. The spirits of the dead mentioned earlier should be underlined for they are very common manifestations of fairy.

From all this it seems that our Anglo-Saxon ancestors had a fairy other-world complete. We are nearing the time when the elves made their first big takeover bid for Christian men's imaginations but before we reach it we must look at Welsh and Irish traditions.

The Celtic Dawn

In the wilder parts of the British Isles the earlier inhabitants still subject to the lighter rule of the Celtic Church and preserved by speaking various forms of their own language had kept and ornamented an alternative mythology. It had been constantly remade by bards and minstrels as it was sung and recited in chieftains' halls, round the camp fires of warriors, by monks in their leisure time,[23] by

---

monster. Layamon mentions both water elves and nicors. Aelf = elf was a common component in Anglo-Saxon names. Alfred, "elf-counsel," is the best known. The cockney pronunciation "Elfrid" is arguably the more correct.

[23] This sort of thing went on even in English monasteries as we know by a sharp note from the English scholar Alcuin who had been called to France by Charlemagne to educate his people and had heard that the Northumbrian monks were telling tales of the Germanic hero Ingeld instead of Christ. "Quid Hinieldus cum Cristo?"

women at the communal washing stones, in the dialects of Britanny, Cornwall, Wales, Scotland and Ireland. Enough similarities remained among the names to suggest a common origin: Mannanan son of Lêr in Ireland is Manawyddan son of Llyr in Wales; Lleu Llaw Gyffes in Welsh is Lugh Lamhfada in Irish. Some of the names are already familiar from inscriptions in Roman times both from Britain and Gaul. A typical family tree is that of Old King Cole:

> Camulus (Gallo-Roman)
> Cumhal (Irish)
> Coel (Welsh)
> Cole (British)[24]

though the descent is more like the spokes of a wheel than *x* begat *y*.

The stories are known to us from manuscripts written by Christian monks from the twelfth century onwards but, because of the nature of the language and other internal evidence, generally thought to have been copied from an earlier source. They tell of heroes, gods, goddesses, hunting, fighting, abduction, hopeless love, incest, betrayal, giants, journeys to the other world, enchantment and all the happenings we are used to in classical myth yet more briskly and with less rationalization as we would expect in stories primarily for recitation rather than quiet reading. All this material was about to be loosed on the imagination of Western Christendom. What it needed was a respectable channel which it found in *The History of The Kings of Britain* by Geoffrey of Monmouth.

Enter Arthur

In knightly tales there's always a moment when the hero going quietly on his way, thinking quite properly of his beloved, comes upon a shield hanging on a tree usually by a ford. Unable to let well alone he unsheathes his sword

[24] Charles Squire, *Celtic Myth and Legend*, pp. 275–7.

and clouts the shield with the force of a J. Arthur Rank gongman whereupon at least one, sometimes several, knights or giants rush down upon him and he's lucky to escape with his life. To touch the field of Arthurian scholarship even ever so gently is to provoke a tourney. However, like the knight, at this point in the journey I have no alternative.

Geoffrey finished his book in 1136.[25] It was in Latin, in prose and it professed to be a history of Britain from the founding of the nation by Brutus, a descendant of the Aeneas who had founded Rome and, therefore, a Trojan. It was important to be on the right side in that war and the right side was the side of love, honor and eventual defeat. Histories were immensely popular. Henry of Huntingdon and William of Malmesbury had both written histories of the English based mainly on Bede and the Anglo-Saxon Chronicle, and there were lives of the saints and ecclesiastical histories. Such works were commissioned usually by noble or episcopal patrons. Apart from an interest in history itself they tended in an oblique way to add up to the human and divine approval of the status quo, of the new ruling house or religious foundation.

Geoffrey's was quite different. Let Henry and William confine themselves to the English, he says, he has a little book in the British tongue on which he will base his history and fill in all the gaps up to the time of Bede from the fall of Troy, about two thousand years. There's some dispute about whether Geoffrey was Welsh or Breton. Those who favour the transmission of Celtic legends into romance literature via the Breton minstrels would like to claim him for Britanny. He seems to me unmistakably Welsh and the whole book to be a piece of revenge propaganda for the Celts who had had their country stolen from them by the Saxons and were now having a little of their own back in seeing their old enemies defeated by the Normans. Naturally he was willing to pay his respects to the Bretons by making Hoel of Armorica, or Little Britain, Arthur's right-hand man, as the Duke of Britanny had been William the Conqueror's, but the fall of Britain following the abduction of Guinevere is too like the fall of Troy for us to think that

---

[25] I have used the excellent Penguin translation by Lewis Thorpe.

it meant that Geoffrey was anything but firmly on the side of the insular British.[26] The decline and Jeremiad after the passing of Arthur is partly because he is now entering ground covered by others and partly because he has lost interest himself with Arthur's exit, for Geoffrey was a novelist. No one has ever found anything that might be "the book in the British language" and forty years after his death it was said that he had made it all up "out of an inordinate love of lying or to please the Britons."[27]

This however was not quite true. What Geoffrey had done was to take a lot of traditional material and make it into a coherent dramatic story on the lines of Livy's history of Rome which he obviously knew well, since the opening of his book is based on it. He had Nennius's *Historia Britonum* of c. 822, the *Annales Cambriae*, the Welsh king-lists and the material to be found in some of the work of the Welsh poet Taliesin and in the prose tale *Culhwch and Olwen*.[28] In his dedication he mentions by name only Arthur of all the kings and adds: "What is more these deeds were handed joyfully down in oral tradition, just as if they had been committed to writing, by many peoples who had only their memory to rely on." This suggests that he intended to tell the story of an Arthur already popular among many peoples.

Culhwch and Olwen bears this out. The hero cursed by a wicked stepmother with love of a giant's beautiful daughter is told by his father: "Arthur is thy first cousin. Go then to Arthur." There is no need to explain to the audience who Arthur is; obviously they all know and this is simply one of the stories which begins with Arthur holding his court and being asked by a young knight for a boon. After a series of adventures, the Celtic equivalent of the labors of Hercules or Psyche, the girl is won, but in the course of it enough

[26] For the main evidence see Thorpe's introduction, op. cit.

[27] William of Newburgh, *Historia Rerum Anglicarum*. Even if it were proved that the accepted version is a rewriting of Hammer's text (see Thorpe, p. 16), which would then be the little book, we still have no source for that other than the sources for Geoffrey's history.

[28] Those who wish to track down the historical Arthur are referred to the Preface to Malory's *Le Morte D'Arthur* by Sir John Rhys. *Culhwch and Olwen* is published in the Everyman edition of the *Mabinogion*.

references have been made to other stories to fill several books of romances. It is generally accepted as having been composed in this form in about 950 when another scribe was copying two references to Arthur into the *Annales Cambriae*.

Nearly a quarter of Geoffrey's book is given to Arthur himself, another quarter to his father and Merlin. Whether such persons ever existed doesn't concern us and indeed the attempt to find the historical Arthur is another manifestation of that childish "Is it true?", thinly disguised as an attempt to fill in the blanks of history, which Geoffrey exploited. But the demand that it should be true, that it should be respectable historically, fulfilled several imperatives. The Church couldn't object to it as a rival nor could Christians feel themselves reprehensible for indulging in such secular daydreams. It lent a cloak of credibility under which people could vicariously experience much like today's "documentary fiction."

In doing so it gave them a remade mythology to express their emotional needs and allowed them to speculate endlessly about love and war.

Geoffrey's book is a piece of consistent euhemerising. Its characters are deities who have been made people. It may be that some of them began as people; Charlemagne goes through a similar process but he wasn't backed by so many characters. Roland and Oliver, his two, became heroes in their turn and attracted romances. Among Arthur's knights we find Urien and Mark, Bran, Balin (Belinus), Gwinas, Lot, all gods known to us from the Welsh mythical cycle of the Mabinogi.[29]

Immediately the history was a bestseller. We have at least fifty contemporary copies. It was translated into several different languages and inspired verse novels and short stories by the great French and German writers of the time, Chretien de Troyes and Wolfram von Eschenbach. It

---

[29] Guinevere herself seems to be simply the Celtic form of Venere, Venus, as in the days of the week where Friday, Italian Venerdi is day of Gwener in Welsh. The connection between Celtic gods and Roman ones doesn't seem to have been fully explored. Surely The Dagda, Irish father of the gods, is Dis Pater, daddy of them all. (N. Chadwick in *The Celts*, p. 170, notes that The Dagda was also called Eochaid Ollathair, father of all.)

was a culvert by which all this "matter of Britain" as it was called could flow into the imagination of the times (and ever since) to give us *Cymbeline* and *King Lear*, *Tristan and Isolde* and *Parsifal*, *The Faerie Queene*, dozens of ballads, poems and the illustrations of Beardsley.

Not unnaturally the characters weren't called gods. They were heroes, knights, elves, dwarfs, giants, fays, magicians and enchanters which are the same but in terms that are inoffensive (at first at any rate) to a monotheism. Over all was cast a Christian tinge. When this didn't seem strong enough the story of the quest of the Grail was worked up from a Celtic original, exalting chastity and devotion to Jesus. For the Church wasn't sleeping. It was simply for the moment overwhelmed in the enchanted, enchanting secular flood encouraged by monarchs like Henry II of England who ruled half France as well and spent the mass chatting and scribbling as if his physical presence was enough.

Why Had It Happened?

The first indications of change are probably to be found in the tenth century in a scrap of Provençal verse on the dawn;[30] in six comedies based on Terence written by a nun, called unlikelily Hroswitha, with love scenes reminiscent of Romeo and Juliet in order (she said) to get them out of her mind; in a Latin lyric:

I was with thee in falseness of a dream.
O far beyond dreams; if thou wouldst come in truth.

It grew with the castles, where for the first time there were communities of lay people with education and leisure, and with the temporary pause in warfare as the Vikings settled down in their chosen countries. It swelled in the eleventh century with a new interest in the classics and in poetry and suddenly it took over the whole region of Provence where there was an outburst of lyric love poetry for singing by professionals and amateur ladies and gen-

[30] Helen Waddell, op. cit., pp. 81–89.

tlemen that exactly parallels the Elizabethan madrigals and sonnets. Attempts have been made to try to explain this phenomenon as if it needed any explanation other than its circumstances. People don't stop falling in love for a thousand years because they are told not to, nor do they stop expressing their love in lyrics. Even Anglo-Saxon has a hint at it.

"Many of us have heard that the Geat's love for Mæthild grew boundless, that his grievous passion wholly reft him of sleep."[31]

Nor do cultural movements spring up overnight. In the eleventh-century manuscript of St. Augustine at Canterbury there is a poem of "The Spring Wherin Everything Renews Save Only the Lover" written in the first person feminine. Somehow it escaped the fanatic's knife that scraped others from the page. It is sometimes argued that the troubadours weren't educated enough to have written poetry but many of them were noblemen and many of them were lay clerics who would have studied in Paris or at the Italian universities. This poem anticipates troubadour lyrics of fifty to a hundred years later which were written from the woman's viewpoint.

The organization of the castle was that of a family where lord and lady stood in loco parentis to the young men who provided the lord's fighting men and clerical staff and the young women who attended the lady. Both young men and women would be themselves the children of good families learning their jobs in apprenticeship: he to fight and rule, she to administer domestically a small village. They would be young, from twelve upwards, living in close promixity with all the heightened sexuality of adolescence. They were expected to make as good marriages as possible to enhance their expectations. The lord himself might be often away and in his absence his lady would govern. Contraception was a thing to come. No man wanted his land inherited by a bastard unless it was his own.

In these conditions a clear social code had to be evolved and was. Manuals were written on courteoisie. You could aspire and serve but it was the woman who set the pace and the limits which your own sense of honor and love

---

[31] *Deor*, trans. R. K. Gordon; probably seventh century.

for her would incline you to accept. Since to arrive was
likely to bring disaster on both of you (both or one sent
home in disgrace or kicked out into a hostile world) the
journey had to be made as elaborate and diverting as possible: the rose, the poem, the sigh. When sex threatened to
sweep away the filigree structure, the girls took to their
knees and the boys to the village maidens who were more
likely to gain by a well conceived bastard than to lose.

To entertain this inflammable group there was the professional minstrel or troubadour who was required to produce an unending flow of songs on the subjects of greatest
interest to them all. At the head was the lady, ma dame as
she is usually called in the poems and sometimes by the
masculine form mi dons (Abelard called Heloïse domina),
derived from the Latin for lord or master. Since early
marriage was the custom the lady would probably herself
be quite young, attractive and the mother of one or two
small children.[32] She would have been married off for
money or title and her husband in any case might be often
away at court, on crusade, hunting, fighting or visiting
other parts of his territory. Yet man and wife were in the
eyes of the Church one flesh and so she too was the lord.
Most important of all she was a young, accomplished
mother-substitute to whom idealized love could be made,
familiar to all readers of Thackeray as Rachel, young
Henry Esmond's mistress. Given this emotional situation
there is no need to look for explanations in the influence of
Arab love poetry or Catharist heresy.

Adultery, real or fantasized, rivalled the love of God in
passion and idealism.[33] If marriage had been only a con-
cession to concupiscence the Church's attitude to this outburst of secular love can be imagined, for all human love
was in a sense adultery since the soul was the sister and
bride of Christ.

[32] The marital career of Eleanor of Aquitaine is a good example:
married at fifteen to Louis VII of France, she bore him a daughter,
was divorced at thirty and married Henry II of England who was
then nineteen and to whom she bore Richard I, John and Henry III.

[33] "Se je vous aim de fin loyal courage
  Et ai amé et amerai toudis,
  Et vous avez pris autre en mariage,
  Dois je pour ce de vous estre en sus mis
    Et de tous poins en oubli?"

I am true love that false was never
My sister mannes soule I loved her so
That I might in nowise from her dissever
Quia amore langueo.

It was this that was at the heart of the agony of Heloïse and Abelard when they met and became lovers in 1118, giving further impetus to the romantic cause by a real life experience that reads like a legend.[34] He was a Breton, from that other, continental, Celtic region where the ballads of Arthur were sung. Geoffrey of Monmouth in speaking of Guinevere's abduction by Modred says: "About this matter, most noble Duke, Geoffrey of Monmouth prefers to say nothing," suggesting that he could say a great deal and the story is well known but not suitable for the pen of the future Bishop of St. Asaph. Perhaps Abelard had heard it sung in his childhood.

The first of the troubadours, as he is called, William Duke of Aquitaine, died in 1127, yet the concept of courtly love was already known throughout France by then. When Charlemagne tells Roland's sweetheart that he has been killed and offers her his own son she says: "These words are meaningless," falls in a swoon at his feet and dies in true romance style. *Le Chanson de Roland* as we have it dates from 1100 though it is said that William the Conqueror's minstrel Taillefer went into the battle of Hastings at the head of the Norman troops chanting it and was rewarded with a grant of land. The minstrel's job wasn't always a sinecure. There is the story of another one who was suspected by his jealous lord, had his heart cut out and served to his lady. Not unnaturally she killed herself by jumping out of the window.

This diversion in pursuit of love has been necessary to explain why the romances, embodying just that theme in almost all its more obvious manifestations and many forms not immediately visible to the uncritical eye, became overnight the most popular literary form in Western Christendom. Suddenly there were fairies all over the place.

[34] For those who don't know the story: they had a son and were secretly married. However, her uncle and relatives refused to believe in the marriage and brutally castrated Abelard while he was asleep. Heloïse became Abbess of the Paraclete; he Abbot of Saint-Gildas.

CHAPTER III

The Elfin Knight

"Fair lady," he answered, "since it pleases you to be so gracious, and to dower so graceless a knight with your love, there is naught that you may bid me do—right or wrong, evil or good—that I will not do to the utmost of my power."

Marie de France, *c.* 1175. Trans. Eugene Mason

It seemed you couldn't go out without falling over them. Two green children were found in Suffolk who would only eat broad beans.[1] They were baptized but the boy pined and died. The girl grew up and married and gave a description of the underground country they had come from. Wisely, she said that the inhabitants were Christians. This was often claimed by or for a fairy. In Marie of France's *Lay of Yonec* the hero arrives in the shape of a great falcon to become the lover of a lady shut up in a tower by an aged jealous husband. When she is alarmed he insists that a priest come to give her communion which he will take, having assumed her shape, to prove he is a Christian and not a devil. As the rest of the story makes clear, he is the fairy king. It is the same problem that confronted Hamlet in his father's ghost: "Be thou a spirit of health, or goblin damned."

Sober chroniclers wrote of fairy hunts, fairy mounds, mermen, fairy wives and a human changeling called Malekin who appeared like a little child in a white tunic eating food left out for her; a fairy commonplace. The Portunes half an inch high were reported from Scotland by Gervase of Tilbury.[2] Giraldus Cambrensis in his *The Itinerary Through Wales* gave an excellent description of both fairies

[1] William of Newburgh and Ralph of Coggeshall both have this story. For beans as the food of the dead see *Black Ship to Hell*, B. Brophy, page 111.

[2] It is often alleged that small fairies are a late invention but they were certainly known in the twelfth century. They appear sometimes in the romances called dwarfs as in the *Lacnunga*. This is a comment on their size and doesn't necessarily imply that they were ugly or comic. We have been too affected by Disney. Compare the present idea of an elf with the elf women who took away Arthur. There are very good reasons why some fairies should be small, but see below.

and fairyland brought back by a child eye-witness. The credibility factor was working overtime to establish factual background to the poets' fantasies.

"These men were of the smallest stature, but very well porportioned in their make; they were all of a fair complexion, with luxuriant hair falling over their shoulders like that of women. They had horses and greyhounds adapted to their size." They were vegetarians, took no oaths because of their great regard for truth and had no public worship for the same reason.

For, if ever, this was the time:

> Of which that Britons speken greet honour,
> Al was this land fulfild of fayerye.
> The elf-queen, with hir joly companye,
> Daunced ful ofte in many a grene mede;
> I speke of manye hundred yeres ago,[3]

not the posited sixth century of Arthur but when he first conquered "the bounds of the empire of Christendom" in literature as Alanus de Insulis declared in 1174-9. Since "their Apparell and Speech is like that of the people and country under which they live,"[4] it was hardly surprising that they appeared in the guise of knights and ladies of the time.

Some writers find it remarkable that there is often no precise mention of fairies in the romances, indeed the word as a noun for a kind of being is a late development; feyrie or fayrie is another word for enchanted or enchantment. It is the whole world that is enchanted as if with a fifth dimension. The lays and romances describe men and women who seem real until suddenly, as if there were a gauze curtain hung before the whole scene which we hadn't noticed until that moment, time and space begin to tremble like a heat dance and we have walked through the border into another realm that is usually just below the threshold of consciousness. In the *Lay of Gugemar*[5] we begin with the usual factual opening giving the young

[3] Chaucer, *The Canterbury Tales*, the tale of the Wyf of Bath.
[4] Robert Kirk, *The Secret Commonwealth of Elves, Fauns and Fairies*, 1691.
[5] Marie de France, *The Lays*, trans. Eugene Mason.

man's parentage and early training at Arthur's court. All seems quite natural except that he is both emotionally and physically chaste for which "men deemed him a strange man, and one fallen into a perilous case." When he has been made knight he goes home to see his family and one day decides to go hunting. They start a stag and Gugemar rides so eagerly after it that he leaves the others behind. Until this point in the story nothing could have been more realistic. It's the upbringing of any young gentleman in the twelfth century. Suddenly the curtain shimmers. The stag has gone and Gugemar sees a spotless white doe with antlers, and her fawn. He shoots at her, wounding her mortally in the leg, but the arrow glances back and pierces his thigh. They both fall to the ground and the doe speaks to him. The transition from naturalism to fantasy is done without any jarring and the supernatural events which follow have our complete submission. There's no need to ask whether the animals are fair beasts or if the ship that sails itself like Coleridge's deadship in *The Ancient Mariner* is a fairy boat. All has changed. The young man, ordinary enough but for his late emotional development, has become a hero. This constant intermingling of the two worlds is characteristic of fayrie, in Barrie's *Mary Rose*, the novels of C. S. Lewis, *A Midsummer Night's Dream*, *Der Freischütz*. It is parallel with those humans in ballad and fairy story who go for a time to fairyland but return to human habitation. Some never come back, like King Herla and his men who went to a fairy wedding and found that three hundred years had passed on their return home. The Fairy King had given him the gift of a little hound and told him that they mustn't dismount until it leapt to earth first. Some of Herla's companions when they heard of the lost centuries jumped from their horses and immediately crumbled to dust. The rest rode on and were eventually seen sinking into the Wye at Hereford in Henry II's reign.[6]

Why Arthur?

It's true that Geoffrey of Monmouth made Arthur respectable by giving him a Latin prose history. What Geof-

[6] Walter Map, *De Nugis Curialium*.

frey did was to catch the already popular[7] Arthurian legend and canalize it. He didn't invent it nor do his efforts totally explain its popularity. Once his book had been published (I use that term in its original sense) other writers could draw freely on the other already existing material. Marie of France says repeatedly that she is using Breton and Welsh lays, both sung and written. It's now generally agreed that she wrote in the second half of the twelfth century for the court of Henry II of England. William of Malmesbury had said in 1125 that Arthur deserved a proper history instead of the false fables of the minstrels. Geoffrey, one likes to think with tongue in cheek, had given it him and warned William off.

A reading of Geoffrey makes the reasons for Arthur's popularity quite clear. He is a folk hero about whom almost nothing is truly known, which allows freedom of invention while the agreed bare bones provide an umbrella under which the stories can proliferate.

Arthur is born of adultery. His father, disguised as her husband, begets him on a lady whom he afterwards marries. There is another child, Anna, more usually known as Morgan La Fee, who is married to King Lot of Lyonesse and provides Arthur with a good nephew, Gawain, and a bad one, Modred. Arthur is crowned at the age of fifteen and begins a series of battles to drive out the Saxons from Britain and then to subdue the neighboring countries. He marries Guinevere but they have no children. Then follow nine years of peace and the holding of a plenary court, to which all his fiefs come, with feasting and sports. In the middle of the festivities messengers arrive from Rome demanding Arthur's submission to the emperor, which he refuses. Leaving Modred in charge of the kingdom he goes with his army to Gaul where he kills a giant and then fights the Romans. Just as he is winning he hears that Modred has made himself king and taken Guinevere. Arthur returns at once to fight Modred whom he kills but not without destroying both armies. Guinevere retires to a convent; Arthur to Avalon to be healed.

Arthur's conception is that of many heroes born of the

---

[7] R. S. Loomis seems to me to have completely made this point in his introduction to *Arthurian Tradition and Chretien de Troyes.*

erotic adventure of a god.[8] It is also a byproduct of adultery which the early medieval imagination found so important. At first he is himself a young hero. Then he becomes a father to his people and, in the period of peace, a catalyst for all the adventures of the new young heroes. It is often remarked that what we might call the Arthur of the middle period does nothing himself. He holds court from which his adoptive sons, his knights, go out with his blessing. In the English version of Geoffrey by Layamon whenever Arthur conquers a new land the king gives him his son to bring up. There is also clearly a strong tradition that Arthur became emperor, though Geoffrey doesn't say so,[9] which both the Welsh romancers and Malory knew.

At this point the story becomes a myth of the rebellion of the sons against the father and the seizing of the mother, familiar as the revolt of Zeus and his brothers and given historical embodiment in the life of Henry II whose sons, egged on by their mother, rebelled against him. In a society where women are married off politically they are likely to be more attached to their children than their husbands, dangerously so. Yet this awakening of the oedipal conflict is disastrous for the family and can only succeed in destroying them all. As Arthur is their father so Guinevere is their mother, obviously still thought young enough to be desirable to the next generation while Arthur seems to age. That no one shall have her she is sent into perpetual chastity. Arthur cannot die for he would have been slain by his own sons. He must pass away with the legend that, like Harold and Sir Francis Drake, he will come again.

Arthur is technically childless in order that the myth can be shifted a little off-centre and therefore given greater credibility and universality.[10] The knights are thus all his sons and the round table a device for keeping them equal in his favor and all bound to him. It's the reverse of the lock of swords which in the English sword dance is used to

[8] Jupiter disguised himself as Amphitryon, husband of Alcmena, for the same purpose.

[9] Presumably because it was a historically verifiable point he knew he couldn't get away with it.

[10] This same device occurs in the anonymous *Lay of the Thorn* where the lovers are clearly brother and sister but given different parents to disguise the incest theme.

kill the father so that no one son is responsible. One thinks of the conspirators killing their political father, Caesar.

After Geoffrey's sober and euhemerizing account, the magical character of Arthur comes more and more to the fore. As we would expect, each writer gave it his own particular slant. Wace, who did it into Anglo-Norman for Eleanor of Aquitaine, emphasized the courtly side; Layamon, who translated Wace, is stronger on the supernatural. It's from him that we get the longest account of the instituting of the round table after a fight for precedence, the account of the elves taking Arthur at his birth (which must be the first reference in English to the fairies at the christening so common in later French stories), a fuller account of Arthur's magic weapons, of the vanishing of Merlin and his return to arrange Arthur's conception, of Arthur's dream of foreboding, of the affair between Guinevere and Modred and the first account of the passing of Arthur that so haunted the imagination of Tennyson and the Victorians.

Layamon knew his audience, not a courtly one but one that could take large doses of explicit fairy. His addition to the story of the birth of Merlin is particularly interesting when we remember the elf-shining Judith. His mother said that when she was in bed: "then came before me the fairest thing that ever was born, as if it were a tall knight, arrayed all in gold. This I saw in dream each night in sleep. This thing glided before me, and glistened of gold; oft me it kissed, and oft me embraced; oft it approached me, and oft it came to me very nigh; when I at length looked to myself —strange this seemed to me—my meat to me was loathsome, my limbs unusual." The shining gold is Layamon's addition.[11]

---

[11] It's often said that Layamon has made his additions from French sources. However that may be, much of his extra material may be traced to English works, particularly the references to magic. Of the strange rectangular pool with the different sorts of fish which Arthur showed Hoel he says unequivocally "elves dug it," a remark straight from Beowulf. The famous ending is very reminiscent of both *Beowulf* and the *Battle of Maldon* in its elegiac tone. It may also owe something to the custom of ship-burial. For this and the following passage see *Arthurian Chronicles*, Everyman 578, p. 145. Layamon's testimony is particularly to our purpose because it gives a strong indication that the partially submerged English-speaking population

The explanation of this apparition[12] that follows in the story is important for a theological explanation of fairy and its connection with demonology and the witchcraft trails:

> There dwell in the sky many kind of beings that there shall remain until domesday arrive; some they are good, and some they work evil. Therein is a race very numerous, that cometh among men; they are named Incubi Daemones; they do not much harm but deceive the folk; many a man in dream oft they delude, and many a fair woman through their craft childeth anon, and many a good man's child they beguile through magic.

For professing such an experience as Merlin's mother had, hundreds of women were later tortured and burned at the stake. Several manifestations of the fairy lover, like the Irish Lovetalker, are to be found in any later folklorist's list of the fairies of the British Isles.

The Pursuit and Meaning of Adultery

In the *Lay of Gugemar* we left our hero, having entered the world of fayrie, in conversation with a white doe. She tells him that she will die and that his wound can only be cured by a woman who for his sake will suffer such pain and sorrow as no woman in the world has endured before. In his turn he must suffer porportionally for her. He binds up his wound, hoists himself onto his horse and follows a path to the sea where there is a ship waiting built of ebony with silk sails. Gugemar goes aboard and finds no sailors but a magnificent bed and while he is resting on it the ship puts to sea. He falls asleep and wakes in a strange harbor to the touch of a beautiful queen who is kept prisoner by

---

was just as interested in the romantic Arthurian material as the aristocratic Normans. There would seem little point in the huge labor of translation otherwise. We can therefore take it that its fairy elements give us a good picture of English belief at that time.

[12] Culled by Geoffrey from Apuleius's *De Deo Socratis*.

her aging husband in a tower. She takes him into the tower and they fall in love.

Of the thirteen lays known to be by Marie of France seven deal directly with an adulterous situation, one indirectly. Probably the most popular story of all in the period was that of Tristan and Isolde and the second that of Launcelot and Guinevere already foreshadowed in the Modred-Guinevere story of Geoffrey. This marital freedom comes straight from the Celtic myths which lie behind the romances. In them we also find the convention that it is very often the woman who desires and makes the first advances.

"I am Rhiannon, and I am being given to a husband against my will. But no husband have I wished for, and that out of love of thee," says the Welsh Persephone who is a woman of wit and intelligence and has come to seek Pwyll for her lover.[13]

The Fairy Queen in making her advances to Sir Launfal is just as plain: "Launfal, fair friend, it is for you I have come from my own far land. I bring you my love."[14] In the same way Thomas of Ercildoune and George Collins, in ballad and folk song respectively, will be solicited by their fairy lovers.

The combination fayrie/adultery is a very important one. In fayrie all the natural laws are reversed or don't apply. But this is simply an image of the real reversal and negation which is of the moral and taboo laws. If we study the subjects of Marie's lays very briefly we shall be surprised by the constant recurrence of some themes and by their undisguised eroticism.

The *Lay of Gugemar* is a story of adultery as is the *Lay of Yonec*: aged husbands shutting their wives in towers; the *Lay of the Dolorous Knight* is about many women's fundamental desire for polygamy: the lady has four equal lovers; the *Lay of Equitan* is an adultery tale of the Clytemnestra-Agamemnon type with the lovers destroyed because they attempt murder;[15] the *Lay of Sir Launfal* is extra-natural with Guinevere's attempted adultery for good

---

[13] *Mabinogion*, Everyman edit., "Pywll Prince of Dyfed."

[14] Marie de France, *Lay of Sir Launfal.*

[15] A similar theme is found in the *Mabinogion* "Math Son of Mathonwy." All three have the bath motif in them.

measure; the *Lay of the Two Lovers* hinges on the incestuous love of a father for his daughter which lies behind all stories of a fatherly test imposed on would-be suitors;[16] the *Lay of the Werewolf* is an engaging homosexual beast story;[17] the *Lay of the Honeysuckle* is part of the Tristram cycle and the other two are lost-and-found-children tales familiar from all mythologies and deeply loved of Shakespeare and Dickens.

It is the kind of subject-matter found in ballads, folk songs, fairy stories and myths and it is particularly suitable to a supernatural setting where the taboos can be broken as easily as the natural laws since we are dealing with a world of fantasy only made credible by occasional realistic trappings. Although adultery occurs in several forms its most common manifestation is that of the knight and the married woman, the medieval metaphor for the goddess and her lover which we are used to in the stories of Venus and Adonis, Astarte and Tammuz, Nerthus and her priest, Helen and Paris, Grainne and Diarmatt.

The social organization of the Middle Ages had other consequences which find artistic expression through the concept of fayrie. If the mother was deeply attached to her children, particularly her sons, so were they in turn to her or her substitute. By the idea of adultery, if not the practice, both sides were able to re-enact the childhood situation as adults. Under the guise of enchantment they could imaginatively break not only the Church's law against

---

[16] Poet and audience would be well aware of this from the many translations and variations of Apollonius of Tyre.

[17] In popular belief (and among some psychologists) there is a connection between bestiality and homosexuality. This idea lies behind Math's punishment of the two brothers (see above) one of whom gets a girl for the other. "Since you are allied together, I will make you fare together, and be coupled, and of the same nature as the beasts whose guise you are in." He makes them first deer, then wild pigs, then wolves, having them change their sex about each time and bear offspring to each other. It is only at the end of Marie's lay that we learn that the werewolf was the king's favorite. When his clothes were privately restored to him "they found the knight sleeping in the King's bed, like a little child. The King ran swiftly to the bed and taking his friend in his arms, embraced and kissed him formally above a hundred times." It's worth remembering that Dante's sodomites circle was well populated and both Henry II and his son Richard Coeur de Lion are thought to have been homosexual.

adultery but through it the incest taboo which it was really hiding.

The original story of Guinevere's adultery as told by Geoffrey is with Modred, her nephew, and this is found in the Welsh mythological substratum underlying the romances. By the Church's laws of consanguinity this is incest.[18] Modred stands in relation of a son to Guinevere as does Tristram to Iseult since she is his uncle's wife. This made it difficult for the fullest emotional exploitation. In the case of Tristram the problem is overcome by the introduction of the magic potion which dissolves the taboo. Iseult is also represented as a young girl married to a much older man, which helps to disguise the basic situation[19] as in Marie's stories of Gugemar and Yonec. Guinevere however cannot be disguised as a young girl. She is the empress and wife of *the* father. By the slight shifting device which I have spoken of before she is given Launcelot for her lover who is Arthur's son by adoption into the familial round table. No original in Celtic mythology has yet been found for Sir Launcelot, unlike almost all the rest of the company, although R. S. Loomis has suggested some links with the sun god Lug.[20] His name also differs from those of the other major characters in that it seems obviously made up. Probably the first record we have of it is in the German form Lanzelot; next as Chretien de Troyes's Lancelot. In both cases it simply means a little spear or lance[21] but the German word for lance is itself an adoption from French. He is named from his attributes both in love and war. His function is to be the queen's lover and the greatest warrior.

Feudal society was based on a system of family units

---

[18] In one version Modred is also Arthur's son by an incestuous relationship with Morgan his sister. This story is exactly paralleled in Welsh myth by the Gwydion/Lleu/Arhanrod tale in *Math Son of Mathonwy*.

[19] Though not the deep resentment for the father.

[20] R. S. Loomis, op. cit., Chap. XXVI. However, I would suggest Lleu Llaw Gyffes as more likely, since he becomes Gwalchmei who becomes Gawain and it's Gawain that Launcelot in a sense replaces.

[21] The Oxford Dictionary of Christian Names in an obscurantist moment suggests a derivation from the German "Lanzo" whose root means land. But "Lanze" is the German for spear and I see no need to look further.

which included adoptive children and servants who stand in a child-parent relationship to the lord and lady. Marriage was sought outside the group for the advantage of the group. Relationships within the group had to be, as far as possible, controlled and canalized harmlessly. Yet the very tightness of the structure made it explosive and obsessive. From this arises the apparent contradiction of the combination of an exaltation in literature of undying and unrewarded service to the lady with a proliferation of adultery fables taking place in a fantasy world of magic.

The Knight Errant

The most common figure in the enchanted landscape is of course the knight himself: the young hero proving himself by his adventures as he pursues the chivalrous ideal in order to be worthy of the lady who has sent him forth. Extraordinary, even absurd, as these adventures appeared to later generations, they are always emotionally convincing. They do not happen in the real world, as Don Quixote proved, but in the imagination. Knight errantry is an imaginative fiction, a fact the poets made quite clear by setting it six hundred years back. It is the story of the ego in pursuit of its ego ideal, told through the imagery of symbol and magic. Seeing an opportunity to canalize this fiction for its own ends the Church raised the call to the Crusades. Only the first call was enthusiastically responded to but it was with an enthusiasm that foundered on the realities of politics and economics. In the late twelfth and thirteenth centuries the crusade songs of the poets increasingly express unwillingness and misery at being forced from home. "Jerusalem you do me great wrong, you who have taken from me what I loved the best; know in truth that I shall never love you, for this it is that robs me of my joy, and often makes me sigh and gasp, until I almost quarrel with my God who has snatched me from the great joy I was in." "Sighing for her I leave for Syria for I must not fail my Creator. If a man fails him in his hour of need be sure that God will fail him." "God does not wish to give me for nothing all the pleasures that I have had in my life, but makes me pay dearly for them . . . Have pity, Love; if ever God did wrong, He does so now in parting our true love."[22]

Already the Church had taken part in the dedicating of a knight and laid its stamp on the concept of chivalry but by doing so it had taken an essentially fictional concept and applied it to reality. The subsequent disillusionment is a recognizable factor in the waning of the Middle Ages. It is paralleled by the Church's treatment of that other side of the fantastic fiction which it suppressed in the witch hunt. By the time that Malory wrote his *Morte D'Arthur* in 1469 knight errantry could again be regarded, in England at least, as quite simply fiction.

The Hunt

Our hero Gugemar set his magic quest in motion by going hunting. In fayrie literature the line which divides this from the other world is often the edge of the forest, a river, the shore. The crossing of this line is the first imaginative breaking of the taboo. Hunting itself is reported from every region and age as a fairy pastime. Partly this is because the fairies are made in human likeness of course and our ancestors were hunters. But the hunt also has a suppressed sexual element known to poets.

> Whoso list to hunt I know where is an hind

> The keeper would a shooting go,
> and under his coat he carried a bow
> All for to shoot at a pretty little doe.[23]

The animals here are not beasts but ladies and so I believe is Gugemar's talking doe. There was no strict feeling that animals were so different from men that they might not change places and in all myth and fairy tale we find humans, gods and fairies constantly appearing under what are usually called totemic forms as animals. It is from this time

---

[22] All from *The Penguin Book of French Verse 1*.
[23] Sir Thomas Wyatt and a popular folksong.

that the elaboration of the simple totem idea into the subtleties of heraldry dates, an idea that the Australian aborigine would have understood perfectly.

The fairy beast and the heraldic one are very close. If a knight chose an animal to represent him on his shield it would be one with which he was connected or which embodied some of his personal attributes. The fairy beast is sometimes a fairy in disguise, like the falcon who fathered Yonec, or a transposed person. If it's a transposed person it may well be that it is so disguised that even the writer, working often from earlier material, won't know what it is. The deer family which Gugemar meets is, I believe, his own family from which he must be cut off before he can be initiated into love. This he does by killing the doe who stands for his mother, the person most likely to resent his growing up and whom, on his part, it will be most painful to leave. His wound can only be cured by a woman who will suffer for him as dedicatedly as a mother would for her child (we are told earlier that his mother had "set all her love" upon him). Not surprisingly the woman he finds is a mother-substitute who will look after him.

In the English poem that marks the apex of Arthurian enchantment, *Sir Gawain and the Green Knight*, the lady who attempts to seduce Gawain is the fairy wife of the Green Knight who is able, like figures in Celtic mythology, to lose his head without losing his life. His daily hunting exploits counterpoint Gawain's pursuit by the lady. Although he doesn't know it Gawain has to refuse the woman to keep his own life.

Sir Gawain and the Green Knight[24] combines three fairy traditions, the Celtic, the romance and the folk, and does so effortlessly, yet by the time of its composition the reaction, the temporary retreat of fayrie, had already begun, as Chaucer points out. The tone of the late thirteenth, early fourteenth century is one of deepening cynicism. Not only the courtly Chaucer, who might be expected to be disillusioned among the everyday jockeyings for power, but his friend Gower, love's servant, was sickened by the corruption of the Church. There are no more elves, says Chaucer, only wandering friars who creep into

[24] Probable date of composition *c.* 1375.

ladies' beds. Gower is particularly angered by the constant bloodshed of holy wars, condemning the Crusades not just for practical reasons or because of their abuse but in principle as unchristian.[25]

The unknown author of *Sir Gawain* writing somewhere in northwestern England is untouched by all this. He moves still in the idealized world of enchantment. He is sophisticated without being cynical and his poem is both brilliantly constructed and rich in imagery. It begins, as we've come to expect, at Arthur's court where he is keeping Christmas, the midwinter feast. Into the court rides a huge knight, green in clothes, hair and flesh and carrying a holly club. Green is itself the most common color for fairy clothing in story after story and still considered unlucky for clothes or furnishings. The green giant is the Robin Hood of the May revels and the Jack in the Green, covered all in leaves, who came to town with London chimneysweeps. His face breaking into tendrils and foliage looks down from cloister bosses. He is John Barleycorn who "became a man" and like the Green Knight was beheaded but "sprang up again and so amazed them all."

He demands a Christmas game. Someone will take a stroke at him and then he at them. Arthur offers but Gawain, in his place, takes the green axe from the giant and cuts his head off. The giant picks it up, gets on his horse and tells Gawain that he is called the Knight of the Green Chapel and that he will expect Gawain to meet him there in a year's time to take his blow. In the following November Gawain sets out for his tryst, going northwards into the Wirral, a forest home of outlaws. At last in a deep wood he sees a fair castle built in the ornate style of the period but described with all the enchantment the artist has given to Saumur in the Duc de Berry's *Book of Hours* or the fairy castle of the Lady of the Lake in which Launcelot was brought up. "It shimmered and shone" between the trees.

Inside he is welcomed by a genial host who says that the place he wants is only a couple of miles away and that

---

[25] But then Gower is a remarkable person prepared to understand and defend brother-sister incest. *Confessio Amantis*, Penguin translation, line 170f.

Gawain must spend Christmas with him and the two ladies, one old and ugly, one young and fair, his wife.
Even when he proposes a game Gawain doesn't suspect
that it's really the Green Knight in disguise. The host will
go hunting on three days and on each day will give his
guest his bag in return for whatever Gawain has gained
that day in the castle. On each day the young lady comes
to Gawain in bed and tries to persuade him to make love to
her. Each day Gawain gives back the kisses she gives him
to her husband but the third day she also persuades him to
accept a magic girdle which will help him in his encounter.
This he keeps.

On New Year's Day with a guide from the castle he
sets out. The guide leaves him at a wild ravine. There is no
sign of any building until suddenly he sees a mound with
four entrances. He knows at once that this is the devilish
chapel. In the folklore of England and Ireland the commonest place for fairy dwellings or the entrance to fairyland is a barrow.

The Green Knight is honing his axe for the encounter.
He makes two feints at Gawain then with the third stroke
nicks his neck so that the blood runs. Gawain leaps away;
his honor, he thinks, has been sufficiently shown. Then
the Green Knight reveals that he is his host and the old
lady is Morgan la Fee who devised the whole thing to upset
Guinevere with the green head rolling under the table.
Gawain escaped two blows because he faithfully gave back
the kisses given him but he kept the girdle and for that his
proud neck was wounded. He returns to court much
ashamed of his cowardice but all Arthur's knights agree to
wear a green girdle too since Gawain insists on wearing his
as a remembrance of his failure.

I've told the story in full because the branch of English
in which it's written didn't become our standard speech
and this makes the poem sadly inaccessible to most people.
(This isn't helped by the orthography and spelling of the
standard texts. There's a good Penguin of a modernized
text with footnotes on obsolete words.) Perhaps because of
its place of composition the Welsh influence is very strong
in the poem. Behind the figures and themes in the foreground stand the shadowy myths of the *Mabinogion*: the
miraculous talking head of Bran, reminding us that Ar-

thur's father was Uther Ben—"wonderful head"; the final encounter between Llew Llaw Gyffes and Gronw Bebyr who had stolen his flower wife; and most of all the story of Pwyll, who is out hunting one day when his hounds drive some others from a kill and in recompense he has to take the place of the king of the Underworld. It includes keeping a tryst in a year's time with a rival to whom he is only allowed to give one blow. Every night in bed he turns his back on the king's wife though during the day he is courteous and affectionate to her. For this piece of loyalty to the king he is eventually given the kingdom.

The behavior of the Green Knight, the king of Anawn and of Oberon in *A Midsummer Night's Dream* shows a consistent tradition: the willingness of the king of fayrie, for that is who they all are, to offer his wife to another, usually the hero and often in context of a blow on someone else's behalf. In *Sir Gawain* there is some interesting doubling up. The host and the Green Knight we know are the same and so, I suspect, are the old and young lady. Morgan la Fee is descended from the Morrigu, the great Irish goddess who demanded Cuchulain's love and when he refused to give it changed shape several times in order to hamper him in his next combat, though finally she became his friend. Some of all this still attaches to Morgan. She is called "the goddess" in the poem.[26] She was known to be a shape-changer and sometimes appears as a hag, sometimes as very beautiful. This gave the romance writers some difficulty which they rationalized away by saying that her traffic with the devil in enchantment and evil caused her to become old and ugly while her brother (sometimes half-brother) Arthur remained young. This duality has similarly given folklorists trouble.[27] The same problem has caused her to split in two in *Sir Gawain*. The behavior of the young lady shows us that she is a fairy woman since they always made the first advances, as their Celtic prototypes had done including the Morrigu herself. Frequently old hags befriended by the hero knight turn out to be beautiful ladies. Everything points to the two ladies being the same.

---

[26] She is so called first by chronicler Giraldus Cambrensis.
[27] See R. S. Loomis, op. cit., p. 102.

We therefore have two parallel situations of a king, a queen and a knave, one in Arthur's court, one in the Green Knight's castle; one good, one evil, connected by the hero. Yet the characters of Arthur and the Green Knight are themselves strangely alike: jovially heroic; and the reputations of Guinevere and Morgan in love are the same.

Gawain is obviously deeply attracted by the lady:

> With welling joy warmed his heart
> With easy courteous smiling they gentled into laughter
> That all was bliss and happiness that broke between
>   them . . .
> Great peril between them stood.

For the lady has come to him in a loose flowing gown that leaves her breast and back bare in the familiar likeness of the harlot which draws on the childhood memory of another offered breast.

> In thin array after a pleasant guise
>   When her loose gown from her shoulders did fall,
>   And she caught me in her arms long and small
> Therewithal sweetly did me kiss
> And softly said, "Dear heart, how like you this?"
> It was no dream; I lay broad waking.[28]

This is the root of the adulterous, incestuous situation and its ultimate sophistication: to be offered the queen by herself with the king's connivance and permission and to return her kisses to him; to suffer a blow in his place instead of the blow you would give him.

Sir Orpheus and the Dead

Hunting is also intimately connected with the dead, with death himself, particularly the boar hunt. In *Culhwch and Olwen*[29] the hero must hunt the terrible wild boar, Twrch

---

[28] Sir Thomas Wyatt, "They flee from me that sometime did me seek."
[29] *Mabinogion.*

Trwyth, and his seven young, before he can gain the beautiful Olwen from her giant father. It's a story on a par with Hercules bringing back Cerberus from Hades. Everywhere the beast lays waste and slaughters. Arthur, appalled, asks his history. "He was a king and for his wickedness God transformed him into a swine," is the rational answer. When at last they catch up with him they can only hold him under the waters of the Severn while they take the instruments of fate, comb, shears and knife, from between his ears, that will sever the life of her father and let Olwen go while the Twrch Trwyth escapes them into Cornwall.

The boar hunt in *Sir Gawain* is the most terrifying of the three chases and well echoes the mythical pursuit. The fairy hunt in which the hunters are after souls is reminiscent of the Valkyries; the Sluagh of the West Highlands, the Gabriel Ratchets of Lancashire, the Dandy Dogs of St. Germans are of this kind.[30] There are many stories, particularly from Ireland, of lost sweethearts seen among the hunting or riding fairies and indeed there's no line to be drawn between the dead and the fairies. This was so obvious so early that Chaucer calls Proserpine the Fairy Queen. Nor is there any real difference between fairyland and the Underworld. By that deep human tendency to what is officially and historically called Manicheanism there are two manifestations of the Otherworld, dark and light, but both are inhabited by the dead and the fairies. I shall say more about this in the next chapter but at the moment I want simply to establish the point so that no one may be surprised by the probably slightly pre-Chaucerian romance *Sir Orfeo* where the classical Hades is fairyland and Pluto King of Fayrie. In an ingenious attempt to localize the whole story, Thrace, Thraciens, is said in the poem to be an old name for Winchester and Sir Orfeo himself King of England.

This charming retelling of a Greek myth provides the most complete survey of fairy belief in the early fourteenth century, with details that continued to be repeated and believed for the next six hundred years, including a description of the Fairy King, of fairyland and the hunt and ride.

[30] K. M. Briggs, op. cit., Chap. V.

Herodias, Eurydice, falls asleep in her orchard and wakes in terror saying that she has dreamt that the Fairy King came to her with all his knights and ladies dressed in white, riding snow-white steeds, and the king himself wearing his glittering crown cut from a precious stone. He takes her to fairyland, his palace, so like the Green Knight's, and then brings her back to the orchard saying that she must be there again the next day and go with him to fairyland for ever. Orfeo and his men try to protect her but she is spirited out of their midst. Orfeo gives his kingdom to his steward and wanders the world as a minstrel, living in the woods like a wild man.

Often on a hot morning he sees the Fairy King out hunting, with faint cries and blowing of horns but not catching any beasts, and at other times the fairy ride and the fairies dancing. One day, among sixty ladies with hawks, he sees Herodias and follows them when they ride "in at a rock." Inside is a fair country, bright as the sun on a summer's day, a flat green plain with a marvellous castle built of gold and precious stones. It's the first unequivocal description of fairyland. At night the stones give off a light as bright as the noonday sun. It might have been "the proud court of Paradise." The porter lets Orfeo in because he is a minstrel. There's a long tradition that the people most often carried away by the fairies are those who can dance and play like True Thomas the Rhymer who became the Fairy Queen's lover. Inside the castle are "folk thither y brought, And thought dead and are not." They are those who seem to have died suddenly; choked while eating, drowned, died in childbirth (a very vulnerable moment), in battle, sleeping or gone mad. Orfeo plays before the king and queen and they offer him anything he asks. He asks for Herodias. The king protests that Orfeo is wild and ugly and she very beautiful but keeps his word, a fairy characteristic. They return successfully to the upper air. The end of the story has been curiously affected by the return of Ulysses but in this case the steward has been more than faithful and all ends happily. There is no point of fairy law in this poem that wouldn't have been acceptable and familiar to an English eighteenth-century milkmaid or an Irish nineteenth-century labourer, testimony to the consistency and longevity of fairy belief.

The probable audience for *Sir Orfeo* is intriguing. In its charm and simplicity the poem is very close to the Lays of Marie of France which we know were intended for a courtly audience. Yet its fairy lore is that of supposedly later country people, very common in ballads and the oral material collected by folklorists. The translation of the Greek myth is totally convincing and without strain once we're prepared to accept Thrace as Winchester. The other striking thing is the completeness of the fairy scene in all its detail. The closest parallels are the ballad of Tam Lin and Lady Wilde's story of Kathleen. Perhaps we are closest of all to an English wood near Athens on a Midsummer's Eve. Obviously the audience were willing to give at least a suspension of disbelief but then so were the readers of *Sir Gawain* at least fifty years later in north-western England.

The New Mythology

"But now can no man see none elves mo."

For Chaucer and Gower the fairies have fled, driven out, says the Wife of Bath, by the great charity and prayers of the wandering friars "thick as motes in the sunbeam."

> Women may go safely up and down,
> In evry bush, or under evry tree
> There is none other incubus but he
> And he ne will doon them but dishonour.

Apart from the chance to have a satirical slap at the lechery of the friars which was always good for a courtly laugh, the implication is that the fairies have lost their hold over people's minds. For "people" we must read "the poet." Chaucer's send-up of the traditional romance in *Sir Thopas*, as clumsy as it is unfunny, makes it quite clear that, on the whole, the Celtic mythology as strained through the fine gauze of enchantment no longer stimulates his imagination.

There are two exceptions to this: *The Wife of Bath's Tale*, which follows on that forerunner of *Farewell, Rewards and Fairies* quoted above, and *The Merchant's Tale*.

The Wife of Bath's story is a romance with a twist but well within the convention that Chaucer has mocked a few tales before. Perhaps he felt that it was so suitable to the character that he couldn't resist it or that it gave a splendid opportunity for a little fashionable misogyny.

One of Arthur's knights commits rape. His punishment is deferred to the queen who says he must die unless he can say what women desire most. After much unsuccessful searching he finds an old crone who in return for her desire (at the moment unspecified) will give him the right answer. They return to court and he tells Guinevere that what all women want is sovereignty over their husbands and lovers.

> In all the court ne was there wife ne maid
> Ne widow that contraried what he said.

As soon as he is freed, the old crone demands that in fulfillment of his promise he shall marry her. Unwillingly he does so but their first night in bed finds him writhing in misery at her poverty, low birth and old age. The first two she disposes of with an appeal to Christian teaching. Then she says she can make herself young and beautiful but he must then run the risk of her being unfaithful, which he won't have if she's old and ugly. Which does he want? Cunningly he says he will leave it to her. "Then have I the mastery of you?" she asks and when he agrees she tells him to pull up the curtain. She is young and beautiful and promises to be faithful as well.

For all the worldliness of the treatment this is simply another tale of Morgan la Fee in her dual role which Chaucer has adapted.

His second story is of an old man married to a young wife and cuckolded by his squire. It's set in Lombardy and introduces the Fairy King and Queen, Pluto and Proserpine. *Sir Orfeo* had already used this transposition but there it could have been put down to the ignorance of the minstrel or his audience. No such excuse will do for the *Canterbury Tales*. Chaucer knew perfectly well what he was doing. He had understood the underlying similarity of all myth. Pluto and Proserpine are simply other names for the same concepts. There's no suggestion that we are in

England and he even tells the story of Pluto's rape of Proserpine in a brief aside. Here again there's a foreshadowing of *A Midsummer Night's Dream*, for the two are wrangling just like Oberon and Titania. They also interfere in the human action in the same way, Pluto restoring the old man's sight and Proserpine giving his wife a ready answer on her tongue when she needs it. One folk detail shouldn't be missed: the well in the middle of the garden where the fairies dance and which we shall find again.

Gower's chief and only sizeable contribution to our fairy saga is the presentation of Medea as a sorceress in the full panoply of *Macbeth*'s witches or Hecate in Purcell's *Dido and Aeneas*, writhing and chanting in strange tongues round her cauldron. The iconography of witchcraft was already fixed.

> She seems no woman, but a fay:
> Such powers to her charms obey,
> She might be called a deity.[31]

Gower too makes no distinction between sorceress, fairy and goddess. Gower and Chaucer were friends. They might well have discussed literary matters; they certainly kept a shrewd eye on each other's work. In spite of their differences, what they have in common is their fancy for what had been called by the French romancers the Matter of Rome, rather than the Matter of Britain. This matter had never entirely lost out to Arthur, and the story of Troilus and Cresseida which Chaucer used to such effect had been itself the subject of a romance, but now it came back with renewed imaginative power, reinforced by Chaucer's Italian travels, by the rise in influence of Italian literature with Petrarch, Dante and Boccaccio, and by a deep passion for that Ali Baba's cave of legends, Ovid's *Metamorphoses* Venus replaces the Fairy Queen as goddess of men's imaginations. The shift is verbal but, as the Matter of Britain had made all Celtic mythology accessible to art, and therefore to men's emotions, so this brought in the divine train

---

[31] *Confessio Amantis*, line 405 in Terence Tiller's Penguin translation. "Reeling, writhing and fainting in coils" was the accepted accompaniment to trance. Layamon describes Merlin going off in terms that would have suited Madame Arcati.

all the manifestations of classical and fourteenth-century Italian enchantment. The elves became little loves, Sir Lancelot, Mars. There was a new vocabulary; a new imagery both visual and literary. To the Italians it was native; to the English exotic. Temporarily the fairies withdrew into their mounds. And only just in time, for the witch-hunters were stirring. Not content with the Albigensian genocide, Lollard-hunting, Jew-baiting and wars against the infidel, the Church was about to turn on the rural holders of fairy beliefs who weren't sophisticated enough to distinguish between art and reality and in whom the credibility factor was soon to be backed up by rack and stake.

The Perfect Hero

> Ah Launcelot, he said, thou were head of all Christian knights, and now I dare say, said Sir Ector, thou Sir Launcelot, there thou liest, that thou were never matched of earthly knight's hand. And thou were the courteoust knight that ever bore shield. And thou were the truest friend to thy lover that ever bestrad horse. And thou were the truest lover of a sinful man that ever loved woman. And thou were the kindest man that ever struck with sword. And thou were the goodliest person that ever came among press of knights. And thou was the meekest man and the gentlest that ever ate in hall among ladies. And thou were the sternest knight to thy mortal foe that ever put spear in the rest. Then there was weeping and dolour out of measure.
>
> Malory, *Le Morte D'Arthur*, Book XXI, Chap. XIII

The epitaph on Launcelot is the epitaph on Hector.[32] In both cases it is the epitaph of a civilization, of a mode of the imagination and of a work of art made by a writer who creates by patching together other men's stories with the gold thread of his own talent so that the whole is a shimmering seamless garment of many colors. Both writers

---

[32] Let anyone who doubts this compare the two passages. What Sir Ector (Hector) says of Launcelot is simply shared out among the cast for Hector. The heroes' attributes are the same.

took the marvelous and gave it an earthly habitation without making it commonplace. Malory's *Le Morte d'Arthur* is the English *Iliad*.[33]

Malory returned to the structure laid down by Geoffrey of Monmouth in his Arthurian chapters and, realizing its fundamental unity, was able to pour into it the variations and individual developments the myth had undergone in the intervening three hundred years.[34] This is the repository of the myth as we know it, visited repeatedly through subsequent centuries by, among others, Tennyson, T. H. White, the librettist of *Camelot* and the unknown purveyors of popular cinema lays and tales retold for children. It contains *Parsifal*, *Tristan and Isolde*, Launcelot and Guinevere, the Legend of the Grail and the life and death of our chief national folk hero.

So great is its attraction that that credibility factor clamors, as it does with the *Iliad* and *Odyssey*, that it should be literally, not simply imaginatively, true. We can't believe that we have made it all up, that the human mind has spun a whole civilization and populated it. Even the stature of its inhabitants and the enchanted air don't stop us from demanding the archeological roots of petty Iron and Bronze Age chieftains. Yet even if, like Schliemann with Troy, we strike lucky digging up Camelot under the glare of the television lights we shall not have found the Arthur of our or Malory's imagination, and only he, like

[33] Comparison of the two throws interesting light on the scholars' vexed questioning on the composition of the *Iliad* (and therefore the *Odyssey*) and who was Homer. Behind both works lie a ramified mythology, popular shorter retellings by other unknown writers and a widespread public enthusiasm for the matter. That Malory used other works in English and French as the bases for his book doesn't make it any the less his. I have considered whether Malory could have been deliberately doing a Homer but it seems very unlikely that he could have read the original Greek text or even a Latin translation of it in its entirety though he obviously knew the stories, as he says. (The *Iliad*'s first printing was in 1488 in Florence. *Le Morte D'Arthur* was finished in 1469.) Still less would he have known the theories of communal or part communal and ballad-based authorship of Homer which weren't suggested for another three hundred and fifty years.

[34] I am aware that the books were redacted separately, probably during different stays in prison but this doesn't mean the final collection doesn't make a whole work informed by one imagination and with one developing and developed theme. For a full discussion of Malory's sources see Vinaver's Clarendon Press Edition, 1967.

Heaven that never was nor will be ever,

is always true.

Sir Launcelot himself is the apex of elfin knighthood. Malory has humanized him so convincingly that we forget that his father was Ban, another form of the god of the talking head, and that Chaucer had said of that other Arthurian knight, his rival

> . . . Gawain with his olde curteisye
> Though he were come ageyn out of Fairye,[35]

siting the whole legend firmly in elfland. In the same way we can easily forget that the prosaic Aeneas is the son of Venus. This humanization has led to an important gap in Launcelot's story. Malory totally ignores the legend of his kidnapping and upbringing by the fairy Lady of the Lake, Niniane. It seems impossible that Malory didn't know of the story.[36] As it is, Launcelot has no childhood. He is first mentioned at Arthur's wedding, when Merlin tries to dissuade Arthur from marrying Guinevere by prophesying that Launcelot will be her lover. Then he is seen as "the young Launcelot" by Merlin, at his father's castle, where we learn that his first name is Galahad and his mother's name Elaine. Suddenly he is the greatest warrior and the queen's lover.

Malory's other principal omissions are the end of the Tristram story and the whole episode told by Chretien de Troyes as La Charette, Launcelot's humiliation when he lost his horse and had to ride in a cart. Malory would have liked to have told that story, he says, but he has "lost the very matter." He gives it in resumé as he does the deaths of Tristram and Iseult but in their case there is no lamenta-

---

[35] *Canterbury Tales: The Squire's Tale.*

[36] There's even a probable reference to it at the end of Book IV, Chapter XXVIII, where the damosel of the Lake in love with Sir Pelleas will only ever let him fight on Launcelot's side. Although Malory often sticks very close to the original he is using he does make additions of his own and sometimes conflates two sources. The last book is based both on the French *Mort Artu* and the English *Le Morte Arthur*. See Vinaver, ed. cit.

tion over a lost source. Perhaps he felt that their tragedy might overshadow the final one if told in full and therefore deliberately included it simply among a list of other tragedies.

Whether he knew the story of the fostering of Launcelot or not, the loss of it does concentrate us on Malory's main theme: the fully grown hero-lover. However, the childhood story gives the valuable psychological case-history background that is often called, pejoratively, modern. This is no more than we should expect from a well worked over mythology. It is surely no coincidence either that Launcelot's unwilling and bewitched betrayal of his mistress is with Elaine, who has his mother's name. It's yet another Elaine whose love he won't requite who becomes the tragic Maid of Astolat, as if the mother who had lost him tried constantly to get him back.

For Launcelot is enchanted by Guinevere, who replaces the fairy foster-mother. She keeps about her under her very real humanity many of the attributes of the fairy mistress. She is barren. Both Launcelot and Arthur have children by other women[37] but none by her. Launcelot suffers madness, humiliation and eventually death because of his devotion which, unlike Tristram's, its parallel, never swerves. Because of it too he doesn't completely attain to the vision of the Grail although, as he knows, he would have done so had his thoughts not been always on her. She seems completely unaging and, by any human reckoning of years, must have been considerably older than Launcelot.

By a mirror version of the magicked conception of Arthur, Galahad, the perfect virgin knight, is begotten in order that the reader (and the teller) may take part as hero in the Grail sequence. The perfect knight, secularly speaking, must be outpointed only by his own son (who is Launcelot reincarnate, as Guinevere recognizes the first time she sees Galahad) and given Launcelot's first name. This doubling means that, in our hero-identification, we are able to have the best of both worlds, to die beautifully when the episode is over and yet return to the queen to take up the adultery theme again. No one who has thought about the ambivalence of dreams will be surprised at the

---

[37] Arthur's is simply mentioned by name, Sir Bohart Le Cure Hardy, but a son of Arthur also appears in the Welsh *Culhwch and Olwen*. Modred may also be an incestuously conceived son.

constant uses mythology makes of doubling up in various ways.

The legend of the pursuit of the Grail brings Christianity into a fictional confrontation with Fayrieland. The first impression we have is that the Church, alarmed by the popularity and basic amorality of the romance, has set up a counter Christianized tale. Instead of the pursuit of ladies' favors and renown in their eyes it is God's favor and a heavenly reward that the knights must seek. Malory, treating the story in the fifteenth century, realizes this antithesis, but since his hero is this worldly Launcelot the adventure is kept down to its necessary narrative without the moralizing accretions of other writers. In *Le Morte D'Arthur* Launcelot comes so close to achieving the quest that it's hard to see what difference there is between his vision and those of Galahad, Bors and Percival who succeed in it completely. Afterwards he returns to the queen and "they loved together more hotter than they did beforehand." Yet this doesn't prevent his dead body giving off the odor of sanctity.

The story of the Grail was undoubtedly very popular all over Europe. It's difficult to gauge the Church's attitude to it. Loomis[38] has said that it was regarded as "inauthentic," whatever that may mean, and makes a very good case for it being of Celtic origin. Apart from the Christian details, the various plots connected with it fit in well with the other romance materials and with their Irish and Welsh forerunners. Also against its completely Christian fabrication is the fundamental structure of the story: the search of the hero for some marvel of fertility and healing, which has innumerable versions in Celtic and Teutonic myth and appears in classical legend as the search for the apples of the Hesperides or the golden fleece or even as Prometheus's theft of the fire flowers for men from the fields of heaven. If the Church did object to it, it must surely have been on the grounds that it was fiction where the equally miraculous lives of the saints were presented as fact. It may have been realized that to countenance the Christianizing of an enchanted world was to make very slight the distinction between one mythology and another, almost to admit in fact that there was none and both were works of art.

CHAPTER IV

Folk and The Faery

And see not ye that bonny road
    That winds about the fernie brae?
That is the road to fair Elfland,
    Where thou and I this night must gae.
                Thomas the Rhymer, Anon.

By setting their scene back in a mythical sixth century of Arthur the poets had been able to enchant the whole world. Fairyland is never here and now: it's always at a remove, and if the remove isn't time it must be place. It's a world of forbidden wishes surrounded by a magic wall of taboo which must be broken before we can enter it, which we do almost always seemingly against our will, "carried away" (the phrase is tell tale) as in dreams. Fairy story which isn't distanced by time is the story of traffic between the other world and this. Those who are taken to be lovers of the Fairy King or Queen are unable to resist. Sometimes they can't find the way out; often they are held by eating or drinking enchanted food. They may be won back by the love of a mortal but if they are turned out by the fairies they are likely to pine and die. This fairyland is the one most familiar to us from ballads and stories.

Breaking the Taboo

The moments of taboo-breaking are all moments of lowered resistance: falling asleep, sickness, being out alone and at night. Sometimes danger is unconsciously yet deliberately courted. The reveller coming home takes a short cut through a wood known to be haunted, past a fairy mound or an old barn. True Thomas falls asleep on Huntlie bank (the name suggests a fairy hill), Janet goes to Carterhaugh and pulls the rose, Clerk Colvill although warned goes riding by the wells of Slane, Fair Isabel goes to the wood to gather nuts: all are to get fairy lovers or win back a lover taken by the fairies. In *Sir Orfeo* the fairy castle was populated by those who had died suddenly.

The third main way of breaking the taboo is for the fairy lover to seek out and deceive the human. The best instance of this is the ballad of *The Outlandish Knight*[1] where the lady who tells the story is courted by an obviously irresistible stranger who persuades her to steal her father's best horses and money and ride away with him to a river, where he tries to drown her as he already has six others. In the *Demon Lover* a former love returns and lures the now married woman to leave all and go away in his ship where he drowns her. Both lovers seem at first to be ordinary humans. The demon lover reveals himself to have been demonic all along; the outlandish knight we recognize as otherworldly only by the title and its alternative *Lady Isabel and the Elf Knight*. In both cases the humans are made to break a moral law: Lady Isabel to steal away as well as steal money, the wife to leave husband and children.

Unlike the hero of Marie of France's *Sir Launfal* these humans are likely to be punished for trafficking with the other world. Sometimes the punishment is Christian. Isabel who has seven children in the greenwood by the fairy Hind Etin,[2] is worried that she hasn't been churched and her children christened and so eventually escapes; Tam Lin, beloved of the Fairy Queen, fears he will be murdered as the seven-year tithe the fairies have to pay to hell; Clerk Colvill, like his successor George Collins, dies after intercourse with a water sprite or mermaid.

It could be argued that Christianity was responsible for this attitude to those who had been carried away, but the Christian explanation is very rare. The suggestion is repeatedly, particularly in stories, that those who go with the fairies are never the same again. Like the sister in *Goblin Market* who ate the fairy fruits, they pine away. This could be discounted as a literary invention if it weren't that the idea is so common in tales like *Cherry of Zennor* and the *Fairy Dwelling of Selena Moor* collected by folklorists. The exception is those who are saved by human love. Sir Orfeo saved Herodias even against the

---

[1] Said by the ballad authority Child to have "perhaps the widest circulation." The English collector, Cecil Sharp, himself noted sixty versions.

[2] Etin is from eoten the Anglo-Saxon for a monster or giant.

grain of the original story; Janet saves Tam Lin but Clerk Colvill dies, even though he has a beautiful wife who loves him, because although he gives her rich presents he doesn't really love her and tells her that he will be unfaithful with any woman he fancies. His deliberate Don Juanry causes strong doubts about his sexuality, reinforced by his return to his mother to die.

The attitude behind all these stories is ambivalent. There is both the strong temptation to break the taboo and the fear of punishment if we do. This is because the concept of fayrie is expressing unconscious wishes that are usually kept repressed. If you indulge them, the stories say, you will never be the same again. Yet many ballads and broadsides told tales of adultery, incest and murder quite openly. Why should it be necessary in some cases to cloak them with a fantasy of enchantment?

I think there are two reasons for this: that the dream atmosphere enables us to experience more deeply, because we have initially suspended rationalization, and that the events which on the surface seem to break conventional morality are acting as symbols for the breaking of a deeper taboo, as the adultery situation of knight and lady in the romances was built upon an incestuous mother and son relationship. It should also be remembered that there are always, whatever society's laws or customs, standards of individual permissibility based on each person's psychological make-up. Although I may think it an excellent system that there should be licensed prostitutes who will satisfy the desire of some people for flagellation, I may find the practice personally distasteful and need to satisfy my own sado-masochistic element with stories of knights being bound and beaten in the service of ladies or by listening to Zerlina sing "Batti, batti."

Time

That we are deep in a barely rationalized world of fantasy becomes even clearer in studying time and enchantment. King Herla's experience of finding mortal time has passed him by on his return from the fairy wedding can be endlessly duplicated from ballads and stories. A day in fairyland may be a year or a century in middle-earth. Occasionally the opposite is true and a year in fairyland may be only a human night. As with time so with space. Puck can put a girdle round about the earth in forty minutes. Witches could be transported through the air with or without something to straddle, as could fairies. Castles appeared and vanished again. Substances lacked their true nature; people might sink into the ground or ride into a hill. All normal physical laws are suspended.

There is a familiar state in which this happens to us all: in dreams. Fairyland is the realm of the unconscious, the dreamworld, duplicated in the conscious in childhood and erotic daydreams. Nothing need obstruct the fulfillment of our wish. We can cross seas, fly, invisibly observe, assume different shapes, juggle time as we wish. Yet fayrie is closer to sleeping than to waking dreams for in waking dreams, unless we are specifically masochistic, our dreams end happily and we are constantly successful. In sleep, where our wishes struggle with censorship and guilt, we suffer the same ambivalence that is noticeable in ballads and fairy stories.

Using the convention of enchantment art, and it doesn't matter whether it is folk or sophisticated, allows unconscious material very free expression untrammelled by the apparatus of credibility. The convention supplies, instead, a framework in which the marvelous can happen, and traditional rules which are recognizable as part of everyone's experience.

The Land of Heart's Desire

Fairyland itself provides the mortals with everything they could wish for, particularly in the way of eating and drinking, in which we recognize the child's delight in those two elemental activities. It is like all the mythological European heavens, and its activities are much the same as on earth except that they never pall. Ambivalence also governs our concept of it. It is without real substance and may vanish at any moment. Its gold will become dead leaves and so will its crystal cups and plates. Its food and drink will be bitter or vapid as soon as enchantment is broken.

Those who inhabit it, however, are quite happy. Only the intrusive human is worried by its insubstantiality. The censor warns that it is unreal and that those who spend too much time there, that is in fantasy, will be unable to return successfully to the real world. Sometimes this idea is expressed by the motif that the fairies may steal the real substance from things, leaving them superficially the same but with all the goodness gone.[3]

The most common site for fairyland was underground, which links it firmly with ideas of the Underworld and the lands of the dead. There is no real distinction to be maintained between them, as *Sir Orfeo* and Chaucer made quite clear and as is reinforced by many stories in which those carried away see dead neighbors or sweethearts among the inhabitants. Here the line between ghosts and fairies blurs. It was the Church which made a theological distinction between them. The ghosts of those who were in purgatory were sometimes permitted to walk since their state wasn't fixed. Devils and angels could come and go freely, and all fairy manifestations were the work or presence of demons. Popular mythology, however, saw them all as basically the same, although sometimes attempts would be made to explain the different classes along lines required by, or thought pleasing to, the questioner. Fairies might become angels or devils or ghosts depending on the degree of sophistication of the questionee, the circumstances related and the attitude inherent in them. A fairy tempting Percival is explained as a demon and disappears in a cloud of smoke, as the whole fairy palace disappeared when St. Collen threw holy water over it. Mr. Noy on Selena Moor saw his dead sweetheart among the fairies.[4]

To hanker for the dead is to live in fantasy. As they are seen again in dreams so they are found among the fairies. The psychological danger of refusing emotionally to admit death is obvious. You are indeed bewitched and your everyday life without substance. You may pine and die. As long as you are so obsessed, particularly by a dead love, you cannot follow the life-preserving instincts, including sex with a new partner. At the same time there is often an

[3] e.g. "The Tacksman's Ox," Keightley, *Fairy Mythology*.
[4] Briggs, *Dictionary of British Folk Tales*, Part 8, Vol. 1, p. 225.

inherent fear of the dead and a feeling of guilt towards them. The fairies may appear malignant and capricious although usually the dead love tries to help the lover in escape and rescue. The feelings of guilt and fear are transferred to the lover's captors. The enchantment which binds is death, and the binding leads to impotence in the living, a freezing of the vital forces.

The underground siting recalls not only Hades but the simple fact that the dead are in the ground. Barrows were fairy mounds because they held the dead, and they made a conveniently rational place for a miniature palace to be if the hill was thought of as hollow. Fairies also lived in wells, trees and water generally, on the tops of hills and in connection with standing stones. However, the very common mention of an underground fairyland also indicates a kind of pun made by the unconscious about itself. The fairies are below the earth as they are manifestations of things usually below the conscious level of the mind.

Our custom of putting the dead in the earth connects death with fertility, an idea spiritualized by Christianity in the text of giving up one's life to save it. "Unless a grain of wheat fall into the earth and die . . ." The pagan version is *John Barleycorn*:

> Then they let him lie for a very long time
> Till the rain from heaven did fall
> Then little Sir John sprung up his head
> And soon amazed them all.[5]

The corpse in the barrow is an emblem of the child in the swollen belly and the seed in the earth, all of which, it was hoped, would spring up to life.[6]

The fairies themselves, as the witch-hunters recognized, were bringers of impotence and infertility. A frequent charge against witches was that they had caused impotence and sterility in men, animals and crops. They were often

[5] Text from *The Penguin Book of English Folk Songs* edited by R. Vaughan Williams and A. L. Lloyd.

[6] The reason I think for so many burials in the foetal position among different cultures. Cf. the use of unamh (weem) a cave, in Scotland for an earth-house or souterrain (Chadwick, *The Celts*, p. 126), a version of "womb."

thought to have stolen a penis by making it invisible to its owner. There is a particularly bizarre story in the *Malleus Maleficarum* of a witch who kept a nest of stolen male members in a tree where she fed them on corn and they waved about like serpents. One afflicted owner who was allowed to go and reclaim his tried to take a bigger one instead and was told it belonged to the parish priest.

An offense to the fairies or a neglect of the proper charms would bring poor crops and murrain of cattle. Hens and cows ceased to yield. This was particularly so if the tribute of a bowl of milk and white bread was neglected or food refused, as in a story where a farmer's wife stopped the fairies stealing milk from his best cow by rubbing its udder with stockfish boiled in brine. The cow pined and died.

With one exception, the brownie, which could in the right circumstances be helpful, the fairies, however it might be glossed over, were associated with bad luck that had to be averted. Among themselves they were generally barren though marriage with a human could bring fertility. They often tried to carry off human children as well as adults, in order to replenish the dwindling fairy ranks. They weren't generally subject to sickness but died after a time much longer than a human life span. It was human vitality and strength which they wanted and tried to draw on. When children were born to them they often sent for a village midwife, once again drawing on human life power.[7] Fairy babies were apt to be weakly, ugly and hairy, recognizable quickly when changelings.

This taking strength from the living is of course another link between the fairies and the dead. Any occasion on which they appear benevolent must be seen as a mirror image of their real nature, an attempt to disarm or mask their power and true intentions by presenting them in apparently favorable colors. If fairies are invited to a christening and one is left out, however benevolent the others may be it is the malignant and neglected who will govern the child's fate. We shouldn't be surprised at this or miss

[7] The most extreme and unequivocal statement of this taking of human vitality is in the stories of the Scottish Boabhan Sith, beautiful fairy women who were vampires and sucked the blood of young men while dancing with them.

the overall significance of the malign element, for both dreams and art work obliquely in order to make the unpleasing palatable. The idea of fairies as pretty, gentle playfellows for children is very late.

Fairy activity was always most feared at times of human or agricultural fertility and every attempt was made either to placate them or keep them away. At births and marriages and at the two big festivals of spring and autumn special provisions were made. Sometimes this appears as if the fairies were giving their blessing, conferring fertility as they do at the end of *A Midsummer Night's Dream*, but this again is a mask. What they are really doing is promising not to blight.[8]

The festivals themselves, of which we have the remnants in Mayday and Hallowe'en, were the inheritors of the Celtic Beltane and Samhain. On both occasions the night before was often spent in the woods, bringing in the May or nutting. Fair Isabel had gone nutting when she was taken away by Hind Etin. The nuts were brought home to be roasted on the fire and the future divined from how they jumped. Hallowe'en is the great night for telling the future, particularly in matters of love, the likeness of the husband-to-be being conjured to appear in a mirror. Both festivals were frowned on by the Puritans for their paganness and for their licentiousness. The night in the woods was a time for free love-making[9] closely connected with the waxing and waning of nature's fertility and clearly meant to encourage it, like the birth fires also lit on these festivals.

Nuts are a traditional symbol of the testicles and "nuts" almost as common a name for them as balls.[10] To be out pulling nuts is itself a euphemism. There is another connected with Mayday which is to give a gown of green.

[8] Compare the Greek Eumenides, the avenging deities whose name euphemistically means "the kindly goddesses" with Robin Goodfellow.

[9] ". . . of fourtie, thre score or a hundred maides gaying to the woode over night, there have scarcely the thirde part of them returned home againe undefiled." Stubbs, *Anatomy of Abuses*.

[10] This seems to be the explanation of "the little nut tree" for which "the King of Spain's daughter came to visit me." The first verse is a particularly accurate phallic description. "A bag of nuts to a bride ensures a fruitful marriage." Briggs, *The Fairies in Tradition and Literature*, ed. cit., p. 84.

> Then she became a silken plaid
> And stretched upon a bed,
> And he became a green covering
> And gained her maidenhead.

Many a green gown has been given.[11]

Puritan fulminations were particularly loud against that "stinking idol" the maypole. Whether they recognized it as a great symbolic phallus related to the wooden phalloi found in Denmark[12] or simply objected to it instinctively and as an unspecified "pagan" thing it's hard to say. The plaited streamers we have become used to are a late (c. 1900) innovation by a Bedfordshire schoolteacher out of, it has been said, Ruskin and Whitelands College.

Those who were slow to take part in May festivals were squirted with water or beaten with nettles, both recognized ways of provoking eroticism. In many parts of the country fertility hobby-horses were out bringing "good luck," fecundity, to women who touched them or who were caught under the horses' skirts. They were accompanied by May Queens impersonating the fertility goddess Tacitus had remarked, sometimes in the form of dolls carried in little green arbors, sometimes by the traditional Betsy, the man dressed as a woman of the folk plays and later pantomime, sometimes by the live prettiest girl in the village. The performance of round dances about the pole,[13] with their in and out chorus figure as in Sellengers Round, is a simple but explicit exposition of the sex act. What was being celebrated was the kind of Spring wedding seen in Swedish rock-carvings of two thousand five hundred years ago.

[11] Herrick, *Corinna's Going A-Maying*. See also *The Green Gown* from Tom D'Urfey's *Pills to Purge Melancholy*.

[12] See particularly the illustrations to P. V. Glob, *The Bog People*, ed. cit.

[13] A tuft of green was often left at the top of the pole as a symbolic head. For the internationalism of this knowledge see Rubens's last letter where he congratulates a friend on planting a maypole in his beloved's garden on Mayday, that is on his marriage, and hopes it will bring forth fruit. The young men's bringing love branches to plant before their sweethearts' doors until all the street "became a path between pale green trees" has the same meaning.

The fairies are constantly found in connection with one or other of the basic male and female symbols. I have already mentioned trees and standing stones, wells and barrows but there is also the fairy ring, and the mushroom or toadstool so much a feature of later fairy lore. Because we don't automatically and consciously think of a penis when we look at a tree, we shouldn't conclude (a) that our ancestors didn't or (b) that there is no unconscious recognition. The manifestations of unconscious symbolism should come as no revelation to those who have read Vance Packard's *The Hidden Persuaders* or studied advertising.[14] The traditional "dirty joke" and seaside postcard trade in conscious double entendre with all the zest of but less poetry than Shakespeare; Nelly Wallace brought down the house nightly with her "I sits between the cabbages and peas."

I labor this point because it's often thought that nasty-minded psychologists invented a preoccupation with sex and saw symbols where there were none. Those who are already alert to the concerns of the folk will need no further convincing but for others I include note[15]. One or

[14] Or indeed those who were tormented in the playground by riddles: John has a thing long; Mary has a thing hairy. John puts his thing long into her thing hairy. Or: What is three inches round, six inches long and all women like it? When you had betrayed young reaction to the rise of these unconscious symbols into your conscious you were told you had a dirty mind and that the answers were respectively a broom and a roll of notes. Two of the first known examples of this in English are Riddles 44 and 54 in the Exeter Book, early eleventh century.

[15] A good quick guide to the use of sexual double entendre is the section "Vocational" in *The Common Muse—Popular British Ballad Poetry from the 15th to the 20th Century*, edited by V. de Sola Pinto and A. E. Rodway. Metaphors for the sex act are: to play an instrument, to mend a kettle, to drive a team, to hunt a rabbit, to give a pill, to plough, to sheath a dirk, to mow, to be a miner and go through all the trades. Any form of work in fact can be turned to the purpose. See particularly the Ballad of the Trades.

Until I labor I in labor lie.

In the same way almost anything may be used as a symbol for the male or female sex organs. Which, depends on its most obvious attributes. A bush is female, a tree male; a hammer male, a kettle female, a muff female, a bolt male and so on. That this can be used to charming as well as erotic effect can be seen in the D'Urfey song

two useful points may be made from the appended ballad. The symbol isn't rigidly consistent. At one time the bird is the penis, at another the child begotten by it and finally young lovers of either sex. The mind plays verbally and visually with the symbol, taking pleasure in elaborating it. Often the symbols are erotically suggestive in a general way without being precise.

> The wind it blew high and the wind it blew low
> And it toss'd their milk pails to and fro

suggests the girls' skirts and hips swinging and yet, because of the mention of milk, their breasts too.[16] Only pails have been actually mentioned but the erotic atmosphere is unmistakably created. It's usually a sign of a more sophisti-

---

using rural symbolism that's the conscious counterpart of the folk symbols. It's particularly well sung by Shirley Collins on TOPIC 12T190.

The Bird in the Bush

Three maidens a milking did go
Three maidens a milking did go
And the wind it blew high and the wind it did blow low
And it waved their pails to and fro.

Now they met with some young man they knew
They met with some young man they knew
And they asked of him if he had any skill
In catching a small bird or two.

Yes indeed I've a very fine skill
Indeed I've a very fine skill
And if you'll come along with me to the younder greenwood
I might catch you a small bird or two.

So along to the greenwoods they went
Along to the greenwoods they went
And the bird it flew in and the bird it flew out
Just above her lily white knee.

So here's a health to the bird in the bush
Here's a health to the bird in the bush
For the birds of one feather they should always be together
Let the people say little or much.

[16] Milk pails are specifically breasts in *The Little Fern*; *The Comcon Muse*, No. 172.

cated hand when the symbol means one thing and one only
as in *The Hunt*, the broadside ballad which hasn't been
through the traditionalizing process (*Pills to Purge Melancholy*) where the play is consistently on the pronunciation
of coney as cunny.

> But all my delight is a Cunny in the Night
> When she turns up her silver hair.

Human fertility is closely linked in the imagination with
that of the earth. Examples have been recorded from
America of couples making love in their newly sown fields
to ensure a good crop. The fairies, however, were felt to
interfere with fertility; to be malign. They had to be driven,
kept or swept away from situations where potency might
be endangered. Puck, taking on this function from the
mumming plays, says he has come with broom before, "To
sweep the dust behind the door." All over Europe folk
plays are attended by sweepers who clear the way like the
whifflers who do the same for morris and sword dances.
For all these are fertility rituals and what is being driven
out is anything that will interfere with them.

The fairies are unreal: they are taboo fantasies, they are
the dead, they are phantoms that suck human vitality and
divorce men from their time and the real world. With his
usual superb insight Shakespeare picks the most real of
them, Puck, to become the sweeper. The folk plays are,
like the mating couples, sympathetic magic; enactments of
birth, marriage, death and resurrection. These are the moments of human vulnerability and therefore the fairies
must be swept away.[17] The plays follow very closely the
Iron Age rock-diagrams in Sweden I have mentioned before.

Although this isn't the place for a full-scale study, something must be said about the folk plays and their relation to
fayrie. It's difficult now to know whether there were originally two plays or only one or hundreds of variations
round the same theme. A comparison with the diagrams
suggests only one, which would contain all the elements

[17] See Spence, *British Fairy Origins*, ed. cit., Chap. XI, for anti-
fairy seasonal practices.

but it would be tempting to divide it into two: the Spring wedding at its appropriate season, and the death and resurrection with the dying of the year at All Hallows or Midwinter. In England the elements are sometimes separated, giving rise to the St. George Play, death and resurrection, collected by Richard Johnson in 1596 and printed as *The Seven Champions of Christendom*, and the Plough Play, the most complete example of which is the Revesby Play written down in 1779.

If it were not for those rock-carvings it would be possible to suggest that these plays were the late invention their language seems to imply. We should, however, have to answer the questions why anyone should bother to make them up so late and how they came to be disseminated throughout Europe. The Swedish diagrams push their basic material back to the period of pre-Classical Greece, nor can one imagine them being invented after the reintroduction of Christianity in Anglo-Saxon times. Even supposing that they were brought to this country by the Teutonic invasion that still gives us nearly fifteen hundred years of survival.

The folk plays, with their sweeping out of evil and their connection with seasons of great anti-fairy activity, enable us to put back the date of fairy presence in this country. They also make an oblique comment on the theory that the folk fairies are degenerate gods. This is most often put forward in connection with Ireland where it's popularly believed that the Tuatha De Danaan, last of the Celtic pantheons, retreated after their final defeat into the mounds, dwindling in size to become the Sidhe,[18] the Irish fairies. Yet the Irish fairies are essentially, and in detail, the same as those of all the other British regions which in their turn are like those of other European nations, particularly the Teutonic. In Ireland the May rites are performed, though the dancing is around a bush, not a pole, on a mound which suggests the celebration of the female principle. The fairies are thought particularly active, stealing girls away with their music, and precautions are taken against them. Since the rites are essentially the same in England, which has no fallen Celtic pantheon, and are

[18] J. F. S. Wilde, *Ancient Legends of Ireland*.

known from the early Swedish rock-carvings, the folk fairies would seem to be autonomous and quite separate and the attempt to explain them as fallen gods a later rationalization like that, also recorded by Lady Wilde, which says they are fallen angels.

If the plays are as early as they would seem to be in their dramatic core they have survived a complete mutation of language and idiom. It's generally accepted for instance that ballads couldn't have been composed before the twelfth century since rhyme, stanza-form and even the language itself in which they are couched didn't exist before then. The same could be said of the folk plays, yet they do exist, although obviously transmuted and no longer even understood by the participants. It's wise when dealing with oral tradition to make great allowance for the continual transmission of material, ideas and structures, even sometimes against reason, and for the almost incredible age of much of it. Nor should we be led by the lateness of the most recent manifestations, Barrie packing the theaters with *Mary Rose* and *Peter Pan* or Andrew Lang's colored fairy books and Enid Blyton's little people, into thinking that it must all be a recent invention or that one mythological system is necessarily ousted by, or a degenerate form of, another. In Ireland, to take the richest proliferation, Celtic mythology, Christianity, fertility cults and folk-fairy systems all flourished side by side, interacting on each other and providing an infinite range of artistic, emotional and imaginative expression.

Pastimes

> Though Amaryllis dance in greene
> Like fayrie queene.

The fairies, except the brownies, rarely worked. If they were forced to they cobbled, as the Welsh Manawyddan had done when Dyfed was laid waste, or were smiths like Wayland. Usually their time was spent between hunting and dancing. Yet although there are many references to their ride there is very little to the catch, for their real prey was human beings. The riding and jingling are for display, to lure and fright, and the wild hallooing through stormy nights is to snatch up the dying like the Valkyries.

Most of all they danced, and the references to this are so many that they couldn't be stacked from end to end of the British Isles. Dancing is the most primitive and common form of communal eroticism. The first act of the bishop of Iceland on converting the country at the beginning of the twelfth century was to forbid the dancing and singing of ballads that passed the long winter evenings. The earliest dances were either round or in a long chain. The fairies' dance, as we know from the fairy rings they footed, was a round. The tradition of this continued even when it was no longer consciously remembered that round dances are usually round something, that stinking idol the maypole or the single cromlech which was the same thing, and had become as harmless as ring-a-roses was thought to be.

Often the fairies' dancing had an hypnotic effect; the mortal was unable to resist or tear himself away, possibly while years passed in what seemed a single night. The fairies were particularly fond of humans who could themselves play, harpers and minstrels like Thomas the Rhymer, partly because such people might be more imaginative but also because to play a musical instrument is a metaphor for masturbation as hunting is for sexual pursuit. Sometimes they taught tunes and instruments to the mortals they caught, which is a way of presenting in a mythological, and therefore artistic form, pleasurable masturbating while under an obsessive fantasy. The fairy time is of course night while we lie in our beds and are carried away by the piping and dance.

CHAPTER V

Dramatis Personae

The king o' fairy with his rout
Come to hunt him all about
With dim cry and blowing
And hounds also with him barking.
                    Sir Orfeo, c. 1300

The ambivalence which we feel towards the dead isn't reserved for them. It's found in our attitudes to other things and people. We are deeply shocked when a dream reveals our resentment or fear of our children or lovers or a desire for someone we hate. We are ambivalent even towards ourselves. This double attitude springs from the baby's relation to its parents, alternately loving and resentful, wanting warmth, food and security, frustrated, angry and fearful when it doesn't get them, jealous of father, siblings and anything else that may claim mother's attention, made guilty by its own fierce reactions.

Since mythologies are the expression of fundamental human conflicts and desires it's not surprising that this ambivalence should be reflected in them and in a historically recurring tendency to explain life in Manichean terms. Fayrie is no exception. What is recognizably the same character appears in manifestations of light and dark, beautiful and ugly, enchanting and terrifying. The Fairy Queen is balanced by the witch; the Fairy King by the devil; elves have their counterpart in demons, brownies in bogies. Our own attitude to what we have invented governs its nature. The most striking example of this is in the evidence from witchcraft trials and the *Malleus Maleficarum*. To the Inquisitors who knew, as Freud knew, "that natural desire which is aroused even in babes and sucklings,"[1] the Good People, as the fairies were often called, were witches and devils; fauns were incubi. In the Scottish witch trials in particular, dealings with fairies figure repeatedly as evidence of guilt. Like Chaucer they had realized that there is no basic difference between mytholo-

[1] *Malleus Maleficarum*, ed. cit., Part II, Question 1, p. 93.

gies, simply regional and temporal variation on the same themes.

The Coarse and Country Fairy

Under whatever name he is hidden, gruagach, urisk, boggart, fynoderee, hobgoblin, Robin Goodfellow, bwbach, dobie, puck, Lob-lie-by-the-Fire, Hob, the commonest fairy is the brownie, a word now irretrievably bowdlerized for us by its association with junior girl guides who presumably adopted it as signifying something small and mischievous and skilfully sidestepped its two most usual characteristics of hairiness and maleness.[2] I shall call him by his most distinguished literary name: Puck, which has an Irish variant, Pooken or Phooka, and a Welsh, Pwcca.

Puck is the English lar, the domestic spirit beloved of the Romans, each of which had one family under its protection and whose shrine was the hearth. Once the prototype has been invented it will accrete stories, variations and sometimes characteristics that attempt to disguise its unconscious origin. This will be particularly true if it offends current taboos. It may take a sudden leap down what seems to the folklorist an entirely false path. The Victorian fairy image is often spoken of as a degeneration. This is to misunderstand the constant changes that a vital concept undergoes, and must undergo, as it adapts itself to the emotional needs of each period. Arthur and his fayrie world are not degraded Celtic gods but recreations out of the body of mythology in their own right. Mythology itself has a legend for it: Venus, goddess of re-creation, born of a severed male member. Proving Puck's kinship doesn't mean a line of descent nor should it suggest the influence of one culture on another. A mythological symbol exists in two ways at once: as a spontaneous projection in answer to a need, and historically as part of a system with traceable

---

[2] I'm aware that there are rare examples of a female brownie, Maug Moulach, the Hairy Meg of the Grants for example, but they are rare and, I suspect, late, and don't affect the argument. Perhaps the Brownie idea was of helpfulness rather than mischief. Apparently it originated in the story *The Brownies* by Mrs. Ewing.

antecedents; that is as a symbol, as the metaphor which expresses it and as the reality that lies behind them both.

The characteristics of Puck are that he is hairy, inclines to brown or red in color and may have goat's feet that link him with the satyrs and fauns. He is able to change shape, although he is usually a bit less than human size. He leads travellers astray, plays tricks, particularly on women, but if a girl sets a bowl of milk for him he will come and labor for her at night, particularly in the churn to make her butter. He is naked and can be driven away by being given clothing. Sometimes he will labor for the farmer.

"Robin goodfellow, he that sweepes the harth, and the house cleane, riddles for the countrey maides, and does all other drudgerie, while they are at hot-cocles."[3]

Any form of work by folk tradition is a metaphor for the sex act. To labor in a milkmaid's churn or to sweep her hearth with a phallic broom need little glossing and to riddle is to shake, in the specific sense of shaking the ash and cinders in a sieve so that the bigger pieces are separated and kept for the next fire. The girl set a bowl of milk by the hearth and lay upstairs in bed imagining a naked hairy man working in her churn. "Hot cockles" was a variant of a game still played by children but also a synonym for female masturbation; cockles because of their resemblance being a term for the labia minora and clitoris.[4] The offering of a bowl of milk is, like Eve's apple, the offering of a breast.

Puck's physical appearance is unmistakably that of the phallus which he is. He has the redness of tumescence, the hairiness of pubic hair,[5] the ability to change shape as a penis does in tumefying and de-tumefying and he is naked. Perhaps the wittiest unconscious touch is that he is dismissed by covering him up. His pranks ware also symbolic: leading astray, causing a fall ("sometimes in likeness of a three-legg'd stool"), spilling liquid, making mischief.

In some stories he is glad to be dismissed by the gift of clothes; in others he goes off in anger: a projection of

[3] Ben Jonson, *Love Restored*.
[4] Partridge, *A Dictionary of Slang*. The most common word for a penis used by mothers to small boys and among schoolboys is winkle. But then the sea-bed is prolific in imagery.
[5] See p. 105 for a continuation of this point.

human ambivalence on the subject. This also appears in the double tradition that sometimes makes him pleased by cleanliness, sometimes angered. The meaning here is that girls who lie abed masturbating or having erotic fantasies are "dirty," in the sense of a "dirty joke," or "foul sluts." The pinching black and blue is related to lovers' pinches but is also a punishment for "dirtiness."

In common with other incarnations of the phallus, cupid, the clown, the satyr, Puck has the mischievous prankish temperament, "into everything and always up to tricks" as the idiom would so rightly put it. It's his phallic nature of cheerful uncaring sexuality that makes him different from the Fairy King and Queen and links him very closely with the European carnival fools and the fool of the English sword dance. Where the folk play has been lost, tradition has preserved the two most important ingredients: the phallus-fool and the mother-Betsy. It was the unconscious recognition of his true nature that made the Church identify him with the incubus.[6]

He has even more distinguished kin.

> He seemed generally small and insignificant, yet, when he was at his full strength, no one could look him in the face without blinking, while the heat of his constitution melted snow for thirty feet all round him. He turned red and hissed as he dipped his body into its bath—the sea. Terrible was his transformation when sorely oppressed by his enemies . . . At such times . . . "His hair became tangled about his head, as it had been branches of a thornbush stuffed into a strongly-fenced gap . . . Taller, thicker, more rigid, longer than mast of a great ship was the perpendicular jet of dusky blood which out of his scalp's very central point shot upwards."

This is a description of the great Irish hero Cuchulain. When he was seven the women of Ulster all loved him so

[6] Etymologically Puck is cognate with fuck through "poken"—to thrust, poke, and "foutre"—to thrust, Fr. from Lat. "futuo"—to have connection. It's correlated too with "fodio" Lat. to dig; poke; Greek Φύτωρ, a father>pater. Pwyll, the Welsh god who would be pronounced in English "pook" is another form. In Swedish "pocker" is the devil.

much that the warriors demanded a wife for him. He too is an obvious phallus and his adventures reinforce this repeatedly. When he dies he does so strapped to a pillar to keep him upright. Confused still by the very real discoveries of the early folklorists who, having laid bare one layer in the formation of mythology, saw everything in its terms, Cuchulain's characteristics and those of other similar figures are usually called "solar attributes." It was thought that sun worship and personification lay behind them.

The identification of the phallus with the sun is a simple extension of the human situation into the natural world. Light fell on mother earth causing her to bring forth fruit. Apollo himself with his bow like Cupid, his association with phallic animal symbols as the dolphin, the mouse (Smintheus), and as Sauroctonos, slayer of dragons and serpents, is easily recognizable. It led to his becoming the cult image of Greek homosexuality with its glorification of the penis as the young male body. "Solar attributes" are simply phallic characteristics translated into natural imagery.[7]

> "Sprinkle a plenty salt on the biscuit, Dan, and I'll eat it with you. That'll show you the sort of person *I* am. Some of us"—he went on, with his mouth full—"couldn't abide Salt, or Horse-shoes over a door, or Mountain-ash berries, or Running Water, or Cold Iron, or the sound of Church Bells. But I'm Puck!"[8]

Kipling's Puck carries on the tradition of realness but there are other phallic images, his lesser brethren, which are more abstracted, further removed from reality. These are the elves, gnomes, pixies, redcaps and the Cornish knockers that live in the mines. Physical descriptions of them usually suggest diminutive Pucks. Their clothing often includes the tell-tale red cap, especially common in Ireland. Many of them are malign. The taboo element is very strong among them for they represent the penis as a barren

---

[7] Compare the Egyptian amulet made from red stone representing the rising sun and the circumcised phallus of Ra.

[8] Rudyard Kipling, *Puck of Pook's Hill* (Macmillan, 1961), p. 9. First published 1906.

fantasy whereas Puck is closely allied to his fertility kin. The Elizabethan writers were aware of this fairy manifestation.

Ioculo: I pray you, you prettie little fellow, whats your name?

3 Fay: My name is little, little Pricke.

Ioculo: Little, little Pricke? O you are a dangerous Fayrie, and fright all little wenches in the country out of their beds. I care not whose hand I were in, so I were out of yours.

3 Fay: When I feele a girl asleepe
Underneath her frock I peepe.
There to sport, and there I playe,
Then I byte her like a flea;
And about I skip.

Ioculo: I, I thought where I should have you.[9]

The creeping into flowers and acorn cups is again a sexual symbol, reinforced by the idea of bees and insects fertilizing flowers, and apparent in our euphemism of "the birds and the bees." When the tulip, most female of blossoms as a cup, most male in its shape, was introduced into England in 1578 it rapidly became the favorite floral haunt of the fairies.

In Scotland there is a form of Puck called the Billy Blind. Billy I take to be a form of Beli, one of the earliest British gods. The "Blind" is because, like Cupid, he wears a bandage over his eyes. He is attached to a family as one might say the household cat, and in ballads is particularly concerned with seeing that matrimonial affairs go well for the girls. His advice cures a young wife in labor bewitched by her mother-in-law. He helps Burd Isobel gain young Beckie.[10] This is the benevolent phallus ensuring fertility. The blindness, symbolized by the bandage, is because the penis is often thought of as blind because it finds its way by touch in the dark. For the same reason one of its most common manifestations is the mole, "The waery wanton

---

[9] *The Maydes Metamorphosis*, Act II, in *A Collection of Old Plays*, A. H. Bullen (1882), Vol. 1.

[10] *The Oxford Book of Ballads*, ed. Kinsley, No. 31.

mowdiewark," which has the added attributes of burrowing and raising pregnant molehills.[11]

The phallus appears in so many different forms in folk lore partly because of the variety of human attitudes to it. When it is thought of as the fertility bringer it will be real and friendly to humans. When it involves fear and guilt in forbidden or infertile fantasy it will be malevolent, murderous like the redcaps who have to re-dip their caps in human blood (a rape or deflowering suggestion), ugly or unnatural. Tom Thumb[12] is a charming little creature particularly favored by the ladies. A fair slim naked little pixy helped a young woman who had married a drunkard and had to put on his clothes and go to work threshing in his place. Every morning she found twice as much done as she had left the night before. Finally in gratitude she made him a shirt which he put on in delight, capering and singing. Then he ran out of the barn and was never seen again.[13] The consistency of the unconscious symbolism in this story is breathtaking.

The English version of Rumpelstiltskin, Tom Tit Tot, gives us an evil little black thing with a long tail which is finally banished by guessing its name. In both English and German versions the girl is married to the king by a boastful parent and required to spin. In return for its services the English impet wants the girl for ever, the gnome-like Rumpelstiltskin wants her child. The penalty for not spinning in both cases is death. These seem to be stories about guilty masturbation fantasies interfering with the reality of married sex and threatening fertility.

A similar idea, incarnate in the ballad of *The Great Silkie*, leads us to the seal people. Seals, because of their very human faces and ways, have become inhabitants of fairyland. They mated with humans, the seal assuming human form by casting its skin. Sometimes troops of them came up on the shore to dance. If you could seize the sloughed pelt of a female it would be unable to return to

---

[11] Ewan McColl, *The Wanton Muse.*

[12] The use of some form of Thomas as a name for the penis (Tom Tit Tot, Tam Lin, Tomalin, Tom Thumb, John Thomas) must have some explanation. Doubting Thomas is the only one that suggests itself at the moment. T. Thumb is Oberon's drummer in 1639.

[13] Bray, *Borders of the Tanor and Tavy.*

the sea. However, the skin must be kept hidden for if it were found the seal wife would slip it on and go back leaving her mortal husband and children. Matthew Arnold's *Forsaken Merman* suffered the reverse of this experience.

In the parallel version of the story, where the seal is male, the skin isn't hidden. The seal is a natural shape-changer:

> I am a man upon the land;
> I am a silky in the sea.

He isn't beautiful but "grimly." He gets the girl with child and when it is born returns to pay her and take his son away.

> And you shall marry a gunner good,
> And a very fine gunner I'm sure he'll be,
> And the very first shot that ever he shoots
> Shall slay both my young son and me.

The relationship with the seal husband is a pre-marriage fantasy which will be dispelled by the first experience of real sex. The gun is the husband's penis.[14] The seal itself is of course a phallic shape. K. M. Briggs in her *The Fairies in Tradition and Literature* tells a modern (1959) variant in which a woman determined to bathe alone at night from a Scottish island and watch the seals was puffed in the face by a big dog seal and nearly pressed to death by the others.[15] She had prepared herself for the experience by passing a place she had been told not to go near after dark by the local people because of its fairy connections and she felt herself followed by the pattering of small footsteps. Yet she continued with her bathe. The real meaning of such stories is often betrayed by an important detail; in the modern story by the dog seal puffing in her face, in the ballad by the one shot that will destroy "both my young son and me."

[14] Compare *Andrew and his Cutty Gun.*
[15] Briggs, *The Fairies in Tradition and Literature*, ed. cit., p. 43.

Changelings

"The thing that everyone knows about the fairies is that they covet human children and steal them whenever they can."[16] On the face of it this seems a most extraordinary idea to have invented to terrorize ourselves with, yet looked at more closely it becomes just the opposite. "Substitutions of children are, with God's permission, possible, so that the devil can effect a change of the child or even a transformation. For such children are always miserable and crying; and although four or five mothers could hardly supply enough milk for them, they never grow fat, yet are heavy beyond the ordinary,"[17] say the authors of the *Malleus Maleficarum*. Sometimes the human child's place is taken by an old fairy, sometimes by a fairy baby which needs human nourishment, sometimes by a stock, a piece of wood shaped like the baby and temporarily animated. Unchristened children are particularly vulnerable.

Occasionally instead of the child it was the nursing mother who was carried off to suckle fairy children or the children were brought to her. There are several stories of such attempts being thwarted but there are many others of the substitute baby being exposed on a dry heap or put in the fire, one of the tests for a changeling. Another was the boiling of water or brewing of ale in an eggshell, when the wizened creature would give itself away by saying: "I am old, old, but never did I see ale brewed in an eggshell." In some stories the human child is brought back or won back by its parents. Lady Wilde has some particularly good changeling stories.

By Elizabethan times the changeling idea had become very popular, perhaps as a reflection of the witch craze but also as part of the period's preoccupation with evil and its motivations. Middleton and Rowley's play of that name isn't really about changelings at all. There is a mock one, Antonio, a man who has disguised himself as an idiot to seduce the asylum-keeper's wife, and the black and vicious

---

[16] Ibid., p. 115.
[17] *Malleus Maleficarum*, Part II, Question 1, Chap. 3.

De Flores who is physically repulsive yet finally irresistible, a murderer and entirely without moral qualms. He embodies the theory of the *Malleus Maleficarum* that inordinate love is devilish and the work of enchantment.

In the matter of changelings the fairies, whether as themselves, witches or devils, bring impotence. The concept of the changeling with all its superstructure of tales is based on procreational guilt. If your child is an imbecile, born dead or deformed or merely ugly, your unconscious will tell you it is your fault. Again the *Malleus* is illuminating: "For God permits this on account of the sins of the parents, in that sometimes men curse their pregnant wives, saying, May you be carrying a devil! or some such thing. In the same way impatient women often say something of the sort."[18] Guilt may take various forms: there was the moment when you didn't want the child, hated its father, thought longingly of an old lover, were tired and spoke harshly, resented its effect on you, and so on. On the man's side all the same guilts may apply in reverse. Then there are the fears of transmitting disease, and old guilts of hated siblings and parents from one's own childhood. The deformed child is all these made manifest.

The first reaction is to disclaim it and with it all that it stands for. It's not mine. This is a substitute for my own beautiful (in all the stories the stolen humans are beautiful) baby. If I throw it in the fire in terror and disgust, it isn't my child I murder but a wooden stock or a fairy which can't die anyway but will fly away up the chimney with a shriek. If the child is born dead, it isn't that I have killed it by not wanting it but that the fairies have stolen it. Such an explanation could also be used to explain the product of adultery where the child was unlike the husband, its presumed father.

From the adult changeling's point of view the idea was just as useful. If I'm not like my parents it's because they're not really my parents; either I'm a fairy or I was taken by the fairies and my parents got me back but I've always been a little different because of it. If I'm not really theirs I need have no filial feeling for them nor feel guilt towards them. On the other hand incestuous feelings aren't guilty

[18] *Malleus Maleficarum*, Part II, Question 1, Chap. 3.

because they're not my real parents nor are my siblings blood relations. If I don't look like my father it's not that I'm a bastard and my mother a whore. The common modern counterpart of this fantasy is the "I'm adopted" one which children often have about themselves, or each other, or, in country districts, that a child is a gipsy or has gipsy blood, the gipsies having inherited many of the fairy traits in the popular imagination: child-stealing and licentiousness chief among them.[19]

Mothers who died from puerperal fever or other postnatal complications were not dead but taken to suckle fairy children: a thought as comforting as that they were in heaven but with the added advantage that they might return. This was a safety valve for the elements of guilt and antagonism in the bereaved husband who may well have been angry about the pregnancy, for any of the dozens of practical and emotional reasons, and at being left with a baby to bring up. The guilt was offloaded onto the fairies whose fault it was.

They were connected with infertility again if the mother's milk was inadequate in quantity or quality. It wasn't that she was a bad mother (lack of milk was thought a sign of shrewishness or unfemininity) but that her milk had been taken from her. Similarly a farmer whose crops had failed or whose cattle had sickened would find a scapegoat in the Good People. The failure in quality is also recorded of food and drink from which the fairies may consume the goodness or foison leaving it to outward semblance the same, a useful ratiocination for explaining both why some people, no matter what they ate, got no benefit from it and why food put out for the fairies didn't seem to be eaten.

King and Queen

The Fairy Queen doesn't change her appearance or her meaning, although she may be sometimes simply a fairy woman or wife rather than specifically royal. Morgan La Fee, Sir Launfal's lady, the queen who carried Tam Lin off

[19] D. H. Lawrence's *The Virgin and the Gipsy* and the various versions of the folksong *The Raggle Taggle Gipsies* for example.

from his human sweetheart Janet, the fairy brides of later tradition, are all beautiful, idealized and forbidden mother-figures, like the queens of fayrie romances. Unions with them are usually infertile. They may, after intercourse, become old and ugly, as in the romance *Thomas of Ercildoune*, or they may be so beforehand or, like Morgan herself, alternate between youth and age or even be split into the old and the young lady of *Sir Gawain and the Green Knight*. The folk fertility manifestation has the same ability. The old woman with the baby and the Spring bride are the same. In Spain they even appear as one, with the girl mounted on the older woman's back.[20]

Usually the Fairy Queen provides for her lovers food and clothing as a mother would. Their carrying off is often attended with conditions symbolic of the breaking of a taboo, "They rode through red blood to the knee," or the enjoining of strict secrecy, and when returned home they often pine away for the unattainable.

Just as common, and in Ireland possibly even more so, are the mortal lovers of the Fairy King. If the queen is a tabooed mother-figure it's to be suspected that the king is the father.[21]

"We are their parents and original," says Titania, attributing all the evils of man, beasts, crops and seasons confounded to the quarrel between herself and Oberon. Quarrelling parents bring just such blights on a child's life. In the romances fairy liaisons are far more kindly treated and they are capable of a happy ending. This is made possible by the guise of fiction and the convention that it was all happening in Arthur's time.[22] In later stories both the Church and the unconscious forbid such relationships because they are much closer to reality and are believed as fact. As with the queen, the fairy man enjoins secrecy and girls deserted by fairy lovers often pine and die.

[20] Violet Alford, *Sword Dance and Drama*, ed. cit., p. 184.
[21] I have never myself heard of an actual case of carried out mother-son incest but I have several of father-daughter. I'm inclined to think the taboo is weaker in the second case though it's obviously something rather difficult to gather statistics on.
[22] This is a clever double entendre the mind makes where an oedipal situation is involved for Arthur's time is necessarily ancestral, that is parental, time.

The story of Cherry of Zennor is a very full account of a Fairy King fantasy with an obvious father orientation. Cherry was hired by a handsome master who took her through a stream, down a dark narrow lane and through a gate in a high wall into a garden where fruit and flowers grew together. A cross old woman, Aunt Prudence, and a little boy came to meet her. Aunt Prudence showed her the ways of the house and left. Cherry was very happy. Every day she had to put ointment on the little boy's eyes. One day she got some in her own eyes which burned so much that she ran to the well to wash them, and there at the bottom she saw her master in tiny shape dancing and being very friendly with diminutive ladies. Presently he joined her in his usual size and they went to weed the garden. At the end of the row he kissed her as he always did but she burst into tears and told him to go and kiss his little midget at the bottom of the well. When he realized that she had been playing with the ointment he said sadly that she must go, and took her to the gate. For the rest of her life she pined and wandered the Downs looking for him and the beautiful garden.[23]

To be hired by a master is to enter into a daughter/father relationship and the journey to the garden is a taboo-breaking as specific as Gugemar's to the forest or True Thomas's to the garden green. The garden is the Land of Heart's Delight, Eden, the mediaeval garden of love: childhood's security and plenty. Aunt Prudence is the cross mother whom Cherry supplants in her master-father's life. By the inversion of dreams, she sees him small whereas it's really the daughter who is too young, or small, for the father. She is jealous. Her eyes are opened and she is banished. For the eyes to be opened is an unconscious metaphor for to understand. She can never have him. He will be at the bottom of her sexuality with people of his own size, that is age. Even to begin to understand is fatal. She can only be with him in the nonunderstanding innocence of childhood.

The pining away which is a repeated feature is the unconscious issuing its warning that childhood fixations mean a sterile life of fantasy. The girls sent back by the Irish

[23] Hunt, *Popular Romances of the West of England*, pp. 102–6.

Fairy King, Finvarra, after seven years as his mistresses, became wise women, spinsters skilled in magic and herbs, set apart from real, that is sexual, life. Humans who grew sickly or quiet or wouldn't take part were thought to be having secret dealings with the fairies or to have had their blood sucked by them, particularly if they were consumptive. Often the punishment for seeing the fairies, or understanding, was to be blinded, and blinding, as in the Oedipus legend, is a form of castration. Usually this was in one eye only; a partial understanding producing only a partial paralysis.

Giants, Dragons, Mermaids

The personae of any mythology divide roughly into the humanoid and the monstrous. The fairy world is no exception. As with the changeling, one is forced to wonder why the human mind should bring forth such terrors like Titans sprung from the blood of the dead father. They are the terrors of childhood produced by that time's fervid and irrational imagination, and the explanation of them is there. Giants and dragons were usually horrific until the nineteenth century, mermaids until Andersen identified himself with one.

The first thing about giants is obviously their size. They are as large to a fully grown human as it is to a baby. They have to be looked up to. They are usually cannibals and often rapists. The story which gives the best clue to their real nature is that of Culhwch and Olwen. The girl must be won from her father, the giant Isbaddon, at the cost of his life. Finn McCool, himself a giant in stature, tried to take a young wife in his old age, Grainne, who immediately fell in love with one of his young warriors, Diarmatt, and forced him to run away with her. Diarmatt pleaded that he couldn't be false to his chief and leader, but she was adamant. These two traditions show the giant as the old fierce father, the cannibal who devours his sons in order that they shan't supplant him. This is the meaning of the frequent cannibalism of giants. The giant must be conquered by the boy Jack. In order to win a bride the hero must overthrow the father, supplant him and destroy his sexual monopoly. In the Irish story the ego preserves itself from guilt by making it the woman who takes the initiative. The Diarmatt story with its homosexual fraternity, the Fianna, devoted to Finn, is full of psychological subtlety. In the end Finn kills Diarmatt. The guilt and the longing for the father are too much for the ego and the son must die.

By the process of taking a part, the most terrifying and yet envied part, for the whole, the father's penis is sometimes itself the giant, described unmistakably as one-eyed and one-footed. The eye was sometimes so baleful that its look brought destruction and it had to be covered by a foreskin eyelid.

In the Arthurian cycle an important story which lasts from Geoffrey of Monmouth to Malory is Arthur's destruction of a giant on his first landing in Gaul before he conquers the Romans and is made emperor. It's after this that he becomes a father to his people; for the son, by replacing the father, becomes a father in his turn and at the mercy of his son. This giant has carried off a maiden and raped her "and hath slit her unto the navel" in forcing her. Then he has taken her old serving woman, who is better able to accommodate him. He is also a cannibal: "he sat at supper gnawing on a limb of a man, baking his broad limbs by the fire, and breechless, and three fair damosels turning three broaches whereon were broached twelve young children late born, like young birds."[24] Fee, fi, fo, fum. The giant snatches up his club (the giveaway traditional weapon for giants) but drops it when Arthur cuts off his genitals. (Arthur has asked him to dress himself, reminding us of the taboo about looking on one's father's nakedness familiar in the story of the drunkenness of Noah.)

In later traditions giants are worsted not by brute strength but by subtlety. The animus is still there and the basic plot of the little one getting the better of the big, but the giant has become stupid in many of the euhemerizing stories that explain natural features like the Wansdyke, Wenlock Edge and the Giant's Causeway. Local giants are sometimes represented as kindly figures helping the natives but clearly this needn't affect their paternal status.

[24] Malory, *Le Morte D'Arthur*, ed. cit., Book V, Chap. V.

The taking of a part, and that the same part, for the whole, has brought forth the dragon. Like giants, dragons frequently carry off and guard maidens: Andromeda, and St. George's nameless piece of "doomed dragon's food." They also ravage and lay waste the countryside, causing the folklorists to think of them as winter, partly, or perhaps even largely, because they come out with the mummers in seasonal rites. However, the seasonal slaying by St. George of a dragon is another metaphor for the slaying of the old man by his sons in the sword dance. The emotional situation is seen reflected in the universal and is given artistic expression in symbol, rite and drama.

> I fought the dragon and put him to the slaughter
> And for that won the King of Egypt's daughter.

The prize for destroying or castrating the father is the female and thus renewed fertility for men and crops, since the aged and infertile old king has continued to govern the food supply and the females, and without the sympathetic magic of human fertility and mating nature will itself become infertile. The penis-dragon must be cut down, as Cronos hacked off his father's penis with a sickle and threw it into the sea, only to become in his turn the cannibalistic old tyrant whom Zeus had to destroy.

Dragons who in Teutonic legends guarded barrows with treasure in them, like Beowulf's last adversary, are of the same company. Perhaps Beowulf died in defeating it because he was himself too old to take over the fertility function. The venom and fire which they breathe out are the equivalent of the giant's evil glance.[25] In the story of the Lambton Worm which appropriately was thrown into a well[26] to grow and at last came out to lay waste, it was the young heir who had to kill it.

Both by tradition and modern dream interpretation the serpent, of which the dragon is a sub-division, is acknowledged as *the* phallic animal; the shape of temptation to Eve, the ram-headed serpent on the Gundestrup bowl that

---

[25] One legend combines both the giant's eye and the dragon: the cockatrice, the small potent serpent self-engendered by an old cock and hatched on a dunghill by a toad. Its eye shot forth a fatal venom.

[26] Sir Bevis in fighting his dragon leapt repeatedly into a well from which he emerged whole to fight again.

Cernunnus[27] is about to thrust into a ring, the beast "more subject to magic spells than are other animals" as the *Malleus* puts it, linking it with the penis. To be turned into a worm was a fate directly connected with a sexual situation. In the ballad of *Alison Gross*[28] the young man refuses to kiss an ugly old witch who wants him for her lover, and becomes an "ugly worm" by a kind of magical making the punishment fit the crime. He's eventually rescued by the Fairy Queen who takes him up in her milk-white hand and strokes him three times across her knee. The witch and the Fairy Queen are both the mother seen under different aspects so it's not surprising that the one can take off the other's enchantment.

This ballad is closely related to another, *The Laily Worm and the Machrel.*[29] In this the change is worked by a jealous stepmother and affects brother and sister, who become a serpent and a mackerel. This time the father effects the rescue but the daughter refuses to regain her own shape, saying that the stepmother has

> . . . shapeit me once an unseemly shape,
> An' ye's never mare shape me.

So close are the two ballads in one part, where the sister, called Maisry in both, comes on Saturday to comb her brother's hair, that one must suspect borrowing or conflation. It seems most likely that a bit of *The Laily Worm* has been adopted into *Alison Gross*, which really has no place for a sister. It may be objected that serpents don't have hair to comb, and this of course is one of the tell-tale details by which the unconscious reveals what it's about. Like Puck's hairiness this is pubic hair.[30]

[27] Is there perhaps a connection between Cernunnus and the phallic giant of Cerne Abbas. Neither the explanation by Ekwall in the *Oxford Dictionary of Place Names* ("possibly from Char, Charn, a derivative of Welsh carn, rock or stones") nor the local story of St. Augustine seems the last word. Nor does the official version of Hercules because of the club.

[28] *Oxford Book of Ballads*, ed. Kinsley, No. 14.

[29] Ibid., No. 16.

[30] Pope of course used this as the basis for *The Rape of The Lock* (see B. Brophy, *Mozart the Dramatist*, Faber & Faber, 1964, p. 90) as did the unknown author of *The Curling of The Hair* (*The Common Muse*, ed. cit., p. 212).

The wicked stepmother of fairy story, of *Snow White* and of *Kate Crackernuts* is well known to ballads. The sexual intricacies of a second marriage where there were already children of the first put a strain on tight-knit family groupings and produced this stock figure like that later one, the mother-in-law of countless jokes. In *Kempion*[31] the girl has been turned into a fiery monster and can only be reclaimed by three kisses of her "ain true love." There are many things left unexplained in this story. Why, if the girl already had a sweetheart, did the stepmother hate her? There's no suggestion that the stepmother wanted Kempion for herself. Yet the girl's behavior to Kempion when he comes to release her, even granted that she's some kind of firedrake, is very cool and concerned only with her own plight. The disenchanting by three kisses suggests that she is another victim of a taboo fantasy, probably an incestuous one and her symbolic going away and coming back between each kiss, "Awa' she gid an' again she came," the breaking of a virginity. The daughter's refusal to resume her own shape (in *The Laily Worm*) probably has the same cause. She cannot have her father and there is no lover for her. Her brother, whose enchantment suggests the same root, since he has taken revenge on his father by killing other men:

> Seven knights hae I slain
> Sin' I lay at the fit of the tree;
> An' ye war na my ain father
> The eight ane ye should be

allows himself to be freed by a woman's touch, although she is his stepmother, and at once appears "the bravest knight, That ever your eyes did see." He has grown up. The ego, which is always identifying with the children in these oedipal situations, often makes an evil witch of the stepmother and ends by punishing her ruthlessly, as the revenant children of *The Cruel Mother* do.

> You'll be seven long years a bird in a tree
> You'll be seven long years a tongue in a bell
> And you'll be seven long years a porter in hell.

[31] *Oxford Book of Ballads*, No. 15.

It's because ballads deal with childhood situations at such a primal level that they have this curious, much commented upon quality of wallowing narratively in fierce passions while seeming unmoved. Initially they are unmoved because what fantasy wants is strong action and the simple but strong gratifications of childhood, not the subtleties of adult sentiment. The use of enchantment is itself an indication of the level in which we are participating. Our parents are the miracle-workers who govern our lives and sex is a magic thing.[32]

Once the mode is established, other plots and matter will be drawn into it and modified into its idiom. This includes the broadside,[33] the historical-minstrel ballad like *Chevy Chase*, the chanty, the Come all ye's, worksongs and goodnights from the gallows. Most effective will be those which are closest to the original childhood emotions. *Queen Jane She Lay in Labor* and *The Bonny Earl of Livingston* are two ostensibly historical ballads which are immensely powerful in the detached idiom because they draw on the child's fascination by birth and, paradoxically, the death that was often its accompaniment.

The girls who were turned into phallic symbols, which expressed their orientation towards the father, lead uneasily to those other tailed females, the mermaids and lamias who were usually death to the men they drew to them. Sometimes the tails were understood rather than expressed.

> I there did espy a fair pretty maid
> With a comb and a glass in her hand.

Yet the tails can't be wished away, and a late comic song *The Man At The Nor*, gives a clue when the mermaid is unequivocally the lightshipman's mother.

> Me father kept the Eddystone light
> And was married to a mer-mi-ad one night

---

[32] The most complete statement of this is *The Two Magicians* (*Oxford Book of Ballads*, No. 13) where the sexual pursuit is through a series of shape changes.

[33] A comparison of *There was a Knight and he was Young* from *Pills to Purge Melancholy* with *Blow Away The Morning Dew* as collected by Sharp would show the process from broadside to traditional.

> And by and by they had children three
> Two were fish and the other was me.

In true tradition the union is virtually infertile since the only human offspring is forbidden by his mother to go ashore, not even to see his sister, the talking fish. Although there are children of a sort they are rather like the crooked products of unions with incubi and the devil, except for the comic-hero who is telling the story. The androgynous figure, I suspect, is a compound of mother and father; the top half alluring, the bottom tabooed because it's the father's tail. This would make another metaphor for the desired but forbidden, and therefore deathly.[34]

One of the most dangerous of the folk fairies is the kelpie or water horse, who often appears as a handsome young man though with tell-tale sand and shells in his hair. His trick is to dive under the sea with a girl he has seduced on his back and drown her. By now this is patterned behavior. Fertility horses accompany seasonal rites, many male fairies have horse manifestations and we ride the night mare[35] as we struggle in sleep with our unconscious desires. The horse seems the most common enchanted animal form in the British Isles and it's no wonder that that ill-fated queen who fell foul of St. Dunstan had changed herself to a mare in her lust. Horses are phallic, licentious and dangerous because they not only symbolize great sexual strength that may carry you away but are also totem animal representations of the father's potency, and as such they are sometimes slain as the hobby-horse in the sword dance instead of the fool or captain.

The list of fairy variations may have been endless, each district producing its own but with fundamental and re-

[34] The harpies were similar phallic-female compounds and so was Oedipus's sphinx. All had the fairy attribute of being thought to have carried off those who had died suddenly. Oedipus's sphinx embodied his problem in its own monstrous shape.

[35] Although the "mare" part of nightmare comes from the Anglo-Saxon mare, mære, a female goblin, it was early confused with a word for a horse, mearh. It already has riding associations in a charm against nightmare in the Lacnunga. See Gratton and Singer, Anglo-Saxon Magic and Medicine (O.U.P. 1952) for the Wellcome Historical Medical Museum. The sleeper is the steed and is ridden bridled through the night.

markably consistent similarities. The underlying meaning of them I have tried to bring out to show the reason for their invention and for their continued elaboration by all the means available to oral tradition, to produce a folk art that would fulfill the needs of the unconscious among semi-literate people.

One or two points should be made finally about the diversity of size. From the earliest records we have for native traditions it's clear, and is now agreed by folklorists, that fairies of all sizes have existed in these islands' imagination for at least fifteen hundred years. The small fairies are the ones that have been in scholarly dispute but the mediaeval chroniclers speak of them, they are known as dwarfs in Welsh folklore and Arthurian romance, and the Elizabethans were delighted by them.[36]

The variety of size has a logical explanation in the variety of situation. As the country became more populated it became increasingly difficult to accommodate a large fairy population unless they were small or invisible like Cherry of Zennor's. Smallness also enabled the Church to overlook them as insignificant. Variations of size and manifestation allowed the mind to play unconsciously yet repeatedly with the same situations and emotions, much as the television series does or compulsively read thrillers or romances. There is, however, an even deeper possible reason. The small fairies may be so because they are metaphors for the external sex organs seen by childhood's eyes, as the concept of shape-shifting and size-changing is motivated by the penis's ability to swell and shrink. Cheerful sexuality unhampered by guilt produced cheerful benevolent spirits; taboo desires produced the enchanting malignity which is far more common.

---

[36] The Eadwine Psalter, c. 1150, has a picture, copied from the Utrecht Psalter, of small winged elves dragging at a man's cloak

CHAPTER VI

The Fairy Queen

Cynthia, into whose hands the balance that weigheth time and fortune are committed.

Endimion, John Lyly

The metamorphosis of Elizabeth I into the Fairy Queen, and by extension of England into Fairyland, began with her coronation, with the procession from the Tower to Westminster which set the pattern for those famous "Princely Progresses" she was to make throughout her reign. Old women pressed forward to give her nosegays, old men wept, the populace huzzaed. There was music, masquing, Latin orations and a gift of a thousand gold marks from the City of London. Thanking the Lord Mayor for it she said: "Whereas your request is that I should continue your good Lady and Queen, be ye assured that I will be as good unto you as ever queen was to her people."

Five pageants were set up on the route through the City "which without any foreign person, of itself beautified itself." To outward appearances they expressed Protestantism, nationalism and that middle-class sobriety which is the basis of capitalism. Yet like another virgin with whom she was later to be paralleled, Elizabeth pondered all these things in her heart where she transmuted those worthy causes into secular, idealized and imaginative manifestations. The fourth pageant at the Little Conduit was of Time: two hills, one green and fruitful, with a handsome youth standing happily under a green laurel tree, the other withered and dead, with a youth in rude apparel sitting mournfully under an arid tree, represented the flourishing and the decayed commonwealth. Father Time emerged from a cave leading his daughter Truth who carried an English Bible which the Queen received and kissed, thanking the City for it and remarking that time had brought her there. The fifth pageant showed Deborah, "the judge and restorer of the House of Israel," and then came Temple

Bar with its two great statues of the giants, Gogmagog the Albion and Corineus the Briton.

It might seem a long way from an Old Testament judge to the Faerie Queene "in whose faire eyes love linct with vertue sittes" but the elements that made one into the other are all present in the pageants: the pastoral, the virgin ruler, the giants out of Geoffrey of Monmouth introducing in their wake all the old dreams of Arthur, Merlin and the enchanted world, even the handsome cheerful youth.

In later years as the Stuarts declined in popularity Elizabeth's reign began to seem even more a lost Golden Age, a fairy time. It was an image she had deliberately embodied and encouraged. To us, taught to think only in straight lines of statesman or bourgeois constitutional monarch, to think of the ruler as an average one of us, her achievement seems almost incomprehensible, only possible for a secular Saint Oscar with his work of art life. What he did she did too but carrying a nation along with her, so that her reign, and that idealized England, became not a series of successful foreign and domestic policies, of pirating and trading cruises, of grimy politics and intrigues but an opera with backcloths by Titian and libretto by Shakespeare, an intricate tissue of art and myth, encompassing every aspect of the national life and playing daily for over forty years. If we fail to understand this we shall find the tributes paid to her mere sycophancy and her tangible achievements inexplicable.

Living as Metaphor

It means, however, that we must try to think in terms of madrigal rather than Lieder, of complex interwoven polyphony instead of single theme with accompaniment. For some reason the deliberate use of fantasy and symbol in thought and in life has become discreditable, usually dismissed under the pejorative "childish." It's recognized that children do have rich fantasy lives and think symbolically, indeed we most of us can remember that it was so, but when we grow up such things are put away, partly perhaps because of some guilty association with masturbation fantasies, partly in order to hold our own in a supposedly concrete adult world. What we don't recognize is that all thought is symbolic and in particular just those areas of thinking from which we have mistakenly copied our yardstick of supposed reality. Mathematics is entirely symbolic, chemistry can't proceed without the use of an elaborate symbol system, both visual, in the rods and globes of chemical structures, and literal, in the CO_2s and H_2Os of the international code. Yet in art and life it is thought to be somehow more real to call a spade a spade, especially when it means a person with a black skin. It's an attitude encouraged by (possibly engendered by) industrial capitalism to keep us stolidly at work, the most far-flung product of the nineteenth-century manufactories and largely responsible for the imaginative impoverishment of contemporary life.

Fortunately for us and for them the Elizabethans had no such inhibitions. They would have found us unsophisticated, and uneducated; our use of language and our thought processes dull and simplistic. They expected not only the language of poetry, but of everyday life, of war, of diplomacy, of seafaring, of religion, to work on several levels. It wasn't that they embellished thought and language with artistic conceits: the images are the thought and we are the losers by our constant process of reductio ad simplicum. As artists we have lost our international symbols while scientists keep theirs. The symbols which could be understood by any educated person all over Europe were the legendary material of the classical world, supplemented by Christian symbolism, medieval history, geography and topography. It worked as a kind of symbolic shorthand, made universal where we can only be parochial, and created the immediate tension between form and content so important in a work of art. To make all the statements on prostitution we would now need a treatise for, Titian had only to paint Jupiter's seduction of Danaë in a shower of gold. Nor was it necessary to rob the symbol of its emotional power by explaining it. It could be apprehended at the level at which art works while the conscious mind was busy with the reference and the eye with its embodiment.

By a similar process Elizabeth became a Fairy Queen whom age could not wither, for people too could be more than we allow them to be except under conditions of stress.[1]

The Virgin Queen

Central to the royal imagery was her virginity, a topic misunderstood by many of her contemporaries and most historians. She was twenty-six when she came to the throne and her counsellors, including Cecil, and courtiers expected her to marry. But already, I believe, Elizabeth and her people had unconsciously rejected the idea although she was to play with it, for diplomatic purposes, and possibly from a dislike of closed doors which many people feel even though they may not want to actually pass through the doors, for many years. Writing to explain her virginity in 1562, three years after the coronation, her old schoolmaster Ascham said: "she resembled Hyppolite and not Phaedra," using the two wives of Theseus as extremes of sexual temperament. The letter was to Sturnius, a scholar of Strasbourg. All Europe was puzzled by the question.

An immensely popular ballad written for the coronation contains the answer. It's called *A songe betwene the Quene's majestie and Englande* or sometimes *Come over the bourne Bessie* by William Birche. In the form of a dialogue between Elizabeth and her lover, Englande, it imitates an earlier religious poem *Quia Amore Langueo* in which Christ is the lover of the human soul.

> E: I am thy lover faire/ hath chose the to my heir
> and my name is mery Englande
> B: Here is my hand/ my dere lover Englande
> I am thine both with mind and hert
> For ever to endure/ thou maiest be sure
> Untill death do us two depart
> E: Oh swete virgin pure/ long may ye endure

[1] The metamorphosis of the hated "war-monger" Churchill into the inspirational leader of the people by accretion of the symbols of John Bull and the British bulldog and by a use of rhetoric and idealization for example.

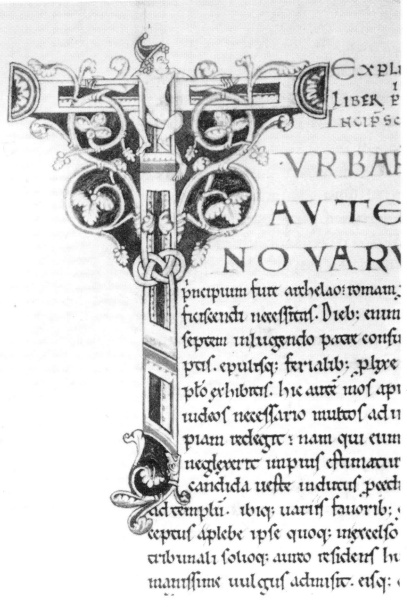

A manuscript of Josephus, late eleventh or twelfth century, Canterbury. It has been suggested that this elf in a Phrygian cap is copied from a sarcophagus. It seems to me more likely a native product and would therefore be the earliest fairy picture in this country. Plate 3 (*above, opposite*), was also produced at Canterbury at much the same time. It is a copy of a much earlier psalter but the English artist has added Phrygian caps to his elves which are not in the original.

These two illustrations show the effect of elf shot. In the upper one Christ's arrows have been confused with it. In the lower the elf with cap and bow has smitten the humanoid creature with various aches and ills.

The idea of the mermaid-siren with the glass is at least as early as the fourteenth century. The art of balancing on a tail was obviously tricky. Plate 5 is from a French paraphrase of the Book of Revelation; Plate 6 from a collection of classical texts belonging at one time to Pope Gregory XI and then to the Duc de Berry.

The conception of Merlin, from the French history of Arthur, thirteenth century. The theological concept of the incubus as expressed in the *Malleus Maleficarum* finds a visual expression. It is interesting to compare it with the English version of the same story in Layamon, where Merlin's father is shining and handsome, not a hairy horny demon. Perhaps this kind of difference helps to account for the comparative lack of witch-hunting in this country.

An illustration to *Sir Gawain and the Green Knight, c.* 1400. The Green Knight holds up his talking head, Gawain holds the axe, while King Arthur (who has drawn his sword), Guinevere and other members of the court look down from the royal box.

The Bible of William of Devon, thirteenth century, in Latin. The manuscript is filled with elf grotesques which seem on the point of metamorphosing even further. This is shape-changing magic.

Beardsley was a constant visitor to the British Museum where he studied for these forms derived from illuminated manuscripts both in concept and in linear treatment.

ROBIN

GOOD-FELLOW,

HIS MAD PRANKES AND MERRY IESTS.

Full of honeſt Mirth, and is a fit Medicine
for Melancholy.

Printed at *London* by *Thomas Cotes*, and are to bē ſold by
Francis Grove, at his ſhop on Snow-hill neere the

The duplication of phallic images in this picture leaves no doubt
of the contemporary attitude to the part demon-part satyr Puck.
From a black letter copy of *c.* 1600. Note Puck's broom and the
ring of small fairies around him. This edition is 1639 and
evidence of his confirmed popularity.

Opposite Titian's painting of the nymph Callisto discovered in pregnancy. This and its companion, Actaeon's discovery of Diana bathing, were painted for Philip II of Spain, husband of Elizabeth I's sister Mary.

The Dutch satire based on it (*above*) shows Elizabeth as Diana discovering the monstrous pregnancy of the Pope. Her handmaidens are the Protestant Estates of the Netherlands. The image of Elizabeth as Diana was international and the Titian original must also have been well known for the caricature to be effective.

Elizabeth watching the festivities at Elvetham, 'when certain stars shot madly from their spheres', from a contemporary broadsheet of the pageant. The mermen are in attendance. Shakespeare could well have read this account before writing A *Midsummer Night's Dream*.

> To reigne over us in this lande
> For your workes do accord/ ye are the hand-
>   maid of the Lord
> For he hath blessed you with his hand.

The image is beginning to proliferate. She is the secular madonna, her lover her people to whom she is also a mother and a ruler. It's tempting to cast Cecil as Joseph.

In 1564 she told the Scottish courtier Melville that she "was minded to end her life in virginity," while offering Leicester as a husband to Mary, Queen of Scots, and in the same year, the Cambridge orator addressing her on the subject during her visit to the university, she cried out: "God's blessing on thine heart, there continue." Yet the problem of succession was constantly thrust before her and once or twice she teetered towards marriage in the hope of a child.

Each time the possibility arose the people showed themselves against it. They rejected Leicester as a murderer, the Archduke of Austria and the Duke of Alencon as papists. Yet these, although important, were not their only motives. They wanted her to themselves. She was "her Majesty our mother," and as such she saw herself, choosing for one of her favorite emblems the pelican which was thought to pierce its own breast to feed its young with its own blood, the symbol she is wearing in the form of a jewel in the so-called "Pelican Portrait." A similar painting is called the "Phoenix Portrait" from a companion jewel which shows a phoenix, symbol of virginity since it reproduced by rising from its own funeral pyre.

These two images lead us from the popular to the educated concepts of her, of which the most common was as Diana, chaste goddess of the moon and the hunt, sister of Apollo and sometimes called Cynthia and Belphoebe. Titian had painted two great "poesie" of her for Philip II of Spain who had been Mary's husband. One showed the goddess rebuking the unfortunate Callisto, a nymph who had been seduced by Jupiter while he was disguised as Diana, the other the huntsman Actaeon who had stumbled upon her secret pool where she was wont to bathe after the chase. So international was Elizabeth's identification with

Diana that a Dutch engraved caricature[2] of the first picture shows the Queen rebuking a heavily pregnant pope as a piece of Protestant propaganda. At home the references are too numerous to cite. They include whole fountains like the one at Nonesuch, statuesque with Diana and Actaeon, Constable's sonnet sequence *Diana* dedicated to the ladies-in-waiting in 1592, comments from chronicles like Sir Richard Baker's "a Diana among her nymphs," Ralleigh's "hunting like Diana" in a pleading letter and a masque, prepared but never performed, in which she was Zabeta, Diana's favourite nymph.[3]

As Cynthia she appears in Lyly's *Endimion* and Jonson's *Cynthia's Revels*, in Barnfield's poem of the same name and in Raleigh's poems which spurred Spenser to figure her as Belphoebe in *The Faerie Queene*. The Queen was, like most of her contemporaries, deeply fond of hunting; so was the goddess. Her ladies-in-waiting were the goddess's nymphs whom, it seemed, she punished as severely for marrying without her consent as Diana did. While not actually changed into a bear like Callisto they were likely to be sent to the Tower or dismissed the court. Nor was her rage always against losing a young male favourite as in the unfortunate marriages of Southampton and Raleigh to maids-in-waiting and in Essex's involvement with Lady Mary Howard. Sometimes it was directed against the ladies themselves since she "doth still much exhort all her women to remain in virgin state, as much as may be",[4] and in the cases of Lady Bridget Manners and Mistress Frances Vavasour there was no question of the Queen being interested in the husbands. It wasn't that she was entirely against marriage. She blessed that of Lord Herbert and Mistress Anne Russell though Herbert had been a favourite from his first appearance at court. However, an interesting

---

[2] Pieter van de Heyden, 1584/5. See plates 13 and 14.
[3] The play concludes with a plea to her to marry:

> Yet never wight felt perfect blis
> but such as wedded bene.

Leicester may have thought better of it and cancelled the performance.
[4] Sir John Harington, *Nugae Antiquae*, May 23rd, 1597, edited T. Pork, 1804.

little incident marred the festivities. Eight ladies disguised as masquers chose eight ladies more to dance the measures. "Mistress Fitton went to the Queen and wooed her to dance. Her Majesty asked her what she was. 'Affection,' she said. 'Affection!' said the Queen. 'Affection's false.' Yet her Majesty rose and danced."[5]

Of necessity she spent a great deal of time, intimate time, with her ladies. She rarely ate in public except on formal occasions, having her food carried into her private apartment. They would bathe and dress her, play cards and dance with her, chatter and play music to her in all those moments when she was not in open court. Foreign correspondents attest their beauty, intelligence and education. Elizabeth didn't care to be surrounded by the ill-favoured of either sex. The relations between the Princess and her ladies in *Love's Labour's Lost* and those of Cleopatra and her women give, I think, a very good idea what their lives and conversation were like.

It was an age that enjoyed transvestism and emotional, if not physical,[6] bisexuality. Before Shakespeare made transvestism popular on the stage in *As You Like It* and *Twelfth Night* there had been several treatments in prose and verse, including the sources for the two plays. A typical plot is Dickinson's *Arisbas* of 1593 where the lost Timodea turns up disguised as the leading choirboy, "loved of all shepherds and liked of all lasses" with the story of Hyalas and Zephyrus thrown in for good measure. Donne has an epistle in defence of female homosexuality supposedly written by Sappho and a great deal of Spenser's *Faerie Queene* concerns the exploits of the Amazon knights, Britomart and Belphoebe, derived from the Italian romances of Ariosto and Tasso. Britomart, like Viola, has to woo a lady in order, we are told, to keep up her disguise. She seems to have been very convincing. This is Amoret who has been

[5] Sidney Papers, June 16th, 1600. Mistress Fitton later disguised herself as a man to keep secret assignations with Pembroke by whom she became pregnant.

[6] Physical bisexuality is difficult to prove since homosexual relations were still illegal and people, not unnaturally, didn't always leave unequivocal records. Jonson, Marlowe and James I were all allegedly homosexual and there is the oft-quoted Latin tag about Elizabeth having been a king and James a queen, supposedly current at his accession.

rescued by Britomart and is afraid that she will have to reward her rescuer in kind. Spenser uses the masculine pronoun suddenly in the last line to show how convincing Britomart's performance is.

> Thereto her feare was made so much the greater
> Through fine abusion of that Briton mayd;
> Who, for to hide her fained sex the better
> And maske her wounded mind, both did and sayd
> Full many things so doubtfully to be wayd,
> That well she wist not what by then to gesse:
> For other-whiles to her she purpos made
> Of love, and other-whiles of lustfulnesse,
> That much she feard his mind would grow to some
>   excesse.[7]

Virginity did not necessitate sexlessness. Diana was goddess of childbirth although chaste. In her aspect as Cynthia or Luna she might kiss the beautiful youth Endimion in his perpetual sleep. Melville had been shocked when Elizabeth tickled Leicester's neck as he knelt before her at the ceremony making him an earl. She flirted outrageously with courtiers and foreign visitors. On first seeing Lord Herbert of Cherbury she gave him her hand to kiss twice "both times gently clapping me on the cheek." She "looked attentively upon me, and swearing her ordinary oath,[8] said, 'It is a pity he was married so young.'" Nor did she content herself with one at a time. In 1579 while Leicester still attended her (although recently married) she was courted by Jean de Simier as proxy for Alencon, inflaming both master and man, while Hatton danced attendance, and Raleigh was new favorite. The list of her conquests is endless since many of them we shall never know about. She used her immense sexual energy to vitalise the whole nation.

Sometimes she was represented as the chaste Venus who

> hath both kinds in one,
> Both male and female, both under one name:

---

[7] Spenser, *Faerie Queen*, Book IV, i, 7.
[8] For the record "God's death!"

> She syre and mother is her selfe alone,
> Begets and eke conceives, ne needeth other none.[9]

The attraction of this symbol is very deep. It gives us a mother whom we may serve as child lovers, an idea perhaps most clearly expressed for the Renaissance by Bronzino's incestuous paintings of Venus and the adolescent Cupid. No father ousts and overrules us. We are all equal yet our competition for her favours and service keeps us all in a frenzy of imagination and activity. No one must be given the ultimate favour, and she must remain ageless as Cleopatra or the Fairy Queen.

Elizabeth's love of dancing was another fairy attribute, shared with the three graces and the nine muses among whom she was often numbered.[10] Another link was her, and the age's, passion for the pastoral so charmingly exploited by England's darling, Sir Philip Sidney, in his *Arcadia*. In the pastoral convention she became Eliza, queen of shepherds and shepherdesses and England an idealised landscape, a temperate Theocritan idyll of sheep and cornfields, piping and mild airs, bordered once more as in a tapestry by the English wood outside Athens.

The pastoral is a form of the Golden Age and the Garden of Eden. Perhaps the traditional English love of gardening and the countryside is the longing for that time when there was mythically only the perfect pair without responsibility, when fruits and flowers bent to their hand and there was only one embargo. But it's also a harking after that mythical fairy England, the country of Spenser's *Shepheards Calendar* and the enchanted forests and plains of *The Faerie Queene*. Fundamentally Englishmen have believed for centuries that England is "not what England seems" but is "the country of our dreams," the idealised pastoral of Handel's *Acis and Galatea*, and if we could all get back to it, find it again, the lost childhood country of Wordsworth and Dylan Thomas, we should be as uncorrupted as when enchantment falls away at the end of all

[9] *Faerie Queene*, Book VI, x, 41.
[10] The eight masquing ladies when Mistress Fitton wooed the Queen to dance were Apollo's muses lacking their ninth. Graces and muses dance about her in the April Eclogue of Spenser's *Shepheards Calendar*.

good fairy stories, *Comus* and *The Tempest,* and *A Midsummer Night's Dream*.

The pastoral Eliza and Diana meet finally and magnificently in the madrigal collection made by Thomas Morley in 1601 while Essex was tottering to his ruin, *The Triumphs of Oriana*. Each madrigal had the refrain:

> Then sang the shepherds and nymphs of Diana:
> Long live fair Oriana.

Oriana was the beloved of Amadis of Gaul, the romance hero cast away at birth and known as the Child of the Sun. The verses and settings are the flower of the English madrigal yet they were written to a woman of sixty-eight.

> Fair nymphs, I heard one telling
> Diana's train are hunting in this chase.
> To beautify the place
> The fauns are running
> The shepherds their pipes are tuning
> To show their cunning.
> The lambs amazed leave off their grazing
> And blind their eyes with gazing
> Whilst the earth's goddess doth draw near your places
> Attended by the Muses and the Graces.[11]

Obviously Elizabeth had the perennial attraction of a Colette or of the great stars of early talkies, Dietrich or Hepburn. One of her costumes, a shawl with a great black spider jewel, even anticipates the classic vamp dress. She made an artistic heyday of literature and music, and a visual magnificence, compounded of tapestry, sculpture, decoration and the portraiture of Nicholas Hilliard, that we can often only guess at from written accounts since so much vanished with the Commonwealth.

The Fairy Background

"The opinion of Faeries and elfes is very old, and yet sticketh very religiously in the myndes of some. But to

[11] John Farmer, *The Triumphs of Oriana*, 1601.

roote that rancke opinion of Elfes oute of mens hearts, the truth is, that there be no such thinges, nor yet the shadows of the things."[12]

> And know you this by the waie, that heretofore Robin goodfellow and Hob goblin were as terrible, and also as credible to the people, as hags and witches be now . . . But in our childhood our mothers maids have so terrified us with an ouglie devil having hornes on his head, fier in his mouth, and a taile in his breech, eies like a bason, fanges like a dog, clawes like a beare, a skin like a Niger, and a voice roring like a lion, whereby we start and are afraid when we heare one crie Bough: and they have so fraied us with bull beggers, spirits, witches, urchens, elves, hags, fairies, satyrs, pans, faunes, sylens, kit with cansticke, tritons, centaurs, dwarfs, giants, imps, calcars, conjurors, nymphes, changlings, *Incubus*, Robin good-fellowe, the spoorne, the mare, the man in the oake, the hell waine, the fierdrake, the puckle, Tom thombe, hob gobblin, Tom tumbler, boneles, and such other bugs, that we are afraid of our owne shadowes: in so much as some never feare the divell, but in a darke night; and then a polled sheepe is a perillous beast, and manie times is taken for our fathers soule, speciallie in a churchyard.[13]

By Shakespeare's time the educated English had largely given up belief in fairies. Chaucer was the great literary father and Chaucer, two centuries before, had consigned them to the past. The process of assimilating classical mythology and combining it with native traditions continued as strongly as ever, as the list above indicates, and indeed was given added impetus by the translation of Ovid's *Metamorphoses* in 1567 by Arthur Golding. No more belief reposed in the Fairy Queen than in Diana; both were free for artistic and symbolic use.

[12] E.K. glossary to *The Shepheards Calendar*, June Eclogue, 1579–80.

[13] Reginald Scot, *The Discoverie of Witchcraft*, 1584, Book VII, Chaps. II and XV.

Among the less educated the belief of course "sticketh very religiously." Reginald Scot was writing on the side of reason against belief in witches and the holocaust of them on the continent. Fairies often cropped up in witchcraft trials but mercifully judges and juries were on the whole sceptical, especially when one Darrell was found to have been cozening by exorcising witchcrafts faked by accomplices.[14]

Fairies were thought appropriate to country places and therefore appeared in some of the entertainments organised for the Queen on progress. In 1575 "the Queen of the Fayry drawn with sex children in a waggon of state" gave her an embroidered gown at Woodstock, and at Norwich in 1578 the children who had been unable, owing to the impromptu nature of the Queen's movements, to present themselves as water nymphs were hastily converted into "Phayries" "as well as might be." They danced and proclaimed themselves as "harmless."

Already in the Princely Pleasures of Kenilworth she had been greeted by the Lady of the Lake from Arthurian legend whom the writer of the commentary to *The Shepheards Calendar* equated with the Greek water nymphs in order to make her more respectable. The Fairy Queen appeared again in the great masque at Elvetham given by the Earl of Hertford in 1591 which closely followed the Kenilworth entertainment but with much better writers. Some of the songs:

> "In the merry month of May
> In a morn by break of day"
> "O come again sweet Nature's treasure . . ."
> "With fragrant flowers we strew the way . . ."

have become anthology classics and anticipate the mood and imagery of *As You Like It*.

The Fairy Queen was Aureola, recorded later as meaning "little pretty golden lady."[15] It suggests the "elf shining" of Layamon but also that this is a small fairy.

---

[14] J. B. Harrison, *The Elizabethan Journals, 1599*.
[15] Lyford, 1655, but probably from Camden, 1605. See *Oxford Dictionary of Christian Names* which has no known example.

I that abide in places under ground
Aureola the Queene of Fayryland
That every night in rings of painted flowers
Turne round and carroll out Elisaes name
Hearing that Nereus and the Sylvane gods
Have lately welcomde your Imperial Grace
Oapend the earth with this enchanting wand
To doe my duty to your Majestie
And humbly to salute you with this chaplet
Given me by Auberon the fairy king.

The Queen was addressed as "Bright shining Phoebe that in humaine shape/ Hidst Heaven's perfection."[16] The form of the Fairy King's name is the same as that used in Lord Berners's translation of *Huon of Bordeaux* (1533–42) which shows him as a dwarf like those of Celtic romance or Alberich the German dwarf from whom the name may be derived. There are various other forms of the name: Oberycom, Oberion, Oboran in Greene's play *James IV*. It was at one time thought that Shakespeare had invented him but Oberion has now been traced to a document of the time of Wolsey.[17] Spenser spells him Oberon in *The Faerie Queene*, Book II, published in 1590, where he forms part of Elizabeth's fairy family tree in the place of Henry VIII. I believe it was from there that Shakespeare took the name for *A Midsummer Night's Dream*.

Scot made no distinction between ghosts, fairies, classical mythologicals and canonical devils. They were all bugs, and interchangeable, as their positions in the list show where the mention of one has reminded him of another by

[16] J. Nichols, *The Princely Progresses and Public Appearances of Queen Elizabeth I*, 1823.

[17] See K. M. Briggs's *Anatomy of Puck* for further documentation. However I am not totally convinced of the Alberic derivation. In a Welsh romance, a version of Erec and Enide called *Gereint Son of Erbin* the author refers to the dwarf King Guivret "whom the Welsh call Y Brenhin Bychan meaning the little king." This could easily be contracted in English into some form of Oberon with no more difficulty than making the Infanta of Castile into the Elephant and Castle. The original text suggests that this was a common name in Welsh for a recognised person, perhaps Herla's little fairy king. Compare the English ballad form *Glasgerion* which James Kinsley suggests is Y Barold GlasKeraint. *Oxford Book of Ballads* note to the poem.

useful association of ideas. To the careful folklorist this adulteration is immensely irritating; to the historian of ideas, attempting to trace and understand the development, disguises and manifestations of a particular fantasy, it is as valid as the native pixie stamped "made in Britain." Before *A Midsummer Night's Dream* itself can be put into context there are two works, neglected by both folklorists and source mongers, which Shakespeare had read and which influenced him in the writing of our greatest fairy play.

Endimion

The England of Elizabeth I was a small world of four and a half million inhabitants, just over half the size of present-day London. The court and intellectual circles were so closely interwoven as to be almost the same. The nobles, men and women, were the patrons of artists and scholars. No one was considered socially acceptable in a society whose queen was a paragon of taste and learning without similar accomplishments. In return literature constantly drew upon or used as artistic material the lives and fashions of the court, following the contemporary mode of idealization.

To our so different view this may seem impossible without the crudest allegory or satire. Constantly, in reading books on the period, one finds the writer apologising for a flattering mention of the Queen, suggesting that she was bored by the entertainments in praise of her and generally trying to brush aside such epithets as "beauteous Quene of second Troy" as meaningless, distasteful or written with the tongue in the cheek in hope of a tip. This is to show as little historical perception as an art historian would in suggesting that Piero della Francesca shouldn't have painted didn't enjoy painting, or painted in a spirit of irony, the Montefeltro Duke and Duchess in triumphal chariots attended by angels and amoretti against their shining domains.

Endimion at least should teach us better. It was written by John Lyly, already famous for his prose works *Euphues*, to be performed by the child actors of St. Paul's "before the Queen's Majesty at Greenwich on New Year's day at Night," the "little eyeases" of Hamlet. It's subtitled *The*

Man in the Moone. Endimion, in love with the unattainable moon goddess Cynthia, is beloved by the jealous Tellus who has him cast into a sleep by the witch Dipsas. Tellus is imprisoned by Cynthia, in punishment, under the guardianship of Corsites whom she suborns to try to carry Endimion away. The fairies protect Endimion and Corsites is changed into a leopard. Cynthia is told that she can wake the sleeper with a kiss, which she does. Tellus is forgiven and united with Corsites; even the witch Dipsas is converted from evil and restored to her husband. Endimion is content to live adoringly beside Cynthia whom he can never possess. There are innumerable sub-plots including a forerunner of the Don Armado character in *Love's Labour's Lost*.

The basic plot as outlined above has certain identifiable historical characters and situations. This doesn't mean that we should expect them to be crudely carried through point by unrelenting point. Like the historical references in Spenser's *Faerie Queene* (discussed later) they may go underground for dramatic purposes. They are allusive rather than explicit. The main one is Cynthia/Elizabeth, by this time such a commonplace that to refer to Cynthia or Diana was automatically to invoke the shadow of the Queen.[18] Endimion is Leicester, Tellus, Mary Queen of Scots, and Corsites, Sir Amyas Paulet who had been given the unrewarding task of looking after Mary in her imprisonment. The central situation takes an added ironic twist from Elizabeth's offer of Leicester as a husband to Mary.

[18] Raleigh's poem composed between 1581 and 1587 and printed in 1593 in *The Phoenix Nest* is a sufficient illustration.

> Praised be Diana's fair and harmless light
> Praised be the dews, wherewith she moists the ground;
> Praised be her beams, the glory of the night
> Praised be her power, by which her powers abound.
> Praised be her nymphs, with whom she decks the woods,
> Praised be her knights, in whom true honour lives,
> Praised be that force, by which she moves the floods;
> Let that Diana shine, which all these gives.
>
> In heaven Queen she is among the spheres;
> In aye she Mistress like makes all things pure
> Eternity in her oft change she bears;
> She beauty is, by her the fair endure.

Clearly it's before Mary's execution, and supports the queen's policy of a settlement with her. The character of Corsites is very much that of Paulet, strong and upright, but his seduction to evil ways is more in keeping with Shrewsbury, who had been her guardian before. The references make for a date of 1585/6.[19] The play may well have been commissioned by Leicester to entertain the queen at the Christmas festivities which were the most important annual diversion, apart from those during the summer progresses.

The play was published in 1591. I believe that Shakespeare read it before writing *A Midsummer Night's Dream* and that it's one of the most important influences on that play, in combination with *The Faerie Queene* and Ovid's *Metamorphoses*. The more precise references will be mentioned in the chapter on Shakespeare's play. One or two structural points can be made here.

Though the character of Endimion remains constant that of Cynthia changes. At one time she is the moon, at another the goddess, at another a more earthly, although always royal, mistress or the abstraction of unattainable chastity. Tellus is more consistent and very close to Spenser's Mary of Scots character in *The Faerie Queene*, the false Duessa, although at times she takes on a certain earthiness as the origin of herbs for witchcraft. For the sake of the comic dramatic convention all characters have to be happily disposed of at the end although this may be a reversal of the historic situation which the play reflects. Not all the characters need have contemporary counterparts though some may have which are lost to us.

The plot elements that the two plays share occur in both main and subplots. The hero of the chief sub-plot is a miles gloriosus character, Sir Tophas, who resembles Don Ar-

[19] If the seduction of Corsites by Tellus is an image of Mary's alleged seduction of her keeper Shrewsbury this dates the work to after 1585 when Paulet took over from Shrewsbury, yet before the Babington conspiracy in 1586 while it was still possible for Elizabeth to be reconciled to her as the play holds out. Cynthia says: "I have laboured to win all, and study to keep such as I have won; but those that neither my favour can move to continue constant, nor my offered benefits get to be faithful, the gods shall either reduce to truth or revenge their treacheries with justice." Act V, iii. The Epilogue is a plea for Elizabeth to shine on them all.

mado in *Love's Labour's Lost* but also Bottom who is famous among his friends for his boasting and his desire to play military roles. But Sir Tophas's wrath is all directed against shooting birds.

"Here is a bird bolt for the ugly beast the blackbird," which suggests Bottom's song about the "ousel cock so black of hue" with which he keeps up his spirits when he is first transformed. Sir Tophas is twice referred to as an ass.

The place of the lovers is taken by the queen's waiting women, Eumenides, a courtier, Endimion's friend, and two pages. A quarrel develops between two of the girls like that between Hermia and Helena.

> Favilla: I cry your matronship mercy; because your pentables be higher with cork, therefore your feet must needs be higher in the insteps: you will be mine elder, because you stand upon a stool, and I on the floor.
>
> Scintilla: Nay you think to be the wiser, because you mean to have the last word.
>
> Samias: Step between them lest they scratch.
>
> Scintilla: I am not angry but it spited me to see how short she was.
>
> Favilla: I meant nothing, till she would needs cross me.

Enchanted sleep is also common to both plays and the transformation of a human into an animal. Above all, the tone of the plays, their combination of romantic comedy with magic, the presence of fairies who sing like Shakespeare's and refer to Cynthia as the Queen of Stars, and the verbal echoes, make *Endimion* a conscious, for Shakespeare, forerunner of *A Midsummer Night's Dream*. It's no more than we should expect. Lyly's reputation was very high and both his diction and structure would appeal to Shakespeare.

> Pinch him, pinch him, black and blue
> Saucy mortals must not view
> What the Queen of Stars is doing
> Nor pry into our fairy wooing.

1 Fairy: Pinch him blue
2 Fairy: And pinch him black.
3 Fairy: Let him not lack
          Sharp nails to pinch him blue and red
          Till sleep has rock'd his addle head
4 Fairy: For the trespass he hath done
          Spots o'er all his flesh shall run
          Kiss Endimion, kiss his eyes
          Then to our midnight heidegyes.[20]

These fairies are diminutives. Corsites calls them "pretty ladies," "nymphs" and "fair babies" which gives a clear idea of Lyly's conception of them, played no doubt by the youngest boys.

Most important to remember is the double meaning of a play not far removed from the court masque. Such a meaning the Elizabethans were used to seeing, indeed expected to see,[21] and I believe no dramatist could have staged a play as similar as *A Midsummer Night's Dream* without certain parallels being drawn, particularly since in 1590 Edmund Spenser published the first three books of *The Faerie Queene* in whom in particular he intended, as his introductory letter to Raleigh shows, "the most excellent and glorious person of our soveraine the Queene, and her kingdom in Faery land."

[20] This song also influenced the fairy song in the *Merry Wives of Windsor* where Shakespeare in a sense parodies his own earlier play with Falstaff disguised as a stag. Discovered he says: "I do begin to perceive that I am made an ass."
[21] The Epilogue points the moral of loyalty to the Queen in the different times when "the malicious seek to overthrow us with threats."

CHAPTER VII

Renaissance: sex and violence

Of faery land yet if he more inquyre
By certain signes, here sett in sondrie place,
He may it fynd; ne let him then admyre
But yield his sence to be too blunt and bace,
That no'te without an hound fine footing trace.
And thou, O fayrest Princesse under sky!
In this fayre, mirrhour maist behold thy face
And thine owne realmes in land of Faery,
And in this antique ymage thy great auncestry.
Spenser, *The Faerie Queene*,

Book II, Stanza iv

To the folklorists Spenser is a non-starter in the fairy field.[1] This is because they are looking for residual beliefs from early native traditions and therefore may miss the most important appearance of the enchanted, enchanting fantasy in a particular period. Undoubtedly to his contemporaries this was Spenser.

The poem was already begun by 1580 during the time while Spenser was staying at Penshurst with Sir Philip Sidney and at Leicester's house in the Strand. It was sent in part to a literary friend, Gabriel Harvey, for his comments which were, on the whole, unfavourable. "If so be the Faery Queen be fairer in your eie than the Nine Muses,[2] and Hobgoblin runne away with the garland from Apollo; marke what I saye, and yet I will not say that I thought; but there is an end for this once, and fare you well, till God or some good Aungell putte you in a better mind." No doubt disturbed by this but not dissuaded, Spenser completed, as far as it is complete, the poem in Ireland, publishing the second three books in 1596.

Consciously modelled on the Italian romance epics of Ariosto and Tasso, it is by Malory out of Ovid, the work of a man so saturated in the symbols and myths of the Italian Renaissance that it seems incredible that he had never been to Italy or seen the great paintings which his work so closely resembles. He is an English literary Botticelli[3] or sometimes a Piero di Cosimo, both at their secular best.

[1] "Spenser used the fays of romance for his allegory but they had already become a little bookish and faded." K. M. Briggs, *The Anatomy of Puck*, Chapter I.

[2] A reference to an earlier poem of Spenser's which Harvey approved of.

[3] This is not an original idea of mine, I wish it were, but borrowed from an excellent book on Spenser: *A Preface To The Faerie Queene* by Graham Hough.

The metamorphosis is complete. Britain is faeryland; Elizabeth is Gloriana, the Faery Queene. "And yet in some places els, I doe otherwise shadow her," Spenser wrote in the dedicatory letter to Raleigh. She is also Belphoebe, "according to your [Raleigh's] owne excellent conceipt of Cynthia, [Phoebe and Cynthia being both names of Diana]", and Mercilla and Britomart although Britomart is one of Gloriana's putative ancestors. She is also called Tanaquil.

The same complexity applies to the other characters. The main nexus is Prince Arthur, begun as Magnificence and Leicester but, after the earl's sudden death in the year of the Armada, combined with the new favorite Essex and Spenser's own patron in Ireland, Lord Grey, and further compounded in the character of Artegall. There are other fairly certain identifications that can be made: Duessa I have already mentioned and indeed James VI wanted Spenser prosecuted for this unappealing portrait of his mother. The other certain one is of the squire Timias with Raleigh and, a possible, Sidney/Calidore in Book VI.

A great deal of time can be wasted in the pursuit of identifications. Spenser made it clear that he didn't intend precision but art in his "darke conceit": "by occasion hereof many other adventures are intermedled; but rather as Accidents then intendments." Nevertheless there is no need to react as some scholars do and behave as though they don't exist or, if they do, must be apologised for. They are the personae of Spenser's dream world, the masked actors through whom his imagination worked. He and his contemporaries were fortunate in being able to treat their public figures as at once more human and more divine than ours but we shouldn't let our envy cloud our artistic appreciation.[4]

Graham Hough has made an excellent analysis of *The Faerie Queene* as a dream-poem[5] with the surrealist organization of *Alice in Wonderland* where time and space are variables along with character and situation. It seems unnecessary to repeat his arguments here and I will take the point as made. One small illustration will do, from a

---

[4] Ronald Firbank, Norman Mailer and Gore Vidal are novelists who have used known people as dramatis personae in this century.
[5] Hough, op. cit.

circumstance already mentioned: Britomart is Gloriana's ancestor yet she meets Prince Arthur who is in quest of Gloriana, the Faery Queene. As in a dream too Spenser begins in medias res. His instinct which he rationalized in his introductory letter was quite right. ". . . a poet thrusteth into the middest, even where it most concerneth him, and there recoursing to the things foreposte, and divining of things to come, maketh a pleasing Analysis of all." (So much for the modern invention of the flashback.)

As in the lays and the early romances there is first a passage of seeming normality opening with one of the most famous lines in English literature. A gentle knight,[6] a lady and a dwarf are outlined on a plain, ambling along. Suddenly the skies are overcast, it begins to rain hideously and they seek shelter in a wood so thick no starlight nor rain can pierce it. When the storm is over they turn back but they are lost in a maze so confusing it "makes them doubte their wits be not their own."

This is familiar ground; the taboo has been broken. The rest of the poem, with the exception of the long section on Ireland in Book V, generally admitted the least successful, and a brief visit to Mercilla/Elizabeth's court, takes place in this wood which in its turn contains bowers, castles, rivers and every aspect of dream landscape.

It also contains every aspect of sex and violence (almost— the qualification is cowardly but necessary) which the human conscious and unconscious throws up, yet all under the aegis of the Lucretian Venus who is love, energy, harmony. Spenser's avowed intention was to write ten books. I suspect he didn't fulfil this not because time ran out, though it's true it did, for four years after the publication of the second part he was dead,[7] but because he had al-

---

[6] That they should be knights is not only a literary harking back to the early romance or even to Spenser's Italian models but a representation of that Elizabethan passion for the tourneys that the nobles played at as part of royal entertainment and as part of the deliberate idealization of their life and times under the image of an Arthurian chivalry that never was. It's impossible to find an uncamp modern parallel except in children's games of Robin Hood or Gerries and British. The camp version is of course the Royal Tournament.

[7] He was caught by the Irish problem, his house sacked and burned and himself forced to flee to England. It can be no coincidence that he died three months later in January 1599.

ready covered the emotional ground. He had already turned aside to write the sonnet sequence *Amoretti* and the two famous marriage odes. There is another magnificent fragment that seems to be part of another book and is known as the "Mutability Cantos" but its dating is unsure.

Those who are forced to read *The Faerie Queene* these days are usually put to the first book from which they never recover and never progress. I would recommend beginning at Book III which is entirely secular and faster moving. Since Spenser never completed his formal scheme there is no straight line which must be followed to a climax, the books are more or less self-contained, although III runs on into IV, and the characters and story can usually be picked up quite quickly. However, for the sake of coherence, which is not the same as subjecting oneself to the experience of a work of art, I will deal with the books in sequence.

The first two are structurally similar. A knight hero is on his quest in company with his super-ego conscience. Book I is about holiness and the taboos are fundamentally religious ones. This makes it, although important to Spenser's contemporaries, less attractive to us whose ethical problems are more political and social. A modern equivalent would concern itself perhaps with the radical politician whose integrity is put in danger by the machinations of power politics, the sort of thing that makes good television drama. It doesn't, I think, work at the same level as the other books and is closer to the allegorizing explanations Tasso had produced before he wrote his own *Gerusalemma Liberata*. This isn't to say that there aren't passages in it which reach down into the unconscious. An important situation which influenced *A Midsummer Night's Dream* occurs when each of the lovers, Red Crosse Knight and Una, mistakes an evil enchanter for the beloved.

Book II however is concerned not with a theological but a psychological state. The knight is Temperance which means that his temptations are to violence and lust. The tone is set by a feigned rape, followed by the discovery of a woman dying in her own self-drawn blood beside the body of her husband while their child dabbles its hands in her bleeding breast. This scene is the work of Acrasia, a Circe who turns her lovers into beasts. Spenser is not against sex, very far from it as he shows in Book III, but this is a sadistic violence which the hero knight Guyon is particularly prone to and it has to be battled against.[8]

Guyon has that chilliness that is often controlled sadism and this is partly why commentators have found this such a difficult one to explain. Whatever an artist's avowed intention his unconscious knowledge will often assert itself, sometimes to the puzzlement of the critic who would like things neatly tied up but always to the benefit of the work of art. Spenser is dealing with psychological make-up. The happenings which befall each of his knights are the fantasies that beset such a psyche. There is a great deal of the Prussian officer-camp commandant about Guyon so we shouldn't be surprised when at the end he destroys the thing that has tempted him.

The other temptation is to self-destruction and there are several instances of this in the book. Riches are offered as a bait too but Spenser quite rightly realizes that they are no real lure to such a temperament and Guyon is unmoved by them. The set-piece at the end is as it were the climax of a masturbation fantasy. The Bower of Bliss is beautiful, otherwise it wouldn't be tempting and it offers the pleasures of voyeurism. The two nymphs who are bathing naked and excite Guyon do so by the old pornographic trick of partial revelation.

> But thother rather higher did arise
> And her two lilly paps aloft displayed,
> And all that might his melting hart entyse
> To her delights she unto him bewrayed;
> The rest hidd underneath him more desirous made.[9]

The other lets her hair loose to cover herself while she rises up. They beckon, blush and laugh,

> And showed him many sights that corage cold could
> rear.

---

[8] The fighting in this book is noticeably lengthy and bloody, many of the characters being variations on rage.

[9] Book II, xii, 66.

Guyon goes on to the heart of the bower where Acrasia and her new lover are lying, having just made love. The picture is of Venus and Mars by Veronese and, like them, they are caught in a net. If Guyon is not to enjoy he must destroy as an orgasm of violence. He has looked on an act in his mind that has excited him to the point where he smashes the image, a piece of psychological rightness that breaks down the allegory. It should be clear that he is not temperance but a striving towards it.

At the beginning of Book III, far from having reached it he falls into violence again when he challenges, and is almost unhorsed by, a stranger. Only his guide saves him from attempted revenge. The alleged theme of this book is chastity by which Spenser means, curiously perhaps to some minds, love which

> . . . of honour and all vertue is
> The roote, and brings forth glorious flowers of fame,
> That crowne true lovers with immortall blis
> The meed of them that love, and do not live amisse.[10]

Spenser therefore has the chance of setting forth all the forms of unchastity and in this book and the next, which is a continuation of it under the virtuous cloak of friendship, he is at his most powerful and lavish. The power is erotic, the lavishness its embodiment in Renaissance mythology under the surreal half-light of enchantment.

The hero of this book is herself a delightful perversion by modern concepts, for she is the warrior maiden Britomart, a shadowing of Elizabeth. Spenser, unlike many of his literary contemporaries, liked women as lovers and equals. The whole mode of anti-feminism is foreign to him. He yearned to recapture the feats of Penthesilea, the Homeric queen of the Amazons. He thinks it a pity women are no longer warriors since they were so good at it, and puts the loss down to men's envy.

> Yet sith they warlike armes have laid away
> They have exceld in artes and pollicy.

[10] Book IV, ii.

All this is obviously complimentary to the queen and as such some people may be inclined to explain it away. This is to put the cart before the horse. Spenser is able to indulge in sincere praise of Elizabeth because of his genuine appreciation of women. Similarly his creation of Britomart can be explained away by reference to his Italian prototypes, Ariosto and Tasso, yet their Amazons are not the same as his and the difference is in the continuing equality of Britomart. She is never put down because she is a woman. The three works[11] each have as a climax a fight between the lovers. Tasso has Clorinda slain by her lover, Ariosto has Bradamante defeated by hers, only Spenser keeps Britomart revealed but undefeated. It's impossible to think of Britomart being *given* in marriage to anyone as Bradamante almost is. Britomart is entirely master of her own fate, stronger than her lover emotionally, as skilled a warrior, both more passionate and more rational. Nor does Spenser make even the customary concessions in physical descriptions. Britomart's is an "angel's face"; Artegall's a "lovely face."

Britomart (her name is derived from Britomartis, one of Diana's nymphs, colored by her Britishness) is a bisexual creation, not the first in English literature for Sidney was writing of a similar happening in *Arcadia* at much the same time.[12] She is all things to all men and women too. When Artegall discovers in the midst of battle that she is a woman he immediately takes her for a goddess and kneels to her. He woos her with "meeke service." There is no suggestion that she becomes a weaker creature in love although she does try to keep him from leaving her. Later (in Book V) Artegall meets another Amazon, Radigund, who subdues him, dresses him in women's clothes and makes him spin. From this state Britomart rescues him. Spenser is in a difficulty with the bad Amazons. His natural instinct is to admire the warrior maids but since they have become the villains and they are being equated with Mary of Scots and

[11] Ariosto, *Orlando Furioso*, 1530. Tasso, *Gerusalemme Liberata*, published 1581, finished 1574. *Orlando Furioso* was translated into English by Sir John Harington, Queen Elizabeth's godson and designer of the water closet, and published in 1591.

[12] *Arcadia* was in circulation from about 1580 although not published until 1590.

her priests he is forced to a verse about the submissiveness of women, utterly at variance with his earlier statements and the fact of Britomart. What has happened is not only that historical allegory has led him astray but that Artegall's psychological make-up has broken through the formal scheme much as Guyon's did.

Artegall likes warrior women who will subdue and even humble him; so much is clear in his first reaction to Britomart. We are involved again in a taboo situation. Indeed all the situations which develop around Britomart are in some sense taboo ones. Women fall in love with her, lovers are jealous of her, Amoret is afraid Britomart will demand the customary reward of a rescuer, and Britomart, to hide her sex, plays up to her.[13]

There is another version of Elizabeth in Book III in the huntress Belphoebe, sister of Amoret, brought up by Diana. Built into her story is an historical episode concerning Raleigh and the queen, where Raleigh appears as the squire Timias. It refers to his falling out of favour when he got Mistress Throckmorton pregnant and married her. The whole episode is told at length under a fiction skillfully and totally convincingly worked into the overall plot so that it can be read without any knowledge of its historic counterpart. Psychologically it's an expression of social disparity in love, a situation Ariosto had also treated but with a happy resolution. Timias betrays Belphoebe, or she thinks he has, and for a time he almost loses his reason and lives like a wild man in the woods. They are eventually reconciled by a bird.

Two more interesting themes take up the rest of Book III. One is embodied in Florimel, a woman of such helpless beauty that she is in constant danger of rape and flees through the book from one horrifying pursuer to the other. Spenser's descriptions of grotesque lechery are forcefully revolting. The other is the story of Hellenore whose husband is a jealous miser.

Many of the knights exhibit the pains of jealousy but always rationally in a context of romantic love. Malbecco is jealous as a form of avarice. When his house is burning he can't decide whether to go after his wife, who is running

---

[13] See Chapter VI.

away with her lover, or put the flames out that are engulf-
ing his money. The money wins. Paridell seduces the wife,
Hellenore, and then abandons her. She is found by the
satyrs and lives with them as wife-in-common. When her
old husband asks her to return with him she refuses:

> And by no meanes would to his will be wonne,
> But chose amongst the jolly Satyres still to wonne.[14]

By the "jolly" Spenser is suggesting that there is nothing
wrong with natural sex. He doesn't condemn Hellenore's
promiscuity, but regards it as a normal state, particularly
for primitive people. It's preferred to avaricious jealousy
and the implied impotence of the husband Malbecco. It
also unconsciously suggests a fable of bestiality. The satyrs
were part goat and very virile; not afraid to spend their
sexuality.

> At night, when all they went to sleep, he vewd
> Whereas his lovely wife emongst them lay,
> Embraced of a Satyre rough and rude,
> Who all the night did minde his joyous play:
> Nine times he heard him come aloft ere day,
> That all his heart with gelosy did swell;
> But yet that night's ensample did bewray
> That not for nought his wife them loved so well.[15]

The two great set-pieces of the book are the Gardens of
Adonis, the perfect celebration of happy, fruitful love and
its opposite the Mask of Cupid, a rout of lust and love
deformed.

Book IV continues and ties up many of the plots of the
previous one. It contains two stories of interwoven lovers,
one with a disguised brother/sister incest theme happily
ended by another brother and sister, and that of Placidas
and Amyas, the devoted friends. Amyas's mistress has been
carried off by a monster who first rapes then devours
women. Amyas himself is held captive by a giant's daugh-

---

[14] Book III, x, 51.
[15] Book III, x, 47.

ter who wants him for her lover but he is rescued by his friend who takes his place.

Book V takes us to Ireland under disguise of fighting the pagans. The historical identifications are at their most precise and the book, concerned with politics and the enforcement of an unfortunate policy which Spenser himself was deeply involved in, lacks the imaginative depth of the earlier ones.[16]

In the final book however all Spenser's abilities are working to the full and straight allegory is left behind except for the continuation of the Raleigh story. The setting is pastoral; the acknowledged theme courtesy. Once again we are in the enchanted wood. Our hero is Sir Calidore, thought to be modeled on that pattern of Elizabethan chivalry, Sir Philip Sidney, and the pastoral episode at the end an image of Sidney's writing of the *Arcadia*. If this is so, and it seems to me a convincing theory based on the way a writer's mind works, it provides a perfect example of all the points I have been making about the osmosis of England into faeryland, and of her aristocracy into elfin knights under the Faerie Queene, as a feat of the idealizing imagination, not simply a piece of stucco flattery. For this episode of Calidore among the shepherds is as artistically successful as, and, I believe, the emotional source for, parts of *As You Like It* and *The Winter's Tale*. The shepherd girls, both lost children, Perdita and Pastorella, are natural sisters[17] but it is in tone and atmosphere that Spenser and Shakespeare are most alike, immeasurables which are nevertheless the features which truly distinguish one writer from another; in their combination of classicism and freshness, of the weary Ovid seen through Renaissance eyes. Nowhere is Spenser more Botticellian than in this book where Sir Calidore comes upon the three graces, the Queen of Love, and Venus's damsels all dancing to the music of a

---

[16] Part of the unsatisfactoriness of Book V may be that Artegall as he is first conceived as Britomart's lover loses all lustre without her. The best parts of this book are those where the, as it were, black Britomart subdues him and the white rescues him, a piece of psychological understanding that has nothing to do with the suppression of Ireland.

[17] Indeed it would seem most likely that Spenser's charming choice of name aurally influenced Shakespeare's.

shepherd's pipe. It seems, as Graham Hough says in his *A Preface To The Faerie Queene,* incredible that he hadn't seen "La Primavera."[18] The piping shepherd is Spenser himself; the fourth grace his new wife. At the approach of Calidore they all vanish like the fairies whom they resemble. There was no distinction in the poet's mind between the two. He too had perceived that they are the same.

The most blatant piece of taboo-breaking that this last book gives us is a return to the theme of lust linked with cannibalism, treated before but now experienced in full as if in defiance of the pastoral idyll. Serena wakes to find herself surrounded by savages who strip her for sacrifice,

> Which as they view with lustfall fantasyes,
> Each wisheth to himself . . .
> Her yvorie neck; her alabaster brest;
> Her paps, which like white silken pillowes were
> For love in soft delight thereon to rest;
> Her tender sides; her bellie white and clere,
> Which like an Altar did itselfe uprere
> To offer sacrifice divine thereon;
> Her goodly thighes, whose glorie did appeare
> The spoiles of Princes hang'd which were in battle
>   won.[19]

The priest lifts his knife, they all shout, bagpipes and horns shriek, the victim wails and at the last moment Sir Calepine, her lover, bursts into the terrifying scene for rescue.

Is this part of fairyland? There are vampire fairies in tradition, and Spenser's "salvage nation," although there is

---

[18] What he may have seen were tapestries showing this scene. Spenser is the most visual of poets and his descriptions of tapestries in *The Faerie Queene* may be the clue to the originals for Shakespeare's descriptions of Venus and Adonis and Lucretia. Did both poets see Venus and Adonis tapestries at Essex House which Spenser describes at length in Book III, i, 34–? If Spenser did go to France in his early adolescence he may have seen the frescoes at Fontainebleau or he may have visited Nonesuch and seen such scenes there. The Lumley inventory, 1590, lists a Venus and Adonis picture among the possessions of Lord Lumley. Leicester's inventory for probate 1588 lists a *Diana* and *Diana with Actacon.*

[19] Book VI, viii, 42.

no description of animal attributes, certainly suggests the obscene goblins of *Goblin Market*. They whoop and halloo with a dreadful glee and swarm about her like flies. Sir Calepine has no difficulty in slaying them in swarms. They certainly suggest that they are less than human height. Serena herself is inclined to "loosenesse" and that is why she becomes their victim. She is bitterly wounded by the Blatant Beast, slander, whom Sir Calidore is pursuing. The squire Timias/Raleigh is another of his victims whom she encounters. Raleigh had already called his wife Serena in a poem. Spenser is referring to the scandal which followed their clandestine marriage and Elizabeth's anger.

As in a dream the figures fuse and separate, vanish and are replaced by others. Mythology, history and faery are all caught up into Spenser's tapestry.

> Whether it were the traine of beauties Queene,
> Or Nymphes, or Faeries, or enchanted show,
> With which his eyes mote have deluded beene.

Through the enchanted wood goes the vision of the Faerie Queene herself, now buskinned as an Amazon, now dancing among her ladies-in-waiting or bathing in Diana's pool or affronting Spain in her shining armor. Some critics have suggested that the Faerie Queene is hardly present, that the title is misleading and in itself a piece of gross flattery. They have not understood the organization of a dream, of enchantment, of figures superimposed one on the other, of that child's garden of Eden presided over by "her majesty, our mother" which became for forty years faerie England.

CHAPTER VIII

The English Wood Near Athens

Ladies and gallants of our court, to end
And give a timely period to our sports,
Let us conclude them with declining night;
Our empire is but of the darker half.
                    Cynthia's Revels, Ben Jonson

All this would have been in Shakespeare's mind when he wrote *A Midsummer Night's Dream* and in the minds of the educated part of his audience. The relative dates of composition make it impossible for it not to be so and the structure of the play confirms it. The first three books of *The Faerie Queene* were in published circulation, the second three probably circulating privately or possibly just published, depending on whether we fix the date for the play's first performance in 1595 or '96. Spenser was at the height of his fame, a friend of Essex and Raleigh and honored by the queen, although he seems to have displeased Burleigh, probably because of the annual pension of fifty pounds awarded him by Elizabeth in 1591.[1]

Given the Elizabethan passion for identification and the currency of Spenser's work contemporaries could not have failed to make the identification Elizabeth/Titania as they made that of Elizabeth/Richard II. This last seems to us far-fetched and without the documentation it's unlikely that it would have occurred to us. Yet the facts are indisputable. The play *Richard II* was performed on Essex's behalf by commission of his supporters on the day before his rebellion.[2] In conversation with the keeper of the Tower records, William Lombarde, in 1601, Elizabeth, when she came to the reign of Richard in going through them with the old man said: "I am Richard the seconde, know ye not that?" Lombarde answered: "Such a wicked imagination was determined and attempted by a most unkind gentleman, the most adorned creature that ever your Majesty made." "He that will forget God will also forget

---

[1] Burleigh is reputed to have said: "All that money for a song."
[2] State Papers Domestic 278: 78, 85.

his benefactors; this tragedy was played forty times in open streets and houses," was her reply.[3] It wasn't until after Elizabeth's death that *Richard II* was published in full with the deposition scene. However, it appears from her conversation with Lombarde that no attempt was made to stop the play.

This seems to have been Elizabeth's attitude whenever possible. Probably she thought it better to ignore comment rather than suppress it since by this method she at least knew what was being said and may have thought it a safety valve.

During the last six or seven years of Essex's life relations between himself and the queen alternated between loving reconciliation and bitter quarrels culminating in his rebellion. "A man of a nature not to be ruled, of an estate not grounded to his greatness; of a popular reputation; of a military reputation," Francis Bacon wrote of and to him, urging him to change his ways. "I demand whether there can be a more dangerous image than this represented to any monarch living, much more to a lady, and of her Majesty's apprehension."[4]

Essex's great friend was the Earl of Southampton to whom Shakespeare had dedicated *Venus and Adonis* in 1593 and *The Rape of Lucrece* in 1594. Between the two dedications the relationship of poet and patron had become much closer. The *Venus and Adonis* dedication is a standard piece of formality. Southampton was the subject of many such in his role as patron of the arts, which might seem strange to us in a young man of twenty but was not at all so to his contemporaries. By the next year Shakespeare's love to his lordship is "without end." "What I have done is yours, what I have to doe is yours, being part in all I have, devoted yours." Without entering into the controversy about whether he was or was not the "lovely boy" of the sonnets and Mr. W.H., it appears that the relationship was a developing one and, by then, beyond the ordinary relations of writer and patron.

Southampton allied himself to Essex's faction further by marrying his cousin. Eventually he was tried and imprisoned with him, although reprieved from execution. He was

---

[3] Nichols's *Progresses*, Vol. II.
[4] October 4th, 1596, *The Elizabethan Journals*, ed. cit.

constantly at Essex House which Essex filled with a group of young courtiers of both sexes and where private performances of plays were given. Southampton was an avid playgoer. Essex was also a patron of, among others, Spenser, as if in this too he was trying to emulate and outdo Leicester, his stepfather.[5] What was clear to all men's minds was that the mantle of chief favorite had passed from one to the other, however Elizabeth might understand and differentiate the relationships.

Essex, unlike Leicester, in his ambition and jealousy brooked no rivals while at the same time forcing others into a posture of rivalry. His tantrums constantly split the country in two: those of his part, those of the other whose leaders were Cecil and Raleigh. Through his association with Southampton Shakespeare was drawn to Essex's side.

The pull wasn't simply one of self-interest. Essex was young, aristocratic and charming. He drew many to him and he provided a glittering circle immediately attractive to a yeoman poet, with gentle blood on his mother's side, and aspirations not only to a successful career in the public theaters but to literary gentility, as his longer poems and "sugred sonnets" show.

Essex was young and a man; Elizabeth an aging woman, to the earlier generation of poets like Spenser, who had known Leicester, the ageless Fairy Queen, but to the younger, colored by Essex's impatience, a subject for envious misogyny. There's no space here to enter into a long discussion of Shakespeare's attitude to women or all his affiliations with the Essex group. But, to summarize: it is in the later plays that women become redeeming daughters, in the earlier, with the exception of the romantic heroines who are there for their plot value and will be successfully put down by marriage, they are fools, schemers and harlots. The romantic heroines are often as sexually equivocal as the sonnets would lead us to expect. Only Portia in *The Merchant of Venice* comes anywhere near Spenser's idea of equality. On the second point it is now generally ac-

---

[5] Some explanation of Essex's behavior might be found in a study of the psychological web of Leicester, Elizabeth, Essex and his mother, Lettice Knollys, herself a cousin of the Queen. It is a complexity reminiscent of Webster and a further comment on the smallness of that educated aristocratic world. That Essex and Leicester were both called Robin is a point not to be missed.

cepted that *Love's Labour's Lost* was written for performance first to Essex and then to the queen, before whom it was played at Christmas 1597, and that it is a highly topical play with the character of Don Armado representing Raleigh.[6]

I believe *A Midsummer Night's Dream* to be a similar play. Like *Love's Labour's Lost* it has no single source and, in form, it is modeled on *Endimion,* written for court production. It bears strong resemblances to court masques and to the two most famous entertainments of Elizabeth's progresses at Kenilworth and Elvetham. It is likely that it was written for a wedding, possibly for that double wedding at Essex House in November 1596 for which Spenser wrote his *Prothalamion.* The play is deeply indebted to Spenser and contains a specific reference to one of his poems, which I will deal with later, and which would have had added point from his being present.

On the queen's Accession Day, always an occasion for celebration and entertainment, in 1595, Bacon wrote a particularly lavish masque for Essex showing his devotion to his mistress's, Elizabeth's, love. Essex was in great favor. There followed the abortive attempt to save Calais and the taking of Cadiz. Essex returned a popular hero. In July the playhouses were closed by order of the Privy Council.[7] This would have given Shakespeare time and incentive to write *A Midsummer Night's Dream* for a private production. By this time Essex was out of favor again, having failed to bring back anything but personal glory from his expedition.

The Other Sources

The critically acknowledged sources for the play are Plutarch's *Lives,* recently republished, for Theseus; Apuleius's *Golden Ass* for Bottom's transformation, combined with Reginald Scot's *Discoverie of Witchcraft* and various retellings of the story of Pyramus and Thisbe.[8]

[6] For a full discussion of this see Walter Oakeshott, *The Queen and the Poet* (Faber, 1960). *Richard II* may have been written, as well as understood, poetically.

[7] Acts of the Privy Council, July 22nd.

[8] G. Bullough, *Narrative and Dramatic Sources of Shakespeare,* I.

Oberon, as I have already said, I believe was taken from Spenser, from Elizabeth's elfin genealogy in Book II. Robin Goodefellow or Puck is from the *Discoverie of Witchcraft*[9] although he also seems, from references in other plays slightly later, to have been a character in folk plays, dressed in calf's skin and with face and hands "coloured russet-colour," that is grey like a ghost, making him another form of the traditional devil with a broom who demands money for the players.

> Money I want and money I crave.
> If you don't give me money
> I'll sweep you all to your grave.

Titania herself is taken straight from Ovid's *Metamorphoses*. In all I have counted twenty-six references to that work in *A Midsummer Night's Dream*. The play is so steeped in it that Shakespeare must have been reading the book just before he began work. There was an English translation which we know he had read before writing *The Tempest* since Prospero's farewell is based in part almost word for word on it.[10] But for Titania he read the original.

The passage[11] is unfortunately too long to quote in full. It's a retelling of the story of Diana and Actaeon. There is the grove in a region thick grown with pine and cypress, the bower with its fountain, the attendant nymphs, Actaeon's metamorphosis into the stag, the flung water drops and the hunting hounds and Diana is called Titania. All these are present, some in disguise, in *A Midsummer Night's Dream*.

How did Shakespeare make the immediate jump from Diana/Titania to Titania/Fairy Queen? Partly it was by common tradition. "That fourth kinde of spirites, which by the Gentiles wass called Diana, and her wandring court and amongst us was called the Phairie (as I told you) or our good neighboures . . ." wrote King James VI in his *Daemonologie* published in 1597. Partly it was from the concept of the triple goddess Diana/Phoebe/Hecate in her

---

[9] Puck is however also in Spenser's *Epithalamion*.
[10] Medea's incantation that Gower had found so exciting.
[11] *Metamorphoses*, Book III, 155.

third manifestation as enchantress, a theory which Shakespeare refers to in the play and which is mentioned in *Metamorphoses* in Medea's incantation.

Diana was Elizabeth, the Faerie Queene was Elizabeth, Cynthia or Phoebe was Elizabeth. Titania was Elizabeth. In *Cynthia's Revels*, Jonson's play performed before the queen in 1601, there is a long speech by Cynthia referring to the late rebellion in detail.

> For so Actaeon by presuming far
> Did, to our grief, incur a fatal doom.

Essex is Actaeon. The giveaway phrase is "to our grief" which is relevant only to the historical happening not to the mythological.[12]

Endimion had been Leicester. Oberon, I conclude, is Essex and the wrangling between the fairy couple is a counterpart to the quarrels between him and the queen.[13] The year 1596 saw the culmination of unnatural weather in a great famine. Titania speaks of it in her famous weather speech in Act II, scene I, ending:

> And this same progeny of evils
> Comes from our debate, from our dissension.
> We are their parents and original

reminding us of "Her Majesty, our mother." The dramatic purpose of the fairy plot is to end the dissension but it's only achieved by trickery, which makes Titania look foolish and submit to Oberon. By the beliefs of the Essex faction Elizabeth was foolish in her favoring of unworthy figures and should have been ruled by the manly Essex. The whole nation was disrupted by their quarreling.

> Oberon: Do you amend it, then. It lies in you.
>   Why should Titania cross her Oberon?
>   I do but beg a little changeling boy
>   To be my henchman.

---

[12] In the next lines Mary Queen of Scots appears as Niobe.

[13] Shakespeare could have found literary precedent for this in Chaucer's argument between Pluto and Prosperpine in *The Merchant's Tale*. See Chapter III.

As in *The Faerie Queene* not every character will have its historical counterpart. The "little changeling boy" may have been a reference now lost to us, someone like her godson Sir John Harington whose allegiance was first to the queen but seemed to have been transferred to Essex when he was with him in Ireland. What it symbolized unconsciously was the succession; the heir that Elizabeth had never had but must adopt and that might be Essex himself. For whatever he might admit even in his own mind, the desire was latent there and realized in such incidents as his identification with the usurper Henry IV and its expression in the dedications, pamphlets and pictures that made him a popular hero. He was young enough to be her son, hers and Leicester's, already in a sense his father. All the overtones of the son-lover and mother-mistress embodied in the myths of the Fairy Queen were present in their relationship.

Puck too may, or may not, have had a contemporary counterpart. Southampton is the most likely candidate because of his relationship to Essex but there's no evidence for this and no need to specify. I can't but think that there was a great laugh at:

How now, spirit; whither wander you?

Burleigh was Elizabeth's spirit. "Sir Spirit," she wrote to him, "I doubt I do nickname you, for those of your kind (they say) have no sense; but I have of late seen an ecce signum that if an ass kick you, you feel it too soon. I will recant you from being my spirit, if ever I perceive that you disdain not such a feeling." The spirit answers that it serves the Fairy Queen and describes its wanderings and work in a satire of Burleigh's ubiquitousness and with a reference to Elizabeth's gentlemen pensioners, but all expressed with a charm that should preclude offence.

It was Elizabeth's habit to give nicknames, particularly animal ones, to those about her. Raleigh was Water, Walsingham her Moor, Hatton her lids or her Mutton, Simier her monkey, the Duke of Alencon her frog, Lady Norris her own Crow and so on. For the Fairy Queen then to be enamored of an ass took on a double meaning.

This brings us to the human characters. If the play meant

on the historical level what I am suggesting, whom are we to understand by Hippolyta and Theseus? Spenser provides the answer. I think it likely that a reading of the first three books of *The Faerie Queene* when they were published in 1590 was the spur to Shakespeare's close reading of Ovid. As the queen is shadowed in at least three different guises in *The Faerie Queene*, one of them the warrior maiden Britomart, so Hippolyta is also Elizabeth. There is a particular verse in Spenser that directly suggests this. It's a description of Belphoebe.

> Such as Diana by the sandy shore
> Of swift Eurotas or on Cynthus greene,
> Where all the Nymphes have her unawares forlore,
> Wandreth alone with bow and arrows keene,
> To seek her game; Or as that famous Queene
> Of Amazons, whom Pyrrhus did destroy.[14]

Elizabeth was often identified with an Amazon, usually Hippolyta. In the verses by Churchyard celebrating the defeat of the Armada she had been called "an Amazonian Quene." Hippolyta is a queen; Theseus only a duke which could be understood in the sense of dux or military leader.

His character is that of an idealized Essex, an Essex as he frequently liked to present himself, as a sober, religious but military nobleman. It was remarked that after his return from Cadiz he was particularly grave and given to sermons. He wrote letters of advice to a lord who was about to travel, sat with one who refused to repent before execution and was apostrophized as "Magnanimous Essex" in a lamentation for Drake. Theseus by Spenser's shadowing method is Essex.

For the lovers there is no need to be precise. However, they do in their complications resemble the affairs of the young courtiers. Essex's sister Penelope was betrothed to Sir Philip Sidney but married Lord Rich, although she continued as Sidney's mistress. Sidney, while continuing as her lover, married Frances Walsingham, who after his death married Essex. Penelope after Sidney's death lived in open adultery with Charles Blount (who had worsted

---

[14] *Faerie Queene*, Book II, iii, 31.

Essex in a duel over the queen's favor) largely at Essex House. By comparison the confusions of the fictional lovers appear simple. Penelope and Frances living in the same house could indeed be said to have been like Helena and Hermia:

> Two of the first, like coats in heraldry,
> Due but to one, and crowned with one crest.
> Like to a double cherry, seeming parted
> But yet an union in partition,

since they had twice shared a man. I don't think that Shakespeare intended a conscious reference but that the knowledge lay at the bottom of his mind and affected this passage which scholars have found hard to interpret. Frances and Penelope literally shared a crest, as wife and sister.

Finally the ass of Titania's dotage, Bottom, the pretentious yokel, is a figure with elements of Sir Tophas, Don Armado and Braggadoccio in *The Faerie Queene*. Again there's no need to specify. The ass could be any fool on whom Elizabeth lavished her favor to the exclusion of Essex. In 1596 Lady Russell had visited Anthony Bacon to try to win him over to Robert Cecil since Bacon was the most staunch of Essex's supporters. Bacon's comment was: "Brame d'ame ne monte pas au ciel." "By God," said Lady Russell, "but he is no ass." "Let him go for a mule then, Madam, the most mischievous beast that is." We don't know if this conversation antedates the play. It might be a reflection of it.

The person I would like to propose is Raleigh. In this piece of literary detection he is my number one suspect. Certain things about him were detested by Essex and a great many others. Whether they were true or not doesn't concern us, only how far they could be said to fit Bottom. His low birth and his yokelish accent, his pretentions to be a poet and a soldier, his vanity, his greed and the fact that he had made money through the queen's favor, his boasting, all rankled with the educated aristocrats, as Essex had once pointed out to the queen at length while Raleigh in his official office guarded the door close enough to hear most of what was said.[15] All this squares very well with Bottom. Quince and company would be probably unspecific members of Raleigh's group although I wonder whether some rival dramatist, Chapman perhaps, might not be glanced at in Quince himself.

All these suggestions should not be taken as any attempt on my part to belittle the play. I hope I have made it quite clear in the previous chapters that the use of an historical layer in a work or as the originating inspiration for a work, particularly at this period, need be in no sense a lessening of it. At the same time a proper knowledge of such an element can illuminate the whole structure. We accept this in paintings; there is no reason why we should apologize for it in literature.

Some Notes

A Midsummer Night's Dream begins with an image of the moon, one of the most recurrent and potent images in the play. It was also one of Elizabeth's most common images, as Spenser and Lyly testify. There is a reference in Sonnet 107 to Elizabeth as the moon.

> The mortal moon hath her eclipse endured
> And the sad augurs mock their own presage

refers to the superstitious fears which attended the queen's reaching sixty-three, in 1596, which was thought the human climacteric because of its perfect number. Shakespeare was, at this time, so imbued with the idea of the Queen-Moone that it's constantly breaking out in the play with unconscious overtones. The remark about the old moon lingering out Theseus's desires "like to a stepdame, or a dowager/Long withering out a young man's revenue" is an echo of the Elizabeth/Essex situation.[16] Hippolyta's

[15] Lytton Strachey, *Elizabeth and Essex* (Evergreen Books, 1940), pp. 37–38. My comments on Raleigh are not to be taken as my estimate of him but as how he appeared to unsympathetic contemporaries of a rival faction. In Spenser he is Tim*ias*.

[16] Essex was extremely extravagant and constantly suing for lucrative posts or receiving hand-outs from the Queen. Such was the system that this carried no dishonor. As the emotional heir apparent it was thought his due. I think there are other acrimonious references to Elizabeth in the sonnets in the remarks on age, painting, wigs, in, for instance, numbers 67 and 68 and such things as:

answer defends the moon with a strong suggestion of Endimion's speeches in defence of the waxing and waning of Cynthia. The "silver bow new bent" at once suggests Diana. Titania is already fluttering part-seen in these first speeches.

The entry of Egeus, his daughter and her two would-be lovers brings in the subject of chastity versus marriage. Again the moon is the symbol of virginity but Theseus speaks against it in a passage very reminiscent of the end of the masque of Diana, not given but published, from the Kenilworth revels, exhorting Elizabeth to marry. It was not a suggestion which would have pleased her majesty but is in keeping with Shakespeare's sonnets on the "get a son" theme.

Hermia's reply causes Theseus to threaten her with Diana's altar. It was generally said that Elizabeth preferred her ladies-in-waiting to be chaste like herself. Hermia must decide at "the next new moon."

Left alone Lysander and Hermia lament together in a kind of litany on the discrepancies that may separate lovers. The matter is a paraphrase of the concerns of the *Metamorphoses*, "the course of true love never did run smooth"; the form is from *Endimion*, the to and fro between Endimion and Tellus on Cynthia.

> Tell.: Why she is but a woman.
> End.: No more was Venus.
> Tell.: She shall have end.
> End.: So shall the world.
> Tell.: Is not her beauty subject to time?
> End.: No more than time is to standing still.[17]

When Hermia swears to be true she does so in images from Ovid. When Helena descants on Hermia's fairness it is in pastoral images from *Arcadia* or Spenser. Later in the scene Hermia and Helena use the *Endimion* antiphonal

---

"Strength by limping away disabled"
"Burn the long liv phoenix in her blood"

I believe that at this time Shakespeare moved in a group where such topics were everyday gossip.

[17] Act II, sc. 1.

form. It leads to another moon image from Ovid: Phoebe beholding her silver visage in the watery glass and "decking with liquid pearl the bladed grass." This introduces the second most potent image, that of water drops, those which Diana threw at Actaeon with such effect. At our first encounter with the fairies this activity will be transferred to them on Titania's behalf, further proof that Diana and Titania are one. Left alone Helena laments on the blindness of Cupid and his childishness. The passage is once again Ovid-derived, with strong affinities with Spenser. Demetrius's oaths are showers reminiscent of Jove's appearance to Danaë as a shower of gold.

Scene Two brings in the mechanicals. Bottom's behavior is noticeably like that of the braggart Sir Tophas in *Endimion* particularly in his "raging rocks" speech. His moving storms also suggests Raleigh's extreme behavior when he was imprisoned by Elizabeth for seducing his future wife. His boasting and desire to play the tyrant Ercles echo Raleigh's vein in his letters and his military persona. The sudden desire to play Thisbe as well could be a cast at Raleigh's all-roundness, as poet, soldier, discoverer, and his aspiring to be a courtly lover. Quince's flattery to persuade him not to play the lion again smacks of Raleigh as does Bottom's concern with his costume. Raleigh was noted for the flamboyance of his dress. Above all it is the aspiration to culture of this yokel that reflects the Essex group's dislike of Raleigh.

I have already discussed the spirit and the mention of Elizabeth's pensioners which open Act II. The trochaic verse form, distinct from the basic iambic pentameters of the rest of the play, which the fairy characters often use is seven or occasionally eight syllabled, ending on a strong beat. Lyly had used it for the fairy song in *Endimion*. It's also used for the witches in *Macbeth*, for Prospero's final speech in *The Tempest* and by Milton for the disenchanting in *Comus*. It seems to be a recognized fairy form, possibly related to the folk play.

The Actaeon myth has affected Puck's account of Oberon's doings. He is a hunter tracing the forests wild. Diana's fountain is also mentioned. Traditionally the Fairy King might be attended by knights but the reference takes on added significance when we realize that one of the chief points of contention between Elizabeth and Essex was his habit of making knights after every enterprise, which she expressly forbad.[18]

The fairy's account of Puck is straight from tradition via Reginald Scot. It's tempting to wonder if Southampton had a reputation for those practical jokes beloved of the Elizabethans; those who paused too long by the pool of a famous house would be suddenly doused by hidden sprinklers while the watchers from the windows fell about with laughter.

With the entry of Titania the moonlight is turned full on. Immediately she and Oberon begin to wrangle. She will not submit. "Am not I thy lord?" Her ostensible reason is sexual jealousy with which they both charge each other. The weather speech which I have already discussed follows. After her description of the evils so well known to contemporaries that the queen issued special edicts to cope with the famine and a booklet was published reminiscent of wartime with instructions on substitutes for beer and flour, there is a further invocation of the moon, "the governess of floods" who "Pale in her anger, washes all the air."

Titania describes the changeling's mother as a votaress of her order, as it might be one of Diana's nymphs or Elizabeth's ladies-in-waiting. Titania's bearing is dignified and queenly. She offers a reconciliation and leaves when Oberon repeats his impossible claim. When she is gone Oberon summons Puck and in a long speech recalls the Princely Pleasures of Kenilworth, the fireworks, the water masque with mermaid and dolphin, making a generally acknowledged reference to the queen, "a fair vestal throned by the west." Cupid loosed his loveshaft at her but it was

> Quenched in the chaste beams of the watery moon
> And the imperial votaress passed on
> In maiden meditation fancy free.

In the published account of the Pleasures where the gods are all invoked Venus charges her son not to shoot while Elizabeth is there. In the masque of Diana, Zabeta is the

---

[18] Her own godson was knighted by Essex in Ireland and fled from her in fear on his return.

goddess's votaress and the attempt is to persuade her to marry. We know that she did indeed pass on in maiden meditation.

The herb itself recalls the magic herbs in Ovid which Medea seeks to rejuvenate Aeson, the herbs in *Endimion* which put him to sleep, the herbs Belphoebe gathers in *The Faerie Queene* to cure Raleigh/Timias. Oberon's herb is very potent. The witch Dipsas in *Endimion* says that she cannot rule affections by enchantment. Only the gods can do that. What Oberon's enchantment is to induce in Titania is bestiality. He lists only animals as objects of her unnatural affection. The queen had already doted on a sheep, a meddling monkey and a frog: Hatton, Simier and Alencon. Puck's boasted speed recalls *Endimion* and Eumenides: "with wings on my legs I fly for remedy" when Cynthia sends him to Thessaly in search of a cure for Endimion's sleep.

The wrangling of Demetrius and Helena echoes the earlier quarrel. Two parallels from Ovid were in Shakespeare's mind: the attempts of the nymph Salmacis to win Hermaphroditus, Apollo and Daphne; and probably his own *Venus and Adonis*. The wood has already had the taboo-breaking effect of enchantment. Helena is unnaturally pursuing when she should be the pursued; Demetrius threatens to rape her.

Puck returns with the flower and Oberon begins his famous speech about the bank where Titania sleeps. It's modeled on the "lunary bank" on which Endimion falls asleep and some of the flowers mentioned, particularly the chaste eglantine, were iconographically associated with Elizabeth.[19] The song Titania's fairies sing is the reverse of the first song in *Endimion* with which they waken Sir Tophas who has had a dream of an owl.

> The clamorous owl that nightly hoots and wonders
> At our quaint spirits.
> What music's best to wake him?
> Bow wow, let bandogs shake him.
> Let adders hiss in's ear.
> Else earwigs wriggle there.[20]

[19] The iconography of Elizabeth is fully discussed in R. C. Strong's *Portraits of Queen Elizabeth I* (O.U.P. 1963).
[20] *Endimion*, Act III, sc. 3.

It's sometimes alleged that Shakespeare began the fashion for the miniature which continued on through Drayton and Herrick but Spenser had already written his *Muiopotmos* by 1590, the story of the butterfly, anticipating Disney by over three hundred years. However, the lullaby gave renewed vigor to the fashion, ensuring the popularity of small fairies at least until Tinker Bell and Rose Fyleman.

When the other pair of lovers enter, the wood has already begun to confuse them. Lysander tries to seduce Hermia who rebuffs him. Puck anoints his eyes and he starts awake to fall in love with Helena; he has indeed forgot his way. Helena describes herself with another image from Ovid, that of the unhappy Callisto, Diana's nymph seduced by Jove, changed to a bear. Hermia herself wakes alone and frightened by a dream of simple but violent sexuality, the serpent eating her heart away while Lysander smiles on, relating back to his attempt to seduce her, and her fearful wish that he had done so, and also forward to her situation.

What has happened is that the lovers have entered the taboo situation of adolescent groups where the love objects become confused and interchangeable.[21] Falling in love with one's best friend's girl or one's girl friend's sister or boy friend's brother is an experience common enough, to judge by the agonized letters in personal columns. Rules within the group have until now tried to discipline such emotions to avoid internecine struggles. There is no space here to go into all the hidden motives, which include latent homosexuality and symbolic incest, only to remark that we should expect, in an enchanted place, the rules to be broken.

With Act III the mechanicals return and provide a contemporary reference in Bottom's qualms about frightening the ladies. In 1594 at the christening of Prince Henry a real lion was to have drawn in a chariot during the masque but was replaced by a "black-moore" at the last minute lest it should frighten or be frightened. Puck enters with his traditional words as quoted by Reginald Scot, "Hempen, hampen,"[22] converted to "What hempen homespuns."

The transformation of Bottom is a parody of the trans-

---

[21] Compare Mozart's *Così Fan Tutte*.
[22] See below, p. 162. Some editions have "hempen," some "hemten."

formation of Actaeon, one to an ass to become Titania's paramour, one to a stag to be destroyed for seeing her naked. There is also a hint of the transformation of Corsites by the fairies to a leopard in *Endimion* and of Raleigh/Timias's transformation to a mute savage by the queen/Belphoebe's wrath. If Bottom is Raleigh then his singing and Titania's pleasure in it becomes a reference to Raleigh's poems to her.

Titania's sharp: "Out of this wood do not desire to go!" contains another *Endimion* echo where Tellus says that she will entangle him in such a sweet net "that he shall neither find the means to come out nor desire it."[23] She behaves as we should expect the Fairy Queen to, heaping her lover with favors as Sir Launfal's lady did but she is also like Elizabeth rewarding her favorites. Raleigh in particular had grown rich at her hand and the "jewels from the deep" would be very appropriate to him. Titania's final speech separates the moon and herself, a device familiar in *Endimion* and *The Faerie Queene,* the moon lamenting the loss of chastity with her watery eye, Titania having her lover led gagged to her bower, a comic effect but in keeping with the injunction given to so many mortal lovers of fairies not to speak of their good fortune. The magnitude and complexity of the taboos broken by the union of Bottom and Titania surely need no unraveling.

Oberon and Puck return for Scene Two, Puck to recount the happenings. In his long speech he says:

And at our stamp here o'er and o'er one falls

which finishes the borrowed Robin Goodfellow quote from Reginald Scot.[24] A great deal is sometimes made of Shakespeare's "countryman's knowledge." I see little evidence of it; for example he is very unreliable on flowers and has put editors to endless footnotes trying to distinguish botanically some plant thrown in for its charming name.[25] I do see

[23] Act I, sc. 2.
[24] Scot: What have we here? Hemton, hamten, here will I never more tread nor stampen. Shakes.: What hempen homespuns have we swaggering here?
[25] See below, Act IV, sc. 1.

evidence of the reader of the back of the cornflakes packet, the subsumer of every scrap of written matter that came to eye and a conflation of fragments into a self-consistent whole. Puck is a literary not a folk creation.

When Demetrius and Hermia enter the unchaining effect of magic is working steadily. Hermia is accusing him of murder. He in his turn, with a side glance at the Actaeon leitmotiv,[26] says he is eager to commit it. These are educated young people behaving with all inhibition gone and moving ever closer to actual violence. With the waking of Demetrius to renewed love for Helena, Helena moves into nightmare, the kind familiar to most of us where everyone is laughing at us. The enchantment and nightmare belong particularly to Helena and Hermia. Neither Demetrius nor Lysander suffer so deeply.

If the experience in the wood is taken as a dream then the two young men's dream wishes are quite straightforward. Demetrius really loves Helena; Lysander is having a temporary desire for the forbidden, his girl friend's best friend. But the girls are in much more complex situations because society denies them the active role and their wishes must be more subtly expressed. Hermia has the common problem of the women's magazines: if I don't sleep with him I may lose him; and so in her dream she does. She is also distressed by her own eroticism. Helena, rejected in life by Demetrius who has transferred his affections to Hermia, has dream revenge on Hermia and the sweetness of being pursued by both young men. Yet her super-ego won't allow her to enjoy it and it therefore presents itself in a form in which she thinks they are laughing at her and that Hermia is attacking her.

The four separate dreams are brilliantly interwoven to make a dramatic whole. The dream atmosphere is never lost. The wood itself sees to that. The four characters run or wander through it, torn and dirtied, seeking each other to woo or fight. For each one the other three are figures in his own dream. The effect should be surrealistic not comic.

The climax comes in Act III, scene 2 when all four of them are brought together. Hermia who is particularly affectionate in her speeches to Lysander is called "a burr, a

---

[26] "I had rather give his carcase to my hounds."

cat, a vile thing," the serpent of her dream. She has disobeyed her father to follow her lust and has run off with her lover. Now her guilt causes her to fear that he will leave her and then no one will want her. It is Helena who is made responsible, for Hermia is guilty towards her for having attracted Demetrius and because her feelings towards him have a certain equivocation which expresses itself in the violence of her rejection of him. She is in her own eyes low and black. She expects that the tables will be turned and Helena draw Lysander from her.

The two young men go off to fight and Oberon charges Puck to lead them apart from each other until they fall asleep and Lysander's proper loving sight can be restored. Puck calls Oberon "King of shadows," a reminder of the idea of Pluto as king of phayrie that Shakespeare would have found in Chaucer and of *Sir Orfeo*. Puck reminds Oberon that night is nearly over in a speech that combines two images from Ovid with the traditional "ghoules and ghostes." Oberon replies that they are "spirits of another sort." Shakespeare intends them to be closer to the classical myths than to hobgoblin and he intends also to underline their harmlessness as was done with the fairies who greeted Elizabeth on her progress. Again the image of Oberon the hunter is invoked. Traditionally there was a strong connection between the fairies and the dead. In *Sir Orfeo* there was no distinction between them but Shakespeare is more interested for his dramatic purpose in the literary than the folk tradition. Oberon, to be kingly and in keeping with his historical parallel, must contrast with the yokel Bottom even if this runs counter to tradition.[27] The references are again to Ovid. The blend of classical and traditional is strongly influenced by Spenser. The lovers, led on by Puck, in his Jack o'Lantern guise, fall asleep. This time Hermia is compared to Callisto in a suppressed image and the scene ends with a proverb Shakespeare had used before, in *Love's Labour's Lost*: Jack shall have Jill.

Act IV opens with the cruel scene of Titania doting

[27] There may also be a contemporary reference here to Chapman and Raleigh's "School of Night" similar to the possible one in *Love's Labour's Lost*, IV, 3. If so, this would be another hit at Raleigh. Chapman's poem on *The Shadow of Night* together with one to *Cynthia*, the Queen, was published in December 1593.

upon an ass. After Bottom's business with Peaseblossom and company, which in its identifying ritual has echoes of the calling-on in the folk plays, he falls into a deep sleep like Endimion. Sleep is constantly used in the play to effect enchantment and to maintain the mirror magic of dreams within the dream. Titania too falls asleep entwined about her clown. Her image of the woodbine gently entwisting the honeysuckle is delightful and quite inexplicable botanically.

Oberon comes forward to anoint her eyes and the Diana/Actaeon story plays behind his speech like the fountain into the goddess's pool. The enchanting water drops stand like tears in the flowers' eyes at Titania's shame. Oberon has the changeling child. He removes the enchantment with "Dian's bud." Only his show of pity takes off from the inherent nastiness of the scene in the complete subjugation of Titania, reduced from her rank of Fairy Queen to a foolish lust which she wakes to repent. A curious reversal of Oberon's boasting about his diurnalness occurs after he and Titania have danced to deepen the mortals' sleep. Puck warns that he hears the morning lark and Oberon answers:

> Then, my queen in silence sad
> Trip we after night's shade.

It seems they must follow the night to the other side of the globe.

Horns sound and Theseus and Hippolyta enter. Much scholarship has been exercised on the famous hound speeches but the explanation is very simple: they are Actaeon's hounds, described at length by Ovid. They won't tear Theseus to pieces for he is to marry Hippolyta but they are psychologically too important an element in the original story to be left out of its Dream metamorphosis. Theseus and Oberon are the conquerors of Diana/Titania/Hippolyta and so the hounds too are mastered and made harmless.

The lovers awake yet they are still under the influence of the enchantment and at first believe they have indeed had separate dreams. Bottom too awakes, as so often the lovers of the Fairy Queen awoke to find themselves alone and "on the cold hillside." So, it was hoped, Raleigh would awake to find himself out of Cynthia's favor and his hopes of preferment a vanished dream to which the upstart yokel had aspired. The reference to the ballad of Bottom's Dream may be to Raleigh's Cynthia poems.[28]

The act ends with his return to his fellows "to discourse wonders." Quince's comments on him fit Raleigh very well.

"Yea and the best person, too; and he is a very paramour for a sweet voice," suggests another jibe at Raleigh's poems to the Queen and Flute's answer: "You must say 'paragon.' A paramour is—God bless us—a thing of naught." Raleigh could never be in the double sense "a thing of naught" for he could never be the Queen's lover in anything but aspiration and fantasy.[29] But a paragon he might well be thought by his friends. He had dreamt of being the Faerie Queene's paramour, taking as his motto Amore et Virtute. What he has is riches from the Queen, "sixpence a day during his life" for playing the fool.

Their play is preferred and Bottom gives them final advice on costume and behavior. "And most dear actors, eat no onions nor garlic; for we are to utter sweet breath, and I do not doubt but to hear them say it is a sweet comedy."

---

[28] Raleigh's verse frequently employed repetition as a device that may also be glanced at in Bottom's speech. Compare too:

> Our Passions are most like to floods and streams,
> The shallow murmur; but the deep are dumb.
> So when affections yield discourse, it seems
> The bottom is but shallow whence they come.

Raleigh had aspired to write a long poem in celebration of Elizabeth of which fragments remain, notably the XI and last Book of the Ocean to Cynthia (see Oakeshott, op. cit.). On arriving in Ireland in 1589 however he found Spenser busy with *The Faerie Queene* and probably realized that to take them both back to England with him would do more to restore himself in Elizabeth's favor than attempting his own epic. Certainly he did bring Spenser back to publish the first three books and to meet Elizabeth, as Spenser makes clear in *Colin Clouts Come Home Againe*.

[29] Compare *Love's Labour's Lost*, Act V, sc. 2.

> Armado: I do adore thy sweet Grace's slipper.
> Boyet: Loves her by the foot.
> Dumain: He may not by the yard.

Garlick was an obscene farce jig, much loved by unsophisticated audiences; so too were jigs about onions, both for their presumed aphrodisiac qualities.[30]

From the evidence of the text as printed in the first quarto it seems as if additions were made to the opening speeches of Act V, possibly for publication. The effect is of a kind of apology for the play. Perhaps it was meant to mitigate the effect of the historical element. Theseus says that the lunatic, the lover and the poet are not to be held responsible for the productions of their overheated imaginations. It might have been thought that the poet had been too apt in giving airy nothing "a local habitation and a name." Cleverly it's Hippolyta who pleads for the truth of the dream.

If the play was first performed for a wedding it's a most baroque structure that has Theseus call for "a play to ease the anguish of a torturing hour." The brief of offered sports gives two subjects from Ovid and one from Spenser. The Battle with the Centaurs is in *Metamorphoses* XII, a curious choice for a wedding entertainment since it tells of mass rape at a wedding feast by the centaurs. That it should be sung by an Athenian eunuch is interesting since the battle is only ended after the death of the invincible Caeneus who had been a girl ravished by Neptune and as part of whose story the incident is told. Caeneus's change of sex has made the singer a eunuch by unconscious metamorphosis in the poet's mind.

The death of Orpheus[31] is also told in *Metamorphoses* XI and is the riot of the tipsy Bacchanals, the second offering. In Ovid it leads straight into the story of Midas which I believe to be the basis for Bottom's transformation to an ass. Two unfortunate happenings overtook Midas. He was given the golden touch which nearly caused his death and he was given ass's ears for saying that the songs of Pan

---

[30] Charles Read Baskerville, *The Elizabethan Jig and Related Song Drama* (Dover Publications Inc., New York, 1965), pp. 292–5. Whether onions and garlic were aphrodisiac or prophylactic (including of the pox) I'm not sure. The jig *Garlick* isn't recorded until 1612 but in a reference that indicates it was older. Certainly the onions were.

[31] There is a poem on this theme by R.B., probably Richard Barnfield, which was registered in 1595. Stationer's Register, iii, 48, Arber.

were better than those of Apollo; for preferring the rustic muse and setting himself up as a literary judge. He was punished for greed and pretentiousness: Raleigh's two vices.

Bearing in mind Raleigh's connection with Spenser who referred to himself constantly as a shepherd,[32] I believe that it's no coincidence that the other rejected offering is one of Spenser's poems, published after the success of the first three books of The Faerie Queene: The Tears of the Muses.

> "The thrice three Muses mourning for the death
>   Of learning, late deceased in beggary."
>   That is some satire keen and critical.

Shakespeare was in a difficult situation with Spenser whose patrons were the queen, Raleigh and Essex. The poem in question, although written before The Faerie Queene and therefore in a sense out of date, had said some biting things about the state of the theatre which Spenser at that time, before the rise of Shakespeare, had criticized for its vulgarity and pandering to low audiences since Lyly's retirement.[33] Each of the thrice three Muses speaks in turn. Thalia's piece begins

> Where be the sweete delights of learnings treasure
> That wont with Comick sock to beautifie
> The painted Theaters ...

Most commentators are agreed that Shakespeare's early work shows a strong influence of Spenser which recedes after 1597. A Midsummer Night's Dream may have been among many other things a piece of exorcism.

Theseus and Hippolyta discuss the value of the kind of entertainment Elizabeth was given on her progresses. Theseus's comments would come most appropriately from the queen who was particularly kind to clerks who shivered and looked pale and were unable to go on with their prepared speeches. At Norwich she called out "Be not afraid,"

---

[32] Raleigh too called himself "the shepherd of the ocean." See *Colin Clouts Come Home Againe.*

[33] I accept Chambers's indentification

to the schoolmaster who had to make a Latin speech and afterwards told him it was the best she had ever heard.

Of the play itself there is little to be said that hasn't already been noticed by academics and producers except to note the continued influence of *Endimion*, particularly its prologue, on the moonshine sequence, where the rhythm of Starveling's "the lantern is the moon, I the man i'th'moon, this thorn bush my thorn bush, and this dog my dog" is modeled on "It is a tale of the Man in the Moon." Theseus's final remark brushing aside the epilogue is in the spirit of another of Elizabeth's after she had been entertained by the Gray's Inn Revellers at court in February 1595 with a masque of Proteus. "Shall we have bread and cheese after a banquet," she said when a measure was danced after the performance.

The mortal lovers get them to bed and the fairies enter to speak the blessing in the fairy meter of *Endimion*. Puck places them firmly as creatures of the night, underlining the curious inconsistency of Oberon's disclaimer and therefore its likely topicality. Diana's drops have become "field dew consecrate" to keep off the "blots of nature's hand." Puck's final speech is a plea that no one shall take offence at the "weak and idle theme." When so many plays dealt with controversial characters and subjects such a device became a defensive reflex. It has been suggested that this speech was added for public performance and both its matter and its meter would bear this out.

Epilogue

Life did not imitate art. Far from the queen being subdued, it was, by a strange fulfilment of the original myth, Actaeon who lost his head and was torn down by his own hounds, among them Bacon who wrote the official account of the rebellion which was then gone over by Elizabeth herself.[34] It was alleged that Raleigh smoked as he

[34] Bacon's part in this shocked Donne who glossed his own copy of the document with a part of 2 Samuel 16:10 which translates: Let him curse even because the Lord hath bidden him. Cf. also *The Courtier's Library*, 27, "The Brazen Head of Francis Bacon: concerning Robert the First, King of England."

watched his rival's execution. He denied it but the balla-
deers were only expressing the popular dislike of him and
approval of Essex, "Our Jewel," "the valiant Knight of
Chivalry" in their lampoons and songs, and he was not
believed.

> Raleigh doth time bestride,
> He sits 'twixt wind and tide,
> Yet up hill he cannot ride
> For all his bloody pride.
> He seeks taxes in the tin
> He polls the poor to the skin,
> Yet he swears 'tis no sin.
> Lord for thy pity![35]

The Faerie Queene herself lived on, "the Mother of
their own times, that took them up from their cradles, and
cherished them in her own bosom,"[36] to appear again as
the immortal Cynthia in Jonson's revels although she was
nearly seventy, during the war of the theaters in which
playwrights and managers satirized each other on the public stage and Jonson made the specific identification of
Essex with Actaeon.

At the Christmas festivities of her seventieth year she
was dancing the coranto. Then gradually as if she was in
truth one of the spirits "that do not die but fade away with
time" she declined to her death, refusing medicine and
food, though her physicians said her body was still youthful and strong and she might have lived much longer. The
"enchanting queen"[37] took with her fairy Albion and the
Golden Age.

[35] J. E. Neale, *Queen Elizabeth* (Cape, 1934), p. 356.
[36] From the prayers officially set forth after the rebellion.
[37] Did a memory of that majesty and Leicester linger in *Antony
and Cleopatra*? Cleopatra's behavior is in many respects that of
Elizabeth, but someone else must pursue that. Shakespeare's silence
on her death was noted by Chettle in *England's Mourning Garment*:

> Nor doth the silver-tongued Melicert
> Drop from his honied muse one sable teare
> To mourn her death who graced his desert,
> And to his laies opened her Royal eare.
> Shepherd, remember our Elizabeth
> And sing her rape, done by that Tarquin, Death

CHAPTER IX

The Enchanter

Where now you're both a father and a son
By your untimely claspings with your child—
Which pleasure fits a husband not a father—
And she an eater of her mother's flesh

Pericles

It's not surprising that a change of ruler should have shifted the fairy emphasis from queen to enchanter since the fairy scene always reflects contemporary preoccupations. King James was himself deeply interested in witchcraft which is hardly surprising either in someone who had Mary of Scots for a mother, Duessa, the bewitcher of so many hearts. The enchanter hovered on the marches between human and fairy, sometimes being simply an alchemist like Prospero, sometimes the product of dubious divine parentage like Comus, as witches too may be village crones or the "blew meager hag," the Cailleach Bheur.

The alchemist was still a half respectable figure, forerunner of both Alistair Crowley and Sir Bernard Lovell. The most famous of Elizabeth's reign was Dr. John Dee, consulted by many, including the queen, and the originator of the strange burning glass that is, along with his wand, often part of the enchanter's equipment, and occurs in Peele's *The Old Wives' Tale*, which may have served as a prototype for *Comus* where the enchanter also has a rationalized glass.

It has also certain similarities with the story of Childe Roland,[1] known to Shakespeare since he quotes it in *King Lear* together with the traditional Fie, foh, fum[2] which Peele also quotes and which can still be heard in the pantomime Jack and the Beanstalk. *The Old Wives' Tale* also

[1] Collected by R. Jamieson, *Illustrations of Northern Antiquities* (Edinburgh 1814).

[2] I suspect fee, foh, fum, rhyming with British or Englishman, of having come from a traditional play of the St. George type:

> Now as I am a British man
> I'll chop thee small as sifted bran

includes the traditional opening: "Once upon a time there was a king, or a lord, or a duke, that had a fair daughter, the fairest that ever was; as white as snow and as red as blood . . ."

The enchanter is called Sacrapant. He has carried off the daughter while in the shape of a dragon. His mother, like Caliban's dam Sycorax, was a witch, called Meroe. Although old he appears young and is in love with the girl Delia. Eventually, as in *Childe Roland* and *Comus*, her two brothers come looking for her but she is under a spell and doesn't recognize them. Sacrapant sets them to work digging as Prospero puts Ferdinand to carrying logs. The hero who finally rescues them all is helped by the Ghost of Jack whose burial he had paid for.[3] Even this condensed version is stuffed with material which was to be exploited in fairy books and pantomime for the next three hundred years.

But the central core of the story is the kidnapping and attempted seduction of Delia by the enchanter. *The Wisdome of Doctor Dodypol*,[4] another magical bran tub as full of curiosities as the *Macbeth* witches' cauldron, tells of a lady carried off by an enchanter who disguises himself as her neglectful husband in order to seduce her. At the crucial moment, just as he has nearly convinced the spellbound woman that he is "him who made thee so long since his bride" her father breaks in and rescues her. The verse has echoes of *A Midsummer Night's Dream* although the fairyland described is that of *Sir Orfeo*.

Twas I that lead you through the painted meades,
Where the light Fairies daunst upon the flowers,
Hanging on every leafe an orient pearle,
Which strooke together with the silken winde
Of their loose mantels made a silver chime.
Twas I that winding my shrill bugle horne
Made a guilt pallace breake out of the hill,
Filled suddenly with troopes of knights and dames

---

[3] A common folk motif for which compare "The Barra Widdow's Son" in Campbell's *Tales of the Western Highlands*, another bran tub with bits of the oriental theme of the girl to be rescued from the Turk and the dead man who helps the hero in exchange for half his winnings, usually his wife or child to be cut in two but reprieved at the end as in *The Old Wives' Tale*.

[4] Anonymous. Acted by the Children of Paul's and published 1600.

> Who daunst and reveld whilste we sweetly slept
> Upon a bed of Roses wrapt all in golde,
> Doost thou not know me yet.[5]

The mis-spelling of gilt in describing the palace is an accident of the period but a curiously evocative one in terms of the psychopathology of everyday life, for fairyland is the palace of guilt. The taboo broken in stories of this type is against father/daughter incest and it lies behind *The Tempest* as well as behind other late Shakespeare plays which hinge on this relationship. Often it's a brother or brothers who make or attempt the rescue, as brothers would indeed be the ones most disturbed by such a situation. The mother is as suppressed in the mythical telling as she would be in emotional fact.

Sometimes the rescue is by the hero, as we would expect since girls grow up and leave their fathers to marry. The great power of the enchanter is a father's dominating influence and his magic the parent's seeming ability in the child's eyes to do anything. The spell with which he binds her sometimes has the effect of a neurotic catalepsy. She is unable to move because of the conflict of desire and fear. Miranda is thrown into a sleep by Prospero; Comus freezes the lady to her chair. Sacrapant and the enchanter in *Doctor Dodypol* both distort the girls' vision.

Milton and Shakespeare refine the raw material of the basic story in accordance with art and credibility. Comus at first glance seems to be a personification of lust as Milton consciously depicts him but his powers are all magic.

> He with his bare wand can unthread thy joints
> And crumble all thy sinews

His rout are "oughly headed monsters." Although for the conscious Puritan wine is evil potion enough and sex itself an enchanting sin, what gives *Comus* its unconscious power is the echo of the other forbidden relationship, and its weakness, for I believe it is a little weak at the dramatic core, is in the lady's failure to be involved except as she is physically bound. One is forced to ask what Comus would have done with her if her brothers hadn't come rushing in to the rescue, his as well as hers.

[5] Act III.

In *The Tempest* the situation is more explicit: the father is the enchanter. The island is the forbidden world of his relationship with Miranda, cut off from the real world and with his familiar Ariel to do his will. Prospero's return and renunciation of magic power are synonymous with his finding a husband for his daughter.

Although as a father he knows this is the right course, emotionally he finds it almost intolerable and his treatment of the selected young man, Ferdinand, is a piece of humiliating sadism rationalized as testing him. The test imposed on would-be suitors by a father is always a disguised incest theme, as Shakespeare and his contemporaries knew.[6] His concern with Miranda's virginity betrays him too. Caliban's great error which turned Prospero against him where before he had been kind, was that he tried to rape Miranda, a no doubt horrifying but not surely unexpected or unnatural desire. Similarly Prospero is terrified that Ferdinand will seduce her, although the rational father in him wishes them not only to fall in love but to love each other. His magic powers are surely enough, since he watches them while invisible, to know of and prevent any serious attempt at seduction.

Miranda's mother is curiously absent. She was "a piece of virtue" presumably dead before the child was three, since Prospero and his daughter were set adrift before she was "out three years."[7] Miranda doesn't remember her mother, only the waiting women. Prospero had already retired to his enchanting preoccupations, giving over the practical rule of the kingdom to his brother. It could reasonably be argued that he was not a very attentive or reliable ruler and a coup d'état was better for the dukedom although such a view wouldn't have been popular with James I, supporter of "the right divine of kings to govern wrong," to whom as was pointed out long ago[8] Prospero bears a strong resemblance.

---

[6] So too is Lear's testing of his three daughters which is why he is so angered by Cordelia's quite correct reply that she will hope to love her husband more than her father.

[7] About the age of Shakespeare's granddaughter at the probable date of composition, 1611.

[8] First by Tieck the nineteenth-century German scholar then by Richard Garnett, see the Irving Edition 1906.

Apart from collaboration, in *Henry VIII* and others, this is Shakespeare's last play. First performed in November 1611, it was repeated in 1613 for the marriage of the Princess Elizabeth (to become the Winter Queen) to the Elector Palatine. But marriage was already in the air when it was written. The young Prince Henry, "the expectation of Europe, the hope of all Britain," was to be married to a Spanish princess. Negotiations, never to be fulfilled, were under way. In 1612 the prince died. A good reason for accepting the authenticity of 1611[9] as the date of a first or early performance is that Shakespeare would have been unlikely to have played with the supposed death of a son and heir as he does if he had been writing the play after the prince's death but for his sister's marriage.

For the uninhabited island itself and the storm, Shakespeare drew on the accounts of the voyage of the *Sea Adventure* in 1609, driven ashore on the Bermudas and miraculously preserved while on a voyage to the colony of Virginia with which his old patron Southampton was deeply involved. The description of the storm in particular is very close to a letter written by Strachey, the governor's secretary, to an unknown lady and probably meant to be circulated by hand among those interested, particularly the London Company of which Southampton was an active member. The district around Cape Cod called Aggawan by the natives was even renamed Southampton.

A further connection with Southampton is through the references in the play to Montaigne's essay *On Cannibals* which had been translated by a friend and protégé of Southampton's, John Florio. If, as seems likely, *The Tempest* is emotionally Shakespeare's farewell to the stage, it's also his farewell to London and his patron. Since his company had become the King's Players and was constantly in attendance at court where Southampton was too, it's impossible that they couldn't have met frequently, although we can't know their precise relationship at this time. But I think we can deduce something from Shakespeare's use of a setting for his last play which particularly

---

[9] This is a scholar's question vexed by the possible forgery of the contemporary revels accounts by one Collier in the nineteenth century.

concerned Southampton who had been admitted to both the Virginia and East India companies just before.

One detail in particular suggests that he had *The Old Wives' Tale* in mind as he wrote *The Tempest*. Apart from certain similarities of theme both plays have a dance of harvesters which is made much of and immediately followed by the enchanter dealing angrily with a plot against his life.[10] In November 1605 had taken place the dastardly plot against King and Commons immortalizing Guy Fawkes. Then in 1610 Henry IV of France was murdered and once again the country was terrified. The House of Commons renewed the oath of allegiance and the British court went into mourning. Kings were at the mercy of common assassins. It has sometimes been asked why Prospero should be so angered by the attempt on his life by Caliban and the clowns,[11] but to contemporary minds base villains and rogues, the ungrateful commoners, could pull down a throne and, for Shakespeare in particular, there must seem to be no similarity to Southampton's attempted rebellion with Essex, which had been an affair of gentlemen. It is the clowns' very baseness that makes their aspirations and threats intolerable.

Ariel and Caliban are the separate poles between which man lies: aery spirit and beast. Both are subject to Prospero. Shakespeare's is an unusual portrait of the wild man who was often used, as in *The Faerie Queene,* as a symbol of the noble savage. Ariel is the kind of elemental spirit conjured up by the alchemists. ("This yeare I began to practise necromancy, and to call aungells and spirits."[12] "He sede that George Dowsing dede aryse in a glasse a

---

[10] Cf. Enter the Harvest men singing, with women in their hands

> *Fro.:* Soft! who have we here? our amorous harvesters.
> Here the Harvest men sing . . .
>> Lo, here we come a-reaping, a-reaping,
>> To reap our harvest fruit!
>> And thus we pass the year so long
>> And never be we mute.

with *The Tempest,* Act IV, sc. 1.

[11] For instance in the introduction to the New Penguin Shakespeare edition.

[12] The Autobiography and Personal Diary of Simon Formen, 1588.

litull thing of the length of an ynche or ther about, but whether it was a spiret or a shadowe he cannot tell . . .")[13] Ariel and Caliban are both extensions of Prospero, his servants. Ariel is sexless, a sublimation ready to assume any form; Caliban is the beastly part that would have raped Miranda. In the language of dream psychology his fishiness[14] is no accident nor is his picture of himself roused to sweet music and falling asleep again and his dream of clouds opening to show riches ready to drop upon him. Prospero's hatred of him is more understandable if he is the unregenerate part of Prospero himself, growing worse as he gets older because more disgusting in an old man. His punishment is to be pinched and cramped: the punishment that fairies give sluttish, dirty maids, the betraying blue-black of the lover's pinch. There is an echo, one of many, of *A Midsummer Night's Dream* in the setting of dogs to hunt Caliban and company, and of the hunted Actaeon.

The relationship of Ariel to Prospero, modeled on that of Puck and Oberon, changes as the play progresses and the Ferdinand/Miranda relationship develops. From an unwilling slave who has to be reminded of past benefits, he becomes "dainty Ariel," "my bird."

> Ariel: Do you love me, master? No?
> Prospero: Dearly, my delicate Ariel.

He can be indulged and employed in the freeing of Prospero from enchantment. His is the spiritualized sexuality of the creative artist, able to pour itself into every different shape, harpy, Ceres, St. Elmo's fire in the rigging, music and all the mischiefs of Puck. All this Prospero is renouncing as Shakespeare was. No wonder "every third thought shall be my grave."

Shakespeare was about forty-six or -seven when he wrote *The Tempest*, King James two years younger, Prospero, if

---

[13] *The Gregory Chronicle*, Camden Society, New Series XVII.
[14] The fishiness is also part of the stock clown like Pickleherring, the rationalization of the symbol being the Lenten fish diet appropriate to when popular entertainments, connected with carnival, were given. But then clowns are themselves as phallic as fish.

we take his comment about Miranda being a third of his life, about forty-five. To us it seems no great age yet Shakespeare only lived another five years and it is his last individual statement. In it there's a triple identification of Prospero, King James (ruler and author of the *Daemonologie*) and the playwright.

He had always thought himself old, even in the 1590s when he was writing the sonnets and couldn't have been more than thirty yet called himself "beaten and chopped with tann'd antiquity" and wrote with horror of when forty winters should besiege his lover's brow and "dig deep trenches in thy beauty's field." After a period of such intense creativity, however, he might well have felt exhausted. It's sometimes argued that life expectancy then was much less than we are used to but this is partly the effect of the very high infant mortality rate on averages before the twentieth century. King James himself, only two years Shakespeare's junior, lived on till 1625; Southampton, boyish to the last, was described in the year of Shakespeare's death as "head of the Malcontents" and died as leader of the expedition to the Low Countries at fifty-two. Shakespeare's great age was emotional rather than physical.

No reading other than that Prospero speaks Shakespeare's epilogue will do unless we are to believe, against all the evidence, that writers work in a compartment unrelated to their emotional lives. That Shakespeare equated the poet's art with enchantment he had made explicit in Theseus's famous comments on "the poet's pen which turns the forms of things unknown," bodied forth by the imagination, to shapes "and gives to airy nothing/ A local habitation and a name." This is precisely Prospero's activity. The characters of the masque are "Spirits, which by mine art/I have from their confines called to enact/My present fancies." The word "art" is used throughout *The Tempest* with a double meaning.

For the most important speech in the play Shakespeare turned again to Ovid, and the source that he chose makes it even more certain that the play is a farewell to the "rough magic" of his art. I have already mentioned that the speech: "Ye elves of hills, brooks, standing lakes, and groves" is based, in some places word for word, on Golding's translation of *The Metamorphoses* and the fascination exercised on mediaeval and later imaginations by Medea.

Medea's spell, ingredients and methods, became the blueprint for all such activities. It lies behind the *Macbeth* witches' recipe. By a piece of, I believe, conscious irony Shakespeare has based his speech which is an abjuration of magic and a farewell to life on a speech begging for "the juices by whose aid old age may be renewed and may turn back to the bloom of youth."[15]

It's as if in doing so he has been forced to invert the whole myth. Prospero, we are to believe, is a good man, Medea an evil woman; Medea and Jason are children trying to restore an old father, Ferdinand and Miranda are restored by Prospero; Medea before this episode meditates on leaving her own island country by sea for exile, Prospero is to return to his from the island; he renounces his arts, she goes on from crime to crime in hers.

Is Prospero's renunciation meant to suggest that such things are evil even though he has used them for good? There seems no reason why this should be so and Prospero noticeably never suggests it. The metaphor has simply become explicit by the end of the play. Interestingly too Prospero's religious position, never contradicted, is remarkably unchristian for a Duke of Milan. The "We are such stuff/As dreams are made on," is a piece of straightforward unbelief like that for which Marlowe was accused. The decision to break his staff and drown his book isn't a theological one. He expresses no thought that his magical dabblings were responsible for his original downfall except insofar as they gave his brother the opportunity to oust him. His people loved him. Gonzalo put some of his books in the boat. But now the period of enchantment is over: Miranda is to be married; the writer renounces his art and retires to Stratford.

[15] *Metamorphoses*, Book VII, 215. Miller's translation of: nunc opus est sucis, per quos renovata senectus in florem redeat primosque recolligat annos.

CHAPTER X

Winged Creatures

Angels with their bottles come,
  And draw from these full eyes of thine
Their Masters water, their own wine.
          The Weeper, Crashaw

Between *A Midsummer Night's Dream* and *The Tempest* a great change had come over the fairies: some of them had grown wings.

> Puck: I go, I go—look how I go—
> Swifter than arrow from the Tartar's bow!

> Ariel: I come
> To answer thy best pleasure, be't to fly,
> To swim, to dive into the fire, to ride
> On the curled clouds.

From Italy Inigo Jones had brought the elaborate stage machinery and costumes for the court masques which became the passion of the royal family, particularly Queen Anne and the Prince of Wales, Henry, as soon as James I became king.

There had been masques for a long time, at least since the fourteenth century. Friends had unexpectedly visited a house wearing masks and accompanied by musicians and torches and bringing presents much as the mummers did on a lower social level, and indeed the one probably developed from the other since, as the dramatic elements became more important in the fifteenth century, they were called "disguisings" and "guisers" is still the word for folk players or dancers in some parts of the country.

At first the hosts joined the performers in dancing, a custom which died out and then was reintroduced in Henry VIII's reign by the King himself on Twelfth Night 1512, "after the manner of Italie." The entertainments given to Elizabeth on her progresses were forms of the masque with song, dance, dialogue and the representation of classical and grotesque figures. Elizabeth herself often took part in the dancing.

What was new was the lavishness of the machinery and staging imported from the Italian theatre where Monteverdi's first opera *Orfeo* had been produced in 1607 in Mantua. Rocky wastes, moving waves, clouds descending with personages, gorgeous palaces became theatrical commonplaces and most of them were designed by Inigo Jones. Perhaps most important in the history of faery was his *Masque of Oberon*, written by Ben Jonson for the young prince to play the Fairy King. Among the miscellaneous drawings of costumes are those for three fairies, one of whom has short wings over the shoulders. This was in January 1611.

In the *Lord's Maske* of 1613 there's a fiery spirit with wings of flames. Iris is of course winged as Shakespeare describes her, and in the volume *Designs by Inigo Jones for Masques and Plays at Court,* which is mainly taken from the Duke of Devonshire's collection, there is an unidentified female masquer with white and gold wings, and a naked mermaid, winged and with dolphin's tails, riding a hippocamp in a drawing which is probably Italian and not by Jones.

Shakespeare had been quick to learn and incorporate the concept of flying, as distinct from the older one of riding, into *The Tempest*. In *A Midsummer Night's Dream* there are constant references to tripping, the distinctively fairy motion related to the dance; in *The Tempest* Ariel "drinks the air" before him, he is a "chick," a "bird," a winged harpy. When he is to be freed it's to the air. He is an aery spirit where Puck is earthy. There are some earthy ones, "the rabble" over whom Prospero gives him power and they are to come "tripping" "with mop and mow." We are in the middle of a changing convention.

The wings had appeared by analogy with both classical and religious figures. Boy Cupid, with his silver and purple pinions as Spenser describes them after Politian, angels and devils and old Father Time had all had them. Milton, by his comparison of his shrunk fallen angels and with bees, suggests that by 1666 he thought of fairies as winged although in his earlier poems he is less sure. Once introduced, wings have seemed so psychologically right that they have become a strong alternative tradition.

By underlining the element of flying in fairy manifestation the wings reinforce its sexual significance, as in dreams of flying and the hallucination of witches who flew to orgiastic sabbats to couple with the devil. At the same time the wings lend credibility as a physical means of flying and later, by close association with angels, a child-like innocence to cover sexual fantasy, an aspect which must wait for fuller comment till a later chapter and the coming of Peter Pan.

Following the fashion confirmed by Shakespeare a period of miniaturization set in. Everything was in little and verse and prose poured out in variation of "In a cowslip's bell I lie."[1] Drayton and Herrick are probably the best known and the most prolific in this tradition, Herrick in particular exploring microscopic sex in *Oberon's Palace*. One of the most perceptive comments on the fairies came from the Duchess of Newcastle, anticipating in metaphor Freud's discovery of the unconscious.

> Who knowes, but in the Braine may dwel
> Little small Fairies; who can tell?
> And by their severall actions they may make
> Those formes and figures, we for fancy take.
> And when we sleep, those Visions, dreames we call,
> By their industry may be raised all;
> And all the objects which through senses get,
> Within the Braine they may in order set.
> And some pack up, as Merchants do each thing
> Which out sometimes may to the Memory bring.[2]

However, such a tradition was no use to 'an aspiring romantic poet, the natural inheritor of Arthurian myth. Where could such a poet in the late seventeenth century find a fairy legend of enough stature and complexity to encompass the full range of his fantasy and yet at the same

[1] See the excellent Chapter V "The Fashion for the Miniature," Briggs's *Anatomy of Puck*, ed. cit.

[2] Margaret Cavendish, Duchess of Newcastle, *Poems and Fancies*, 1653.

time give him the benefit of the credibility factor? Only in the Bible. *Paradise Lost* is our longest and greatest romance work of science fiction.

Milton had been considering and rejecting possible subjects for many years before he wrote *Paradise Lost* in order to write a "great English poem." The hot favorite for a long time was to be taken from the legendary history of Britain and include the familiar material from Geoffrey of Monmouth and Malory. To do this he had studied the sources, writing a prose *History of Britain*, published after *Paradise Lost* in 1670. He had also read Ariosto, Tasso and Spenser and was filled with the spirit and practice of enchanted literary chivalry. In 1639 in his Latin epitaph on his friend Charles Diodati, who had died while Milton was abroad, he sketched out the plot for his great English work.[3]

By the next year he is not so sure. In a list of possible subjects several versions of *Paradise Lost* are explored in the form of a drama. A year later in 1641 he is hesitating between epic and drama but has put off the attempt while the country is unsettled and during further study.[4]

In retrospect it's possible to see that although Milton's conscious mind was undecided the unconscious had made its choice. Indeed if his nephew-biographer Edward Phillips was telling the truth he was shown part of the drama in the 1640s which was later incorporated into the epic.[5] However, it's possible to take the choice even further back, to a poem Milton wrote when he was twenty-one, in 1629, *On the Morning of Christ's Nativity*. All the machinery and imagery of the later poem is there.[6] What is different is the point of view.

The hero of the early poem is King-baby. The poet's emotional identification is with the holy child. Interestingly Milton himself was born in December and the poem begins:

---

[3] *Epitaphium Damonis.*

[4] *The Reason of Church Government.*

[5] The lines in Book IV beginning "O thou that with surpassing glory crowned," 32–41.

[6] It would be perfectly possible to do a verse by section comparison between the two but this is not the place for it.

This is the month . . .

He was, as I've said, just twenty-one, about to be reborn into the adult world. He was a clever, beautiful young man, eminent in his college, seemingly with everything before him. Next year his younger brother joined him at Cambridge. Suddenly all wasn't well. Milton had been destined for the Church. Finding himself at variance with official religious policy he refused to take orders and left Cambridge. The policy was Laudian Anglicanism yet Milton had managed until that time to subscribe publicly to the necessary Articles of Religion and did so in July 1632 on taking his M.A. with a signature at the head of his college list.

He refused to take any other profession and went to live with his parents at Horton. His father protested in some form but clearly Milton won.[7] He wanted to be a poet. He had already shown this in his sonnets on Shakespeare and to the nightingale but he was afraid that time was passing and he had achieved nothing and indeed appeared immature to the outward view.[8] He lived at Horton until his mother's death[9] when, he says, "I became anxious to visit foreign parts." His brother had returned from Cambridge, married, and was also living in the same house.

In 1638 Milton set out for the continent, going first to Paris and then on to Italy. He had letters of introduction to smooth his path and was at once taken up by the academics and literati. He had probably the happiest, fullest time of his life. It lasted fifteen months during which he saw above all Florence, Rome and Naples, fell in love, attended concerts and soirées, saw galleries and antiquities, met Galileo, Hugh Grotius, Cardinal Barberini, the elderly Marquis of Villa, Manso, patron of Tasso and Marini, and the famous singer, Leonora Baroni.

The impact on Milton was stunning. He had come from rural seclusion into a sunburst of artistic and noble society where he was admired for his looks, intelligence and verse. I believe however that the greatest impact was visual. Italy

[7] *Ad Patrem*. There is also a self-justifying letter to an unknown friend who seems to have enquired what he was doing with his time.

[8] Sonnet on reaching Twenty-three.

[9] *Defensio Secunda*, 1654.

was in the ebullience of full baroque. Bernini was already in high favor and had just done a bust of King Charles I. Pietro da Cortona and Sacchi were at work on the Palazzo Barberini where Milton was taken to hear the famous Leonora sing.

I suspect that Milton had never seen anything like the riot of painting and sculpture, particularly of a religious kind. His father was a Puritan with a repugnance for graven, or painted, images. Milton was brought up to the "Blest pair of sirens . . . Voices and Verse" but not to the visual arts. That he acquired some appreciation of them in Italy, I think appears in the *Apology for Smectymnuus*, 1642: "For as none can judge of a painter, or statuary, but he who is an artist, that is either in the practice or theory, which is often separated from the practice and judges learnedly without it." He was an artist in another medium and had learned to judge learnedly.

It's this sudden immersion in Italian baroque which I believe accounts for the poetic mode of *Paradise Lost. On the Morning of Christ's Nativity* is a baroque poem and is generally recognized as such but it is literary baroque, derived from Marini and anticipating Crashaw's poems like *The Weeper. Paradise Lost* is visual baroque translated into words. On the ceilings of the Palazzo Barberini Milton would have seen Pietro da Cortona's "Allegory of Divine Providence" and Sacchi's "Allegory of Divine Wisdom." He could also have seen Pietro's "Battle of Issus" as an inspiration for the war in heaven and, in Florence, his "The Golden Age" which seems a model for the charming scene where the animals play before Adam and Eve. The figure in the tree might have suggested Satan.

He would no doubt have joined in the fierce contemporary discussion of classicism versus baroque, personified by Pietro and Sacchi who maintained that "a picture should be likened to a Tragedy, which was the better when the greatest effect was achieved by the smallest number of players."[10] This was to be Milton's problem, translated into literary terms of baroque epic or classical drama. In the event he wrote both but the influence of Sacchi appears

[10] Quoted in Waterhouse's *Italian Baroque Painting* (Phaidon, 1962), p. 58.

in *Paradise Lost* as well as in *Samson Agonistes*. His "Vision of S. Romuald" has the patriarchal repose of Adam's conversation pieces with Raphael and Gabriel. The "Allegory of Divine Wisdom" with its globe, ethereal throne and light piercing the darkness recalls the setting in heaven and Milton's invocation of his muse Urania. Pietro, wishing to crowd his scenes and induce a feeling of magnificence, preferred the epic structure of painting.[11]

Not only painting but statuary too impressed Milton. The figures of *Paradise Lost* are three-dimensional, with space around them. The polished flesh of Adam and Eve is in Bernini marble and as lustrous as the statue of Apollo and Daphne or Pluto and Persephone that might have served as model for one of Milton's most famous similes:

> Proserpin gathering flowers
> Herself a fairer flower by gloomy Dis
> Was gathered.[12]

The riotous baroque energy is everywhere too both in description and in action.

> His fair large Front and Eye sublime declar'd
> Absolute rule; and Hyacinthin locks
> Round from his parted forelock manly hung
> Clustring, but not beneath his shoulders broad;
> She as a veil down to the slender waist
> Her unadorned golden tresses wore
> Dissheveld, but in wanton ringlets wav'd
> As the Vine curls her tendrils[13]

The particular baroque concentration on curling hair is sculptural.

Yet above all it was the baroque angelic image that lodged in Milton's mind's eye. He couldn't have seen, he was too early, the most charming of Bernini's angel figures, although it seems almost impossible that he didn't.

---

[11] Wittkower, *Art and Architecture in Italy 1600–1750* (Penguin, 1958), p. 171. The controversy became open in a dispute in the Academia di San Luca in 1636.

[12] Book IV, 268.

[13] Book IV, 300.

> And now a stripling Cherube he appears
> Under a Coronet his flowing hair
> In curls on either cheek playd, wings he wore
> Of many a coulourd plume sprinkl'd with Gold,
> His habit fit for speed succinct, and held
> Before his decent steps a Silver wand.[14]

There is nothing there that wouldn't equally fit a fairy prince. The wand is a definite link between angel and fairy but more appropriate to fairy, although Bernini's St. Theresa angel carries an arrow. The silver wand is presumably meant as a sign of peaceful intention but its magical overtones are very strong.

I think Milton was well aware what he was doing and that that was the meaning of his comment that he was pursuing "Things unattempted yet in Prose or Rime." He knew quite well that they had all been attempted in painting and sculpture (what else for example is the decoration of the Sistine Chapel?) and he was setting out to retranslate them into an epic as if he had been given a palazzo to ornament. This accounts too for the, to many people, surprisingly visual nature of this blindman's[15] poem. He was remembering with peculiar intensity the revelations of that happiest period.[16] In this other sense the poem is aptly *Paradise Lost*. The paradise is not a natural but an artificial one. The picture of Eve going out with her simple rustic tools to her unnecessary but charming labors is as idealized as Egeria in a Claude landscape.[17]

Even though Milton couldn't have known the full flow-

[14] Book III, 636. "Succinct" I take to mean caught round and up, with or without a belt, to give the characteristic Bernini angelic drapery as if in flight with bare legs and feet.

[15] His sight began to fail in one eye about four years after his return.

[16] Italy was consciously in his thoughts in the constant references to Galileo in the poem and his problem about which cosmological theory to use. In Book V there is a description of Raphael flying through heaven between ranks of angelic choir to the gate that opens on golden hinges and below Earth with the Garden of Eden: a perfect ceiling painting. Immediately this is likened to Galileo's moon-gazing.

[17] He might also have seen early examples of Claude's work though the pastoral was already so much his mode it would probably have made less impression on him.

ering of Bernini's angel forms there were plenty of others for him to base his descriptions on, including the bronzes on top of the baldacchino in St. Peter's. It's likely that he saw the Guido Reni "St. Michael," painted for another member of the Barberini family, a copy of which was probably the "St. Michael" sent to Henrietta Maria,[18] and it would therefore be pointed out to a visiting Englishman. He would have seen Pietro da Cortona's crowded "Apotheosis of the Barberini" and probably Lanfranco's "Assumption of the Virgin" with its circle of cherubs, and his other angelic shapes in Florence and Naples.

The worsening political situation caused him to return home where the Horton ménage broke up, his father going to live with Milton's brother in Reading while John himself moved to London. Delighted as he had been with Italy his Protestantism had been unaffected although obviously attempts had been made on it by the charm of Cardinal Barberini, an indefatigable contriver in the cause of restoring England to the Catholic fold, by Manso, and, Milton alleged, by the threats of English Jesuits in Rome. As if to prove how little he was seduced, or in guilt that he had been unconsciously so far, Milton began immediately pamphleteering against episcopacy.[19] In 1642 the Civil War broke out and the following year Milton's father was forced to leave his Royalist son in Reading and join his Republican one in London. At almost the same time Milton married a girl from a Royalist family who left him after a month, which caused him to fling himself into renewed pamphleteering, on behalf of divorce.

Finding that the Cavalier cause was going badly his wife returned to him in 1645. In 1646 King Charles was taken prisoner. In 1647 Milton's father died. Two years later the King was executed and Milton published his defence of the execution. He was appointed Secretary for Foreign Tongues to the Council of State. By 1652 his blindness was complete. In 1658, before the death of Cromwell, he began

[18] See M. Levey, *The Later Italian Pictures in the Collection of Her Majesty the Queen* (Phaidon, 1964), p. 17.

[19] He was at great pains to make his religious position clear in Italy, too great pains I think. From a later letter to Carlo Dati with the volume of early poems it seems that the Italians were very tolerant of his views and he asks them to be so again.

Paradise Lost which he finished and first published under the Restoration.

I have given this run-through of his life until the writing of *Paradise Lost* because I think these facts are important in understanding the poem. In deciding on the subject-matter of his epic Milton hovered between two main themes: the mythical history of England with its fairy manifestations, and biblical history with its supernatural equivalent. Fundamentally, as mythologies, there is no difference between them. This Milton's unconscious understood. His conscious mind, because of the nature of and need for the credibility factor in fantasy situations, chose the second with its weight of biblical conviction.[20] For fairy knights we have angels, for Arthur, God the Father, for Camelot, Heaven. Magic is symbolized by diabolic or heavenly power which can, as in dreams, overleap time, place and shape. He was helped in all this by those baroque works of the Counter-Reformation that had burst upon his newly opened eyes with the force of a birth only a few years before they began to dim for ever. Cut off from these revelations by the Civil War and encroaching darkness he must have lingered over them, constantly re-creating them in words into the fabric of the poem and binding them by the narrative thread that was mythologically and personally an image of his own unconscious concerns. The result is a baroque web of childhood fantasy unequalled in English literature. In compounding fairy and angel Milton helped to underline the necessity of wings for airy spirits. From this time on elf becomes a separate earthy species, related to gnome, goblin, dwarf while the fairies soar in company with their angelic counterparts, completing the transformation Inigo Jones had begun.

[20] In his commonplace book where he made notes of reading and themes he copied out several quotations from authors questioning the authenticity of Arthurian material.

CHAPTER XI

Paradise Lost

> it was all
> Shining, it was Adam and maiden,
> The sky gathered again
> And the sun grew round that very day.
> *Fern Hill*, Dylan Thomas

By popular belief the fairies were often rationalized as rebel angels who didn't fall all the way when they were turned out of heaven.[1] Even to the unlettered mind they could seem to be much the same thing. Representations of good angels when put into words betray themselves as sublimated versions of goblins: for the hairiness substitute the crisped locks and downy wings, for the redness the traditional white-wash, for the mischief, the making of music, that other metaphor for intercourse. The angel is another attempt not to let our conscious Right know what our unconscious Left is doing. In a study like Bernini's St. Theresa with the angel, the repressed intention bursts through the symbol. Baroque energy is sexual energy. The apotheosis or going up to heaven is a metaphor of orgasm. In the seventeenth century the human mind, not to be deprived of its unconscious food, found in biblical subjects a manna that would nourish it while it waited for the refreshment of the Age of Reason.

Paradise Lost is baroque too in its structure. Ostensibly it's about "Man's first disobedience." That is only the foreground leading perspectively, like Pietro da Cortona's Barberini dome, to Satan's disobedience and to Milton's, and thence to the universal disobedience of all children. For beneath the grave exterior of the blind devotional Puritan writer is a naughty child banging its spoon on the table and screaming with frustration and jealousy. The Miltonic mask which has deceived generations of critics began by deceiving himself. The breaking of taboo by enchantment applies here too. The taboos which the poem breaks are

[1] Briggs, *The Fairies in Tradition and Literature*, Chapter 17 Human Opinions.

against infantile sexual curiosity, sibling and parental jealousy and primal disobedience. Milton states his theme quite clearly. What he didn't, *couldn't* know, was that he was writing so close to himself. To have recognised it would have led to collapse of his personality and of his image of himself. No blame attaches to him for this failure of understanding in a pre-psychoanalytic age. We should be grateful that he made great art out of it although I suspect that it may have demanded the sacrifice of his eyes as well.

It was Hazlitt who first recognized Satan as the true hero of the poem. By extension we recognize Milton's unconscious identification with him. In a poem written to him by the elderly Neapolitan marquis, Manso had called him, if he hadn't been a Protestant, "Non Anglus, verum hercle Angelus," an old pun but one which I think stuck in his mind. Milton's grandfather had been a staunch Roman Catholic recusant. It was his father who had turned Protestant, and in his middle age his brother was to follow the Stuarts back into Catholicism.[2] Milton's religious position was thus in a sense one of disobedience.

He was not by nature a puritan but highly sexed and deeply sensuous. Only his violent anti-authoritarianism was reforming and that was as inimical to the Presbyterians as to the Papists. His renowned temperance in food and drink was the Danegeld of a man aware of his own artistic and emotional sensuousness.[3]

Politically Milton was a regicide and his advocacy of king murder has made him unpopular with following generations. His attitude contrasts strongly with that of his fellow republican, friend and helper, Andrew Marvell, like Milton a great admirer of Cromwell but author of the famous and generous lines on Charles's execution:

---

[2] This is not quite proven but I think it very likely.

[3] The other implicitly autobiographical Milton hero, Samson, betrays himself through "lust" but this isn't the only instance of this conflict in Milton's work. At one time when his first wife seemed unlikely to come back to him he attempted arrangements for a bigamous marriage. His real worry about alcohol was that it inflamed his passions (*Comus, Samson Agonistes* and *Paradise Lost* all have this fear). In the context of friendship it was acceptable, see the sonnets to Lawrence and Skinner.

He nothing common did nor mean
Upon that memorable scene
But laid his kingly head
Down as upon a bed.

There is nothing generous in Milton's writings on the same subject. He accuses Charles of three things in particular which Satan accuses God of: he says that he is guilty of the innocent blood of those he caused to rebel against him and that he brought in foreigners (Irish) and relied upon evil counsellors. Charles is here acting as a political father upon whom Milton projects his personal childhood wrongs. The King is being accused for making the people rebel and for having favorites, as a father might be accused by a son for turning him against him by preferring another child. This is Satan's position. He is made to rebel by God's announcing the preferment of the Son, Christ, over the angels. Satan says that they are older than the Son and he himself was "of the first, if not the first Archangel." His wrath against Adam is also against a new son.

When his brother was born Milton had been for seven years the only boy. His sister was two years older. Several other children had not lived. Now there was a new son, called, significantly, Christopher. John was an excessively good child, learning everything he was asked and often sitting at his books till midnight from the age of twelve which gave him headaches and, he believed, weakened his eyes. It sounds as if he was guiltily compensating for something and trying to win his father's love. Milton is always quick to rationalize but sometimes he slips up. In one place he says his father destined him "from a child to the pursuits of literature" and in another to the Church. Ad Patrem shows that his father didn't so easily accept the substitution of one for the other. He was himself a well-known composer but at the same time a successful scrivener to which the nearest equivalent today would be a solicitor-cum-broker. It was his money which kept John for much of his life.

There are at least two lost paradises in the poem: Adam's and Satan's. Satan has lost heaven. Milton, I suspect, felt he had lost the child's heaven of being the worshipped young and only son when his brother was born.

The exchanges between Father and Son in Book Three are as between lovers. The Son has the feminine meekness of Eve. Again in Book VI:

> He said, and on his Son with Rays direct
> Shon full: he all his Father full exprest
> Ineffably into his face receiv'd.

The deaths of the other babies who threatened him can't have escaped his infant notice. After so many lost children the parents would doubly cosset and idolize the baby Christopher. It would be only natural for John to wonder if this one would die too and to fell guilty at the thought.[4] It was after Christopher had joined him at *Christ's*[5] that John found himself unable to continue there and went back home to leave again for Italy when Christopher returned as he would in about 1637.

Christopher was a conformist and a good son. He was enrolled at about seventeen in the Inner Temple. It seems to have been thought better that his father should live with Christopher and his wife in 1639 perhaps because John wasn't married or perhaps because, in spite of a difference in religion, he preferred to. The rebellion in *Paradise Lost* is against a father with, on the other hand, a good son, for Milton to alternately identify with and be jealous of in his satanic persona.

Christ, the good son, is deeply loved by his father but has usurped from him the power of creation. It's he who makes the universe and who defeats Satan. The image isn't a simple one, partly because an oversimplification would make bad art, partly because unconscious motives are never unmixed. Milton wished to be a poet. His father

> . . . fraught
> With envie against the Son of God, that day
> Honourd by his great Father, and proclaimed
> Messiah King annointed, could not bear
> Through pride that sight, and thought himself impaird
> Deep malice thence conceiving and disdain.
>
> Book V, 611–

[5] Milton's father's college was Christ Church, Oxford.

was a composer. In his poem to his father about this desire
to be a poet Milton says that he and his father have divided
Apollo, god of poetry and music, between them.[6] Milton
sang and played himself yet he didn't wish to compete with
his father as a composer. He wanted to create for himself.
In writing of the creation of the world he has, as it were,
created it and become the Son-creator. As a child Milton
would be envious of his father's power to create yet wish to
copy and surpass him both to gain his favor and to be
revenged on him for creating things other than John.

The basic myth of the Garden of Eden is about infantile
sexual curiosity as *Oedipus Tyrannus* is about the oedipal
situation. It's expressing the questions about what do parents do and where do I come from. Satan raises one of
these questions too.

> ... rememberst thou
> Thy making, while the Maker gave thee being?
> We know no time when we were not as now;
> Know none before us, self-begot, self-rais'd
> By our own quick'ning power ...

Satan is a voyeur child watching the first parents making
love.

> ... aside the Devil turned
> For envie, yet with jealous leer maligne ...
> Sight hateful, sight tormenting! thus these two
> In paradis't in one another's arms ...

Adam has a complete birth fantasy in which he is born
only of a father, a concept which seems to suit Milton very
well. Then Eve is born of him. Milton doesn't shirk the
implications of this. Eve is Adam's daughter as well as his

Ipse volens Phoebus se dispertire duobus,
Altera dona mihi, dedit altera dona parenti,
Dividuumque Deum genitorque puerque tenemus.

Literally "Phoebus himself willing to divide himself in (or between)
two, gave some gifts to me, others to (my) father, and we hold,
father and son, the divided God."

spouse.[7] Milton's conscious reasoned attitude to sex is that it is right and proper. His emotional attitude is mixed. The result of eating the apple is that they know evil and the principal evil is shame. There is no difference in their love-making before and after but that suddenly they think it shameful. Their knowledge is of lost good and innocence. Milton believed "that if unchastity in a woman, whom St. Paul terms the glory of man, be such a scandal and dishonor, then certainly in a man, who is both the image and glory of God, it must, though commonly not so thought, be much more deflowering and dishonorable." Therefore he tried to keep himself chaste. Like St. Paul too he thought it was better to marry than burn. Marriage, "conjugal love," is the way to deal with concupiscence. It should be no wonder then that he married three times. He had to have a sexual outlet that was theoretically acceptable to him. His greatest affections were reserved for men. Naturally he rationalized this by saying that they were "the image and glory of God." One of the charges brought against him by the pamphleteer Salmasius was that while in Italy he was a practising homosexual. This I think is the emotional rather than the factual truth.[8]

Satan himself is a shape-changer. The angels as a species share the fairies' ability to assume any size or disguise. Like knockers they work as miners to dig the minerals to build the baroque palace of Pandemonium which, although it rises from the ground in traditional style, is distinguished from the fairy palace of Heaven, which is made of jewels like Oberon's fairy mansion or that Sir Gawain saw in the

[7] There is another example of father/daughter incest in the poem, Satan with Sin, the dark side. Satan gives birth to Sin without any female help as God to the Son. At the root of this is a desire by the child to have a child by its father. That it appears in a black and a white form is another example of the ambivalence of emotion on this point. This is a further use of baroque structure: the Father impregnates the Son who creates the world; the Son creates Adam from whom he takes Eve; the Father has created Satan who brings forth Sin like a dark Athena; Satan and Sin bring forth Death; Sin and Death mate and produce a brood of monsters. It's a baroque mirror of incest like Bernini's famous stage production which showed two theatres opposite each other, one full of mirrors reflecting the live performance.

[8] The factual material in this chapter and Chapter X is from W. P. Parker's biography. The conclusions are my own.

Green Knight's wood. The angels themselves are compared to English elves when they shrink their bodies so that they can all get inside it. Satan's best-known metamorphosis is into the phallic snake but he also has Cuchulain's power of swelling himself up for battle and of seeming to burn like a comet. He is often described as a tower and retains much of his beauty although fallen.

In Rome or Florence Milton probably encountered one or more of the stage representations of biblical material which were popular, particularly in carnival time, in the streets and at the Barberini palace. The two which have the closest resemblance to *Paradise Lost* are Landi's *Sant' Alessio* 1631 with the devil, panoramas of heaven and hell and other worlds, and Andreini's *L'Adamo* 1613 with the Creation, Temptation and Fall. The character list of this is very close to at least two of Milton's synopses in his commonplace book. I think it very likely that he read the play while he was there and in particular the preface to it. "But if it is permitted to the painter, who is a dumb poet, to express by colors God the Father under the person of a man silvered by age . . . and to figure the divine messengers or Angels in the shape of winged youths; why is it not permitted to the poet, who is a speaking painter."

The dispute between Sacchi and Pietro da Cortona turned on the distinction between epic and dramatic painting. Sacchi's appeal was to Aristotle for decorum, a limit to the number of characters and a preservation of the unities. This the Italian dramatists neglected with results which must have been close to the English mystery plays and would seem old-fashioned to Milton. In his preface to *Samson Agonistes* Milton invokes Aristotle, decorum and the unities. For the multiple scenes of *Paradise Lost* he wisely chose the epic. This was the artistic problem he meditated in the long years while he was writing prose for the Commonwealth. It meant the application of the theories of visual artists to a literary problem. In choosing epic he freed himself for flight of fantasy and so wrote our first real work of science fiction.

Throughout the poem one is conscious of the subject he rejected: Arthur and his knights. Not only are they used for similes but they are present in the warfare in heaven and in the general chivalrous deportment of the angels.

God is a grieving Arthur confronted in the fall by the ruin of what he has built through ingratitude and lust. There are dozens of references to magic and its characters.[9]

It's in his creation of, and voyaging through, the universe that Milton invents science fiction. Satan doesn't need a space ship, he is magnificently winged, but his journeys through chaos buffeted by winds, seeing the earth far off, landing on the sun and passing through the nine spheres anticipate the flood of twentieth-century travel and yet are only a logical extension of Puck's putting a girdle round about the earth. It makes no difference that Milton uses the old Ptolemaic cosmology. He himself was inclined to think it might be false but for the artistic necessity of total conviction an established geography was required. Even those who believed the Copernican theory at this date would have found it extremely difficult to visualize in detail and use as familiarly as a map of England, as Milton uses his universe. He is, he says, "likening spiritual to corporeal forms" like Andreini's "speaking painter." But "is it true" as well as art needs a credible background and the old system provided this.

Eve's lamentation over Paradise sounds like a Vaughan lament for lost childhood and so betrays itself.

> O flowers,
> That never will in other Climat grow,
> . . . how shall we breathe in other Aire
> Less pure, accustomd to immortal Fruits?

Perhaps, though, the building of the bridge to earth from hell, reminiscent of Celtic and Norse myth, and the final metamorphosis of the fallen angels into serpents, writhing and hissing like the nest of witch-stolen members in the *Malleus Maleficarum*, with the monstrous figures of the

---

[9] Death is a "goblin." Pandemonium is lit by "suttle magic." The fallen angels engage in disputes "with a pleasing sorcerie" like the Italian academics. The night hag and Lapland Witches dance "while the labouring moon eclipses all their charms" and so on. The influence of *A Midsummer Night's Dream* is strong throughout *Paradise Lost*. When Satan meets Abdiel in battle in Book VI Abdiel greets him, "Proud art thou met?" and he answers, "Ill for thee." Milton has unconsciously put him in the position of Titania warring with her "lord."

hag Sin and Giant Death, are enough to convince us that
we are in fairyland if we had any further doubt.

Finally Adam and Eve, Milton, and we with him, are all
cast out. This has no happy ever after; just the opposite:

> though sad
> With cause for evils past, yet much more cheered
> With meditation on the happy end

At best a resignation. The taboo is restored. The cherubim
descend like ghosts or Jack o'Lantern, will-o'-the-wisps

> Gliding meteorous, as evening mist
> Risen from a river o'er the marish glides
>   . . . High in front advanced
> The brandished sword of God before them blazed
> Fierce as a comet.

I can think of no better description of the barrier reared
against looking back into our childhood unconscious, with
the fears of what we may find there and our sorrow at
our supposed loss of being the loved center of our world.

> They, looking back, all the eastern side beheld
> Of Paradise, so late their happy seat,
> Waved over by that flaming brand; the gate
> With dreadful faces thronged and fiery arms.
> Some natural tears they dropped . . .

Satan has become the epitome of lust: the plumed serpent; the Son, a social worker providing clothes for the
feckless. Ahead is nothing but the drudgery and solitariness
of life where the babes in the wood will give each other
what little comfort they can. Eve at least has Adam. Adam
has really nobody since he has lost his father. It is an
ending as black as Grimm.

CHAPTER XII

Enchanting Satire

"Where sleeps my Gulliver? O tell me where!"
The neighbours answer, "With the sorrel mare."
A. Pope

What happens to the fairies in an age of reason? Do they disappear completely or simply go underground? As extra-rational creations to embody taboo subjects they might be expected to vanish. Yet the taboos don't necessarily vanish nor the emotional situations to which they apply. Reason in a pre-psychoanalytic age may, because of the mind's constant attempts to rationalize away things that it doesn't want to look at, work as repression.[1] The repressed material will have to find other ways of disarming reason in order to be expressed. We would expect a greater subservience to credibility, which does happen, and the lifting of the material into the level of conscious wit, including satire.

By laughing at something we are able to experience it without rationally endorsing it. This is the method of Pope and Swift. At the same time the social comment in their works is the form which the credibility factor takes. The reason is able to work at the social criticism while the unconscious matter slips in unnoticed. Wit itself is energized by the tensions between the thing expressed and its expression. It's a form of metaphor and it is by metaphor that the unconscious works as we know from our own dreams.

In the eighteenth-century countryside the fairies remained much as they had for several hundred years and were to go for the next one hundred and fifty. The great age of the collectors had begun both in England and Scotland and those without the creative ability to tell stories for themselves were able to enjoy the release of the fairy convention under the scientific guise of collecting and preserv-

---

[1] On this and other relevant aspects of eighteenth-century background see Brigid Brophy, *Black Ship to Hell*, Part III The Emancipation of Reason.

ing. A myth doesn't have to be believed, in any simple sense, for it to do its work. The most famous of the early collectors was Bishop Percy with his *Reliques* which has many enchanted ballads.[2]

In adapting themselves to the town the fairies produced, apart from the novels of Jane Austen,[3] the two most important works of Augustan English: *The Rape of the Lock* and *Gulliver's Travels*.

The rationalizing guise which Swift adopted is the traveler's tale which had become immensely popular in an age of exploration before the invention of the seagoing clock, which made it possible to fix, on Cook's later journeys for instance, longitude as well as latitude. Until then it was very easy to get lost and there was still enough unknown globe to get lost in. Defoe had given the genre new impetus with *Robinson Crusoe*, published seven years before *Gulliver's Travels*, and Johnson and Voltaire were to keep it going with *Rasselas*, and *Candide*, among other adventures.

These are only part of a convention which stretches back through the *Tempest* to *Huon of Bordeaux*, knight errantry and the *Mabinogion* and forward to space travel. In each age the marvelous journey takes on a contemporary idiom, literary and rational. I don't know whether any folk idea of The Little People had reached Swift in his Irish childhood but that is what, rationalized, the Lilliputians are.

Each of the tales begins in the same way: a build-up of nautical detail, some of it seriously criticized in Swift's day for its inaccuracy; shipwreck or marooning on an island or peninsula and a plunge into the other; an opening like *The Tempest* or *Gugemar*. The first voyage has the longest opening. After this Swift can rely on association to do the transition from the natural for him. Gulliver swims ashore

[2] There is a sense in which collecting had never stopped and therefore can't be said to have begun. Tottel's *Miscellany* (1557), The Playford collections (1650 onwards), D'Urfey's *Pills* (1661 onwards) lead directly to Allan Ramsay's Scottish collections from 1724 (*The Tea Table Miscellany*), David Herd, 1776, James Johnson and Burns, 1787–1803, and on through Scott, Sharp, etc. At the same time antiquarians like Aubrey and Grose helped to fill out the non-vocal side of folklore. Broadsheets also continued to be produced until the nineteenth century.

[3] For *Northanger Abbey* see below.

and, exhausted by his efforts and half a pint of brandy, falls asleep. Wayfarers returning from the inn late at night are traditionally liable to go to sleep under a tree and wake to fairy happenings.

When Gulliver wakes he is tied, the rational equivalent of being spellbound and the little creatures swarm over him shooting him with arrows that are like fairy pinches or elf shot. As in fairyland too there is no real time except by moons. Gulliver's watch is incomprehensible. The little creatures are willing, eager indeed to feed him. In each of the voyages Swift makes much of the food, a topic that after Crusoe would be of great interest and on which he could exercise his ingenuity, but it should also be remembered that food plays an important part in fairytale, particularly in keeping the captive in fairyland. The sting of the arrows is cured instantly by a healing ointment also familiar among the fairies. Perhaps the closest analogies to Gulliver among the Lilliputians are in William of Newburgh's story of Herla and the Fairy King and Huon's treatment by Oberon.

Instead of a Fairy King we have his Imperial Majesty. The diversions of the pigmy court are described to satrical point, the qualification for office being the ability to perform on the tightrope, and Gulliver arranges a miniscule joust. Reflections of Lilliputian morality, way of life and social organization, although intended by Swift to score points off the contemporary situation, are well in the tradition of writers on fairy matters and particularly the accounts of visitors to fairyland.

> His dress was very plain and simple, the Fashion of it between the Asiatick and the European; but he had on his Head a light Helmet of Gold, adorned with Jewels, and a Plume on the Crest. He held his Sword drawn in his Hand, to defend himself, if I should happen to break loose; it was almost three Inches long, the Hilt and Scabbard were Gold enriched with Diamonds. His voice was shrill, but very clear and articulate . . .

To anyone who has come this far the parallels should be clear, but particularly the helmet and sword wand.

The punishment that is suggested for Gulliver, apart from execution, is the fairy one of blinding. He is asked to interfere in the war between Lilliput and Blefuscu as mortals were sometimes asked to take part in fairy matters, Herla to the wedding, Huon to be ruler of fairyland after Oberon. That they are never called fairies needn't fool us. Neither were many of the mediaeval supernaturals, including Arthur and Merlin. The Little People of the Isle of Man "are small persons, from two to three feet in height, otherwise very like mortals."[4]

The books of travels form a single work. Having been among fairies Gulliver moves to giantland. The only magic that we expect of giants is their size and so it has never been disputed that the Brobdingnagians are giants. The third book, in many ways the least artistically satisfying, moves into science fiction. Swift invents the flying saucer and the computer. He anticipates *Back To Methuselah* in the immortal Struldbruggs, although in a black Swiftian version, and journeys through Gulliver to the magic, specifically so, island of the dead. The bittiness of this book indicates that he is never really caught up in the fable but simply tossing off a series of ingenuities and pet hates.

In *A Voyage to the Houyhnhnms* he is back in deep water. The Houyhnhnms are horses who keep Yahoo humans as their beasts of burden. This is still an anticipation of science fiction but the fable is properly explored. Perhaps it owes something to legends of centaurs. Certainly Arthur C. Clarke's story, *Second Dawn*,[5] with its highly developed other-worldly Atheleni, who are like unicorned kangaroos, and Phileni humanoids, owes a great deal to it. But as I have said earlier the horse is a common fairy or enchanted form. Gulliver on first seeing two of them thinks they are enchanters in disguise.

The travels present a surface of reasoned anger against the follies and vices of human kind shown up by belittling and by comparison. But if they are indeed fairy stories we have to ask what this is concealing and what are the unthinkables that are finding expression through this means.

One of the first things that must strike the unwary reader

[4] Sophia Morrison, *Manx Fairy Tales*.
[5] *Expedition to Earth* (Sidgwick and Jackson, 1954).

who opens the complete edition after happy years spent with the children's book, Disney film and family pantomime is Swift's playing with the ideas of shit and piss and his basic disgust and yet fascination with these two functions. It would be possible to justify the instances in the first two books by saying that having conceived the fiction it is as important to know how these two activities were taken care of in the changed Alice-like situations of too little and too big as to know how Gulliver ate and clothed himself, but this argument won't account for the concentration of interest in the fourth book. For all their moral and intellectual failings it is the sheer physical nastiness that overwhelms Gulliver and the reader in the Yahoos. When he first meets them they assault him, some of them climbing up into a tree "from whence they began to discharge their Excrements on my Head: However, I escaped pretty well, by sticking close to the Stem of the Tree, but was almost stifled with the Filth, which fell about me on every side." When he picks up a three-year-old cub (child) he observes "the young Animal's Flesh to smell very rank" and "while I held the odious Vermin in my hands, it voided its filthy Excrements of a yellow liquid Substance, all over my Cloaths."

Returned to England Gulliver is unable to bear the smell or touch of any humans, particularly his wife: "having not been used to the Touch of that odious Animal for so many Years, I fell in a swoon for almost an hour." The smell of a female Yahoo in heat he finds particularly disgusting. However, it would be a mistake to think it is only this famous last book that has this side to it.

The climax of Gulliver's stay in Lilliput and the reason for his danger is that he put out a fire in the queen's apartments by peeing on it. This is a classic schoolboy joke. It's really about potency. A child often confuses the sex organs and act with their defecatory equivalents.[6] Some such confusion had taken place at some time in Swift's childmind making him unable to physically consummate any relationship. I wonder whether he owed it to

[6] This isn't helped by inaccurate diagrams in sex instruction books. A friend's small daughter told her father that she believed he used his penis to shit with since in the book there was no rectum and anus in the male diagram only in the female.

an experience among servants from whom upper-class children used to assimilate such a lot of garbled information. It would account for both the horror and affection he felt for them. In the travels the two creatures who are kindest to Gulliver, are said to love him, are Glumdalclitch, his ten-year-old giant nurse, and the servant sorrel nag.[7]

To be able to put out a fire by peeing on it is a metaphor for the sex act, made in this case more specific by the fact that it is the queen's apartments and that he says he "voided in such a Quantity, and applied so well in the proper Places." The queen is incensed and vows revenge for this symbolic rape.

It is really Gulliver's penis which has grown so large. To amuse himself the Emperor commands him to stand with his legs apart while a section of the army marches through.

> His Majesty gave Orders, upon Pain of Death, that every Soldier in his March should observe the strictest Decency, with regard to my Person; which, however, could not prevent some of the younger Officers from turning up their Eyes as they passed under me. And, to confess the Truth, my Breeches were at that Time in so ill a Condition, that they afforded some Opportunities for Laughter and Admiration.

This betrays a fear of castration, echoed in the suggestion of blinding, and again in the later book when it is suggested for all Yahoos, and implies that his penis has become his Person. It also shows an exhibitionist boasting.

[7] For the horror see *Directions to Servants*. Swift was carried off for three years by his nurse when he was a year old to England. His mother sent telling her not to bring him back until he "was better able to bear it. The nurse was so careful of him, that before he returned he had learned to spell" and could read any chapter in the Bible. I didn't know Swift's account of his childhood when I wrote the paragraph to which this note refers. It seems ample corroboration, particularly since Glumdalclitch and the sorrel nag teach him their languages. The affection shown him by his nurse was, he says, "very unusual." But why, he must have wondered, wasn't he with his mother but with servants. Was it because he was dirty, like them?

Among the giants Gulliver is also a penis but this time a Tom Thumb the Mighty, particularly pleasing to and cared for by the ladies who provide him with soft lined boxes and get him to perform tricks. His benefactresses are nevertheless very disgusting to him. The maids of honor stripped themselves off in front of him.

> Their Skins appeared so coarse and uneven, so variously coloured when I saw them near, with a Mole here and there as broad as a Trencher, and Hairs hanging from it thicker than Pack-threads; to say nothing further concerning the rest of their Persons. Neither did they at all scruple while I was by, to discharge what they had drunk, to the Quantity of at least two Hogsheads, in a Vessel that held above three tuns.

They stripped him and put him in their bosoms where he was disgusted by the smell. One of them set him "astride upon one of her Nipples; with many other Tricks, wherein the Reader will excuse me for not being over particular." They are using him for their pleasure.

The most horrifying piece of misogyny is the description of a nurse's breast, while suckling a child, in the gigantic close-up. Swift as a rational being liked women. He thought they should have the same education as men. He was continually surrounded by an adoring intellectual harem. Physically though he was quite unable to cope. Disgust and fear of castration obsessed him. In the quilted boxes they offered him he was in danger of being stifled or destroyed. Even a female monkey treated him as its baby.

Among the Houyhnhnms Gulliver conceives a great devotion to his master.[8] I have said that the horse is a phallic symbol in itself in the literature of enchantment and it's therefore not surprising that there is an oblique and horrified reference to homosexuality in the fourth book. "I expected every Moment, that my Master would accuse the

---

[8] In his account of his childhood Swift says he liked to impersonate characters of a lower social level such as an "ostler or waggoner's boy" or "footman to a great lady." This too I didn't know before writing this section. The connection with horses is remarkable. This is what Gulliver is to the Houyhnhnm master.

Yahoos of those unnatural Appetites in both Sexes, so common among us. But Nature it seems hath not been so expert a Schoolmistress; and these politer Pleasures are entirely the Productions of Art and Reason, on our Side of the Globe." A strange slip has happened here. Art and Reason are, by Swift's usual canon, goods. Why then are they said to produce the "unnatural Appetites"? The Houyhnhnms are creatures of reason. The word is a whinnied anagram of hominus and puns aurally on who-in-him.[9] Swift was particularly addicted to word games. At the end of the book Gulliver says he could be content if the Yahoos would be "content with those Vices and Follies only which Nature hath entitled them to." He instances pride as *the* unnatural one and says the Houyhnhnms didn't recognize it among their Yahoos but he could see it. It looks as if it has been unconsciously substituted for the other unnatural vices.

Gulliver would like to stay in the rational male world of the Houyhnhnms but he is cast out to return to his odious wife. The Yahoos are not fit to be anything more than servants and they only pretend to virtue and reason. But above all they are physically disgusting, particularly the women. Gulliver is able to tolerate the sea captain better than his own wife. His real horror is that he has "copulated" with this filthy animal.

Swift's information about his life makes the *Voyage to Brobdingnag* the most overtly autobiographical of the tales. It reflects the baby Swift carried away to an island of giant, because adult, servants, aware that he was different from them and no doubt made much of. Did he have a fantasy of being flown home by a seagull to his mother? It seems a likely childish idea. The experience of being carried away has been responsible for the plot of the travels. Perhaps the female figure to whom he returns each time is emotionally his mother. If so it would account for his disgust at having "copulated" with her. An interesting supporting detail to

----

[9] Many of the names in all the books break down into sense by analogy or anagram, e.g. Laputa = Putala, the island of thought, from Latin "putare," but there may also be a suggestion of "putana," prostitution. Brobdingnag contains the elements Big-and-rob, Lilliput suggests both Littl(e) and politi. I leave readers to play with the others but remark Flipman and Resselder in Book I.

the childhood basis for this story is that Gulliver is put in a baby's cradle when he arrives among the giants; baby being the contemporary word for doll, first recorded from 1700.

The matter-of-fact and plain style of the book is derived from Swift's usual literary practice and *Robinson Crusoe* which itself hovers on the fairytale border. (All stories which become pantomimes should be suspected as members of the genre, including the *Babes In The Wood* which supposedly began as an historical incident like the stories of Arthur and Robin Hood.) The plain style is a credibility device deliberately employed by Swift who was anxious to pass the travels off as genuine. He apparently succeeded. The first edition, bowdlerized a little by the publisher, sold out in a week. The manuscript had been delivered cloak-and-dagger to the bookseller by night, dropped from a carriage by a friend and purported to come from a cousin of Lemuel Gulliver. Arbuthnot when let into the secret congratulated Swift on being so happy a man at his age to be able to write such a "merry book." Lilliputian poetry in short lines became the rage as miniature fairy poetry had in the seventeenth century.

Swift himself was not happy. He had wanted to "vex" not "divert." The book, as he says, in the prefatory letter to the second edition, had not removed those vices from the Yahoos which he so deplored. But it had done its work as a fairy story in expressing unconscious experiences which, however exacerbatedly personal they were to Swift, are nevertheless common to millions of children in some degree.

The Sylphs

To many critics it has appeared that Pope only included his supernatural spirits in *The Rape of the Lock* as a piece of prettification, as one might decorate a teacup or a tombstone with cupids, and that they have nothing to do with "real fairies." Such an opinion is an insult to a careful and great artist and leads to misreading of the poem on a superficial level. Had Pope not intended the spirits to be important he would never have made them such a vital part of the machinery nor explored them at such length. We must allow him to have known what he was doing.

The mistake arises from three causes: the comparison of the sylphs with figures in a masque, which is fashionably reckoned lightweight stuff; a misunderstanding of the ambivalence and prevalence of putti in rococo art; and the idea of Pope as a waspish mocking sophisticate.

In his introductory letter Pope says he has used the Rosicrucian doctrine of spirits as a basis for his supernaturals. This treats them as elementals, as the Ariel of *The Tempest* is treated and as he appears again in *The Rape*. The system is a rationalization of well-known types that are common in British mythology: Sylphs, Gnomes, Nymphs and Salamanders. Sylphs are flying fairies; gnomes, earthy elves; nymphs, water fairies, and salamanders, will-o'-the-wisps. Like many fairies they are connected with the dead, indeed are dead beauties like Sir Orfeo's wife. The kind of spirit a woman will be in afterlife is governed by her temperament on earth. Termagants become salamanders, prudes are gnomes, "soft yielding minds" become nymphs and "light coquettes" sylphs. The amusing orderliness hides a serious point.

Credibility is provided by the wealth of witty descriptive detail; by the worldliness of characters and setting. The social comment works like Gulliver's maps and nautical terms. Ostensibly it's a story of a daring young aristocrat snipping off a girl's ringlet. Under the fairy aegis this works as a metaphor of rape and castration. In Pope's case it is difficult to decide where the line between conscious and unconscious should be drawn. I am inclined to make it between rape and castration.

Pope consciously equates folk fairies, angels and elementals. He knows, as well as Chaucer knew Proserpine was the Fairy Queen, that they are all the same. Ariel himself is a sylph. He is also an incubus, who explains to Belinda about adolescent fantasy, and the fairy lover who can be hers as long as she is a virgin.

> A youth more glittering than a birth-night beau,
> (That ev'n in slumber caused her cheek to glow)

The sylphs keep their charges chaste by offering them constant variety. What seems levity in the girls and fickleness is simply a way of not getting in too deep. Ariel warns her in a dream, but nevertheless an erotic one, that she is in danger. As soon as she wakes she forgets the warning in preparing herself for the sex war.

> Now awful beauty puts on all its arms

Meanwhile the baron has prepared himself to steal the two locks of hair that Belinda cherishes at the nape of her neck. He wants them because they hold him captive, enslaved in chains by his lust. The transposition is clear. To free himself from Belinda's sexual power over him he must have her.

> With hairy springes we the birds betray,
> Slight lines of hair surprise the finny prey.

The symbols the poem uses betray the real fear. Fish and bird are the penis; the hair is pubic hair. This last symbol is made specific in Belinda's cry after the deed:

> Oh hadst thou, cruel! been content to seize
> Hairs less in sight, or any hairs but these!

The would-be lover is afraid of being caught, of the devouring female sex organs that terrify D. H. Lawrence's heroes.

Belinda goes by boat down the Thames. The winged spirits, "fays, fairies, genii, elves and daemons," hover over her in protecting canopy. Ariel's fears are divided between the material and the spiritual; a metaphor of the whole poem where the trivial is symbol of the serious, the flawed china-jar of the broken hymen.[10] Above all he is afraid of rape. Fifty spirits are to guard the petticoat.

> Oft have we known that seven-fold fence to fail
> Though stiff with hoops, and arm'd with ribs of
> whale

The dressed girl is a maiden besieged in a tower, constantly under assault for the prize of her virginity, the rose in the mediaeval love garden of Guillaume de Lorris.

---

[10] See B. Brophy, *Mozart the Dramatist*, p. 90.

At Hampton Court Belinda meets two beaux whom she wishes to engage in mortal combat at cards, one of them the baron. She beats them after a brisk skirmish but lucky in cards is unlucky in love. Helped by one of the other belles with a pair of scissors the baron severs the lock. Ariel, in vain trying to rouse her to the danger, looks in her heart and sees an earthly lover. At once, like all fairy lovers including the Great Silkie and the Fairy Queen herself, he is defeated. Real sex disperses fantasy. Belinda has unconsciously fallen in love with the baron and will acquiesce in his castration of her. One of the sylphs "too fondly interposed" and is cut in half. Pope restores him much as Milton's angels airy substance was restored. In a baroque mirror-image of the female thighs closing about the penis to cut it off the "glitt'ring forfex" encloses and divides the lock.

Belinda screams; the baron exults. With precise touch Pope underlines the importance of "unresisted steel," traditionally anathema to fairies. Ariel deserts her weeping and in his place comes the gnome[11] Umbriel. Deeply shocked Belinda becomes a prude. She too fears the castration of intercourse. Yet secretly she wants a lover.

Umbriel visits the Cave of Spleen where the dark goddess lives among her Boschlike grotesques, the personified madnesses of thwarted sex. He is the black Puck, full of evil mischief. The goddess herself owes, I believe, a great deal to Hecate in Purcell's *Dido and Aeneas*. She is the "wayward Queen" as the witches who work the anti-love mischief in Purcell's opera are the "wayward sisters." The gnome takes a phial of tears and a bag of sobs and sighs to confirm Belinda in her misery and rage. He symbolizes that sexual frustration and resentment that the baron's symbolic castration has caused in Belinda.

Back on earth Belinda's friend Thalestris is fanning her anger by harping on the public disgrace. It might be thought that if the baron had actually raped her it would

[11] Pope was very much in fashion with this word if the Oxford Dictionary is right in recording its first use as 1712. *The Rape of the Lock* in its first complete edition is 1714. Perhaps the lexicographers mean Pope. The word comes from Paracelsus and is synonymous with pigmy and dwarf. It has accreted some of the associations of gnomic.

have been worse but no. The humiliation, the reductio ad absurdum of the beauty, is what hurts. Had he seized the pubic hairs it would have been better. Thalestris's beau Sir Plume asks the baron to return the lock, dimly realizing the insult but in his stupidity not the true nature of the baron's triumph.

Clarissa, the one who in a sense had begun the trouble by lending her scissors, exhorts Belinda, and all women, to compliance and submission.

> Curl'd or uncurl'd, since locks will turn to grey;
> Since painted, or not painted, all shall fade,
> And she who scorns a man must die a maid;
> What then remains, but well our power to use
> And keep good-humour still, whate'er we lose?

No applause greets this statement of the traditional position of women. It is part of Pope's brilliance to make it clear that he doesn't subscribe to this view, though without intruding personally, and to make this character so consistent that it's now clear why she lent the scissors. She is the kind of woman who constantly stabs women's emancipation in the back with her darning needle.

Angered, the women fall to the sex war in earnest. Umbriel claps his wings with pleasure and the sprites look on or goad the combatants. The weapons are those of *Lysistrata*, the withholding of favors, the killing by denial. Belinda makes the baron impotent with a flung pinch of snuff, the gnomes directing the grains so that he discharges noisily, futilely and humiliatingly. Finally she threatens him with a bodkin and all demand the restoration of the lock which can no longer however be found. Some think it has gone to the lunar sphere, repository of all idle fictions, but Pope sees it changed to a comet by the immortalizing power of the Muse which is the only power to defeat physical decay.

Women are made the sexual victims of men by a society that denies them everything except physical beauty. Freed from the body those of any spirit become masculine in their activity, only the submissive like Clarissa remaining female as water nymphs. Thalestris will undoubtedly become a salamander.

> . . . spirits, freed from *mortal* laws, with ease
> Assume what sexes and what shapes they please.

Pope is in direct line with traditional views of fairies, and
of angels as Raphael had made clear to Adam in *Paradise
Lost*. Any girl of spirit has a masculine spirit even if it's a
prudish gnome. Only the flesh differentiates women and
men and in doing so castrates women. Ariel, Belinda's
particular familiar, is male. He is her spiritual penis. The
sylphs, although often called by female names, presumably
those of their flesh, are "he."

> Whatever spirit careless of his charge
> His post neglects . . .

At the cataclysmic moment one of them is cut in half. In
Thomas Stothard's illustration to the 1798 edition this
sylph is in the form of a putto clinging to the fated lock.
At this moment Ariel sees himself betrayed and Belinda's
spiritual penis is snipped in half with the lock, as Sampson
was made impotent by the loss of his hair. Rage restores
her and the airy substance. Belinda is too spirited a girl to
be easily reduced.

The mutual fear of castration leads to the sex war. It
isn't Belinda's fault. Society expects nothing from her except to be beautiful and gives her neither education nor
activity. Her intelligence and energy can only find expression in a game of cards, which she plays with such brilliance that she could have led armies, with her masculine
spirits seated on each card. It isn't the baron's fault either.
He can only defend himself by attacking.

In the fairy machinery Pope has been able to embody
that controversial thing: the female penis. In the Cave of
Spleen he shows himself aware of sexual ambiguity.

> Men prove with child, as powerful fancy works,
> And maids turn'd bottles call aloud for corks.

It's impossible to decide how conscious Pope was of this
embodiment but as with so many writers it may simply be
that his unconscious has worked unerringly on his behalf
in using fairy to treat a taboo subject.

CHAPTER XIII

Gothick Horror

Angela: Father! Father! Stay for heaven's sake!—He's gone. I cannot find the door.—Hark! 'Twas the clank of chains! A light too! It comes yet nearer! Save me, ye powers! What dreadful form! 'Tis here! I faint with terror!

The Castle Spectre, M. G. Lewis

By the end of the eighteenth century reason and satire had been inundated by the Gothick. In terms of faery, this means that taste for the horrifically supernatural which continues in the novels of Dennis Wheatley, in the endless collections of ghost and macabre stories and in horror films dripping with the ketchup of vampires, putrid with green flesh of ghouls and sound-tracked by screams of virgins and rumbling vaults. The paraphernalia and settings of the genre have hardly altered by a bat's leathery wing brush against the unsuspecting cheek in two hundred years. Recently there has been an even deathlier resurgence to prove that we are as willing as ever to terrify and punish ourselves with black magic.

The rise of the species which is usually dated from the publication of Walpole's *Castle of Otranto* in 1764 needs some explaining for it was a complete reversal of a strongly flowing tide by which men hoped to set the world on an evolutionary road to reason and happiness. By 1759 it had already become clear to two of the best minds of the century, Voltaire and Johnson whose *Candide* and *Rasselas* appeared in the same year, that the fruits of enlightenment were a long way off, that the world was full of the corrupt and the stupid, and that it was best to set oneself the limited aims of work, common sense and one's own comfort as far as possible[1] thereby making the best of the possible world.

Such a resolution required great courage and made no concessions to the demands of the imagination and the unconscious. It was these two which were now to backlash

[1] This is how I interpret Voltaire's irritatingly opaque "il fait cultiver notre jardin" and Johnson's ultimate paragraph.

into the Gothick. I have said that the movement began with the publication of *The Castle of Otranto* but this is only to say that the novel dropped into prepared soil which made it possible to shoot up overnight into its fantastic popular form. It is not, as has sometimes been suggested, a product of Teutonic gloom imported into this country, but a perfectly acclimatized native growth. Its idiom may be in terms of the Black Forest or the wolf-ravaged Apennines but this makes it no less indigenous than *Rasselas* which is set in Abyssinia and Egypt.

The ground was first prepared by a revival of religious guilt and of a personal god. Wearied with religious wars, reformation and counter-reformation, rational thinkers had moved into a position of Deism, a belief in a Supreme Being or first principle combined with a general acceptance of the Copernican universe suitably expressed in Addison's hymn: "The spacious firmament on high." In the thirties John Wesley began his movement to repersonalize Christianity by awakening a sense of sin and a longing for personal salvation. It had enormous success largely, at first, among those who had insufficient education and resources to make life tolerable in a period when aspiration far outstripped the technological ability to give those things to more than a few, at the expense of the rest, and when at the same time the country was entering the first stages of industrialization and undergoing a big population explosion.

> Weary of wandering from my God
> And now made willing to return
> I hear and bow me to the rod:
> For Thee, not without hope, I mourn:
> I have an Advocate above
> A Friend before the Throne of Love.
>
> O Jesus, full of pardoning grace,
> More full of grace than I of sin,
> Yet once again I seek Thy Face;
> Open Thine Arms, and take me in,
> And freely my backslidings heal,
> And love the faithless sinner still.

Thou know'st the way to bring me back,
My fallen spirit to restore;
O for Thy truth and mercy's sake
Forgive, and bid me sin no more;
The ruins of my soul repair,
And make my house a house of prayer.

The stone to flesh again convert,
The veil of sin once more remove;
Sprinkle Thy Blood upon my heart,
And melt it with Thy dying love;
This rebel heart by love subdue,
And make it soft and make it new.

Ah, give me Lord, the tender heart
That trembles at the approach of sin;
A godly fear of sin impart
Implant and root it deep within
That I may dread Thy gracious power,
And never dare offend Thee more.

I have given this example from Charles Wesley's hymns in full rather than any of the better known ones, like *Jesus, Lover of My Soul*, another web of intensely eroto-masochist imagery, because it reads like a miniature Gothick novel. There is the blood, the ruin, the guilt, the trembling sensibility, the disguised sexuality, the veil, the father who is lover and judge. Yet Charles Wesley died in 1788 and had begun his evangelism before his brother.

Another element in the Gothick was its love of nature and setting up of an antagonism between nature and art. Emily, the heroine of Mrs. Radcliffe's *The Mysteries of Udolpho*, at the opera feels "how infinitely inferior all the splendor of art is to the sublimity of nature." This too was a native product owing more to the poetry of James Thomson and "Ossian" Macpherson than to Rousseau. It began that strand of anti-urbanism and anti-intellectualism still characteristically English. In Mrs. Radcliffe, as in Wordsworth, nature is an ennobling force to be delineated in page after page. It needs no education to be able to appreciate it and since it appears pure and impersonal the worship of it is thought to have no impure, that is sexual, overtones. In the same way it was thought right to apostrophize Jesus as a lover who would "Keep me pure within."

This concern with purity contrasts with the morality of the upper classes expressed in *The Rape of the Lock*. It is particularly related to women, and the attitude to them of Walpole and Mrs. Radcliffe plots their declining position as the century progressed. The difference between say Mrs. Millamant in *The Way of the World* and Emily is that between a person and an object. Emily no longer has any self-determination even against her aunt's husband. She can do little except weep and faint, both of which she does with wearying monotony, a trembling soul prepared to give up her lover because she can no longer esteem him on someone else's word. The all-important word comes from the Count de Villefort, who reminds her of her father. We do not know whether Millamant and Belinda have fathers. They are thought capable of standing by themselves and making their own decisions. As for playing cards with two men, discussing the physical side of marriage or threatening a man with a bodkin in a rage, Emily would die from offended sensibility and delicacy.

This acute softening of the feminine image which was to persist for nearly a century and which is begun upon in Richardson's *Clarissa Harlowe* is another aspect of the paternalism which is at the root of the Gothick. It is particularly a product of the aspiring middle classes. In a time when the lower classes were being called to repentance the middle classes couldn't be left behind. They had no titles to confer but could improve their connections if they had money by marrying their daughters into the aristocracy as long as the daughters were perfect, unsullied and pleasing objects.

As the process of involving thousands of women as cheap manufacturing labor advanced, the population grew and living conditions declined, it became more and more important to differentiate the masters' womenfolk from the brutalized and degraded women workers. They had to seem a different species, incapable of work or any kind of coarseness. Ideally they should be incapable of independent thought since a man accustomed to rule hundreds of workpeople expected also to be master in his home.

For nice women sex became unthinkable, for nice men synonymous with lust. It was alleged that some owners ran their factories like harems, while attempts to improve the workers' minds or conditions, especially attempts by themselves, were linked with Jacobinism. After the terror of the French Revolution this idea was given further impetus. The workers were, psychologically, brutal children rebelling against the father-master in an attempt to usurp his place.

In France this had expressed itself in regicide, the murder of the king father. Regicide is always a horrifying deed, symbolic of more than itself. The English had already performed it. They had been saved from the worst emotional consequences by having Cromwell to put in the king's place but in France there was no single person and the children were left to squabble among themselves, getting deeper and deeper into violence as they tried to distract attention from that first sin. Father God was also dethroned and an attempt made to dechristianize the country.

Confronted by this the British aristocracy and middle classes made common cause to keep the British Jacobins from following suit. Repressive measures against them from Pitt,[2] moral condemnation, a renewal of religious fervor, was against the French invoking patriotism, and an overall determination to keep everyone in his place, allied all the forms of paternalism. The Gothick movement, in architecture and art but above all in literature, is an expression of the unconscious obsessions which this situation both provoked and repressed.

> . . . the French Revolution has made us shrink from the name of philosophy, and has destroyed, in the more refined part of the community (of which number I am one), all enthusiasm for political liberty. That part of the *reading public* which shuns the solid food of reason for the light diet of fiction, requires a perpetual adhibition of *sauce piquante* to the palate of its depraved imagination. It lived upon ghosts, goblins, and skeletons (I and my friend Mr.

[2] For much of the background material to this chapter I am indebted to E. P. Thompson's *The Making of The English Working Class* (Gollancz, 1963).

> Sackbut served up a few of the best), till even the
> devil himself, though magnified to the size of Mount
> Athos, became too base, common, and popular for
> its surfeited appetite,

wrote Peacock in 1818 in *Nightmare Abbey* giving the
conscious reasons for the fashion for the Gothick.

In the terror that followed the French Revolution England saw a reenactment of the violence and intrigue the
Jacobeans had drawn on in contemporary Italian life as
they saw it. These two strands, particularized as Shakespeare and the Latin South, reappear as part of the Gothick idiom. Walpole in his preface to the second edition of
The Castle of Otranto invokes Shakespeare as his inspiration. He has deliberately written an attempt to combine the
two kinds of romance, ancient and modern because "the
great resources of fancy have been dammed up . . . Nature
has cramped imagination."

Ossian had used a miraculous Celtic setting. The mediaeval was supplied by the unfortunate Chatterton who
faked antique poems under the guise of a long-dead monk,
Thomas Rowley. Chatterton died after his nine days' wonder in 1770. By all accounts he must have begun impersonating Rowley in about 1765, at about the time that
Percy published his *Reliques of Ancient English Poetry*
with its emphasis on chivalry and supernatural ballads.
This impersonation introduced one of the most important
stock characters into the genre: the monk.

From the first the fairies, as distinct from faery, were
included as part of the setting along with the other infer-
nals, and enchantment was a necessary part of the machinery even if, as in *The Mysteries of Udolfo*, it was rationalized away at the end of the book. *Northanger Abbey*, by a
piece of baroque structuring, is a rationalization of a rationalization allowing Jane Austen to make her comment
on reason and sensibility and the roots of everyday terror.[3]

---

[3] Jane Austen's niece Caroline remembered her telling them "delightful stories chiefly of Fairyland"; "her fairies had all characters
of their own." They sound French-derived and this would have been
quite possible. There is a sense in which many of her novels are
fairy stories: *Sense and Sensibility = Toads and Jewels; Pride and
Prejudice = Cinderella*, etc.

Walpole believed he had created a "new species of romance." Manfred is its usurping villain whose only son is killed on his wedding day by a monstrous black plumed helmet very like that which, in stone, was part of the tomb of the family's tutelary saint, Alfonso. Manfred hates his daughter Matilda and is tired of his wife Hippolita, who does seem a tiresomely submissive pious lady. He decides to put her away and marry his dead son's betrothed, Isabella. When he tries to seduce her she resists, saying such a match would be incestuous. As he persists the portrait of his grandfather steps from its frame in warning. Isabella escapes and is joined by a young peasant who has been accused of bringing about the bridegroom's death by sorcery and imprisoned by Manfred under the helmet. Meanwhile the servants have seen a monstrous mailed foot and leg which they believe to be that of a giant. Manfred now says that he has scruples about his marriage since he and his wife are cousins.

A trumpet sounds outside the castle; the monstrous black plumes quiver like live things. The knight of the gigantic sabre has come to demand the return of Isabella to her father Frederic and of the principality of Otranto which Manfred has usurped from him. Isabella has taken sanctuary in a nearby church but Theodore, the young peasant, has been caught and imprisoned. Matilda tries to free him but he has fallen in love with her and refuses at first to go. She persuades him and he too goes to the church where his father is the priest. Isabella has fled. Theodore goes after her to protect her and by a misunderstanding severely wounds her father Frederic, who is really the knight of the gigantic sabre. He is carried to the castle where he falls in love with Matilda. The two fathers decide to take a daughter each. A giant hand is seen and then a skeleton in a hermit's robe which tells Frederic to give up Matilda.

Manfred, mistaking his daughter for Isabella, whom he thinks has an assignation with Theodore by Alfonso's tomb, stabs her. Matilda with her dying hand joins those of her parents together. Theodore is revealed as the lawful heir of Otranto by the apparition of the dead Alfonso, "dilated to an immense magnitude," and finally persuaded to marry Isabella since with her he could talk about his dear Matilda and "forever indulge the melancholy that had taken possession of his soul." In this melancholy he is the forerunner of Goethe's hero young Werther whom he anticipates by over a decade.

The apparition which the servants describe as a giant is, in company with folk giants, as I have said earlier, a father; in this case a usurped one, as all fathers are ultimately displaced by their sons unless they devour them first. The real hero in the sense of the figure with whom the reader unconsciously identifies, is Manfred, and Walpole underlines this by a sudden explanation of Manfred's temperament: "Manfred was not one of those savage tyrants who wanton in cruelty unprovoked. The circumstances of his fortune had given an asperity to his temper, which was naturally humane; and his virtues were always ready to operate, when his passion did not obscure his reason."[4]

Like Hamlet he is plagued by a ghost, the spirit of his grandfather as well as by the dead Alfonso. Each time language and situation echo *Hamlet* very closely. In the second appearance there is an exchange with his wife Hippolita very close to the scene between Gertrude and Hamlet. The young Theodore appearing suddenly is so like Alfonso that Manfred thinks it is his spectre. This gives us a clue to the real nature of Hippolita. Emotionally she is Manfred's mother and this is how she is portrayed. She has borne him two children yet he accuses her of unfruitfulness. The story he tells Frederic is that he fears their marriage is incestuous.

Matilda is devoted to her mother. Isabella calls her her mother: "my own mother—I never have known another. —Oh! she is the mother of both! cried Matilda. Can we, can we, Isabella, adore her too much? My lovely children, said the touched Hippolita." In trying to marry Isabella, Manfred is hoping to marry his daughter because she is both his son's intended wife, and his wife's daughter in love. Matilda herself he hates because the blood taboo is too strong to be overcome. Matilda on her side loves Theodore because he looks like Alfonso, her mother's emotional husband by whose tomb Matilda is instructed by Hippolita

---

[4] Horace Walpole, *The Castle of Otranto* (Oxford English Texts), p. 30.

to pray. Dying she barely mentions her lover who is distractedly trying to arrange a deathbed marriage, in which he doesn't succeed. She calls continually for her mother and father and the deathbed scene, to become so familiar on stage and page for the next hundred years, is all piety and family passion.

The bonds of family, loosened by rationalism and greater sexual freedom after the restoration of Charles II, were tightening again to culminate in the obsessions of Victorian melodrama, the terrors of *Hatter's Castle* and *East Lynne*. The emphasis on paternalism, purity and the family carried over into adult life the basically incestuous loves of childhood. Fairy tale and fantasy were the obvious ways of expressing these otherwise inexpressibles. This could still be done even when the main character constantly warned himself against superstition as Emily does in *The Mysteries of Udolpho* and when supernatural happenings were ultimately explained away. The explanation and warning is yet another device of credibility.

In Matilda and later Emily we have the introduction of the super-refinement of female innocence which leads to the nineteenth-century obsession with children, purity and death, and to a new fairy form: the gauze-winged and robed girl-fays so despised by folklorists who see them as a degeneration of an earlier earthier type rather than a new creation to meet particular psychological needs. Flying, the wand, transformation, and reward and punishment are all important attributes of this type. The wings become enormous, spiritualized labiae sometimes framing the body, sometimes sprouting above it. Long unbound hair flows over the shoulders. The whole image is a representation of the female external sex organs bathed in luminosity, enchantingly erotic as in J. Simmons's picture of Titania painted in 1867 (see photo insert). Her wand will transform you and the world and grant your wishes. She is the good fairy of the pantomime and the *Blue Fairy* of Disney's *Pinocchio*. The surreal Swiftian version of it is Magritte's grotesque torso with the elements transposed to make a face.

Mrs. Radcliffe's novel is told through the eyes of the innocent girl, Lewis's *The Monk* through the villainous Ambrosio and the young Antonia. All three of these most famous of the Gothick novels deal with a disguised father/ daughter relationship. I have already discussed its form in *The Castle of Otranto*. In *The Mysteries of Udolpho* the girl is carried off to the castle by her father's sister who has married the corrupt Montoni. The first part of the book is taken up with the close relationship between Emily and her father before his death; the second with her attempts to free herself from her black uncle, who is a reverse image of her father. Mrs. Radcliffe is too constantly aware of the proprieties for uncle to try to seduce niece directly. Instead he tries to force her into various marriages which will pay his debts. Emily is taken away from her young lover on the model of young girls carried off by the fairies as if she cannot really have him until she is freed from her dependence on her father.

Lewis admitted himself in a letter to his mother that Mrs. Radcliffe's book had influenced him in *The Monk*. The other influence is Goethe's *Faust*. Lewis must have read or had read to him or discussed parts of it while he was staying at Weimar to learn German. There are too many similarities for them to be accidents. In particular there is a scene with a magic mirror in which Faust sees Margareta and another in which Ambrosio sees Antonia which by its flagrant eroticism provoked such a moral outcry that it was cut from later editions. *Faust* was not published until 1808; *The Monk* in 1795.[5] Faust is older than the girl; Ambrosio is specifically by the use of religious idiom her "father." To enjoy her he has to kill her mother and rape the girl in a tomb after he has drugged her into a semblance of death like Snow White. Her own wishes partly coincide with his. Although her mother warns her against him Antonia can't quite believe he is evil.

Like Faust, Ambrosio is a respected local doctor who falls through lust and love. The machinery of the book is

[5] This isn't the place for an extended discussion of all the parallels between the two works. A reading of them both will surely convince better if anyone doubts my assertion. The only other explanation is that Lewis had read Goethe's *Faust* source book. He does refer specifically to the legend in one place but he also translates the poem *The Erl King* and uses it as a basis for a piece about elemental spirits acknowledging his debt to Goethe.

the most supernatural of these three Gothick horrors. There is the devil himself, and a succubus which disguises itself as a woman disguised as a novice to bring about the monk's downfall. The moment of revelation is an early piece of camp drag. " 'Father!' continued he, throwing himself at the friar's feet, and pressing his hands to his lips with eagerness, while agitation for a moment choked his voice; 'father!' continued he in faltering accents, 'I am a woman!'." As the succubus becomes more assured of Ambrosio it becomes more masculine in its manners although remaining very female in body. "But a few days had passed since she appeared the mildest and softest of her sex, devoted to his will, and looking up to him as a superior being. Now she assumed a sort of courage and manliness in her manners and discourse, but ill calculated to please him." He finds himself regretting the submissive youth Rosario.

Antonia kneeling before a statue of St. Rosalia to say her bedtime prayers expresses the view of fairies as dream tempters which was to appear in many Victorian fairy paintings, particularly those of J. Anster Fitzgerald.

> Yet may not my unconscious breast
> Harbour some guilt to me unknown?
> Some wish impure, which unrepent
> You blush to see, and I to own.
>
> Chase from my peaceful bed away,
> The witching spell, a foe to rest,
> The nightly goblin, wanton fay,
> The ghost in pain, and friend unblest.
>
> Let not the tempter in mine ear
> Pour lessons of unhallowed joy;
> Let not the nightmare wandering near
> My couch, the calm of sleep destroy.
>
> Let not some horrid dream afright
> With strange fantastic forms my eyes

The theme of the book is temptation through supernatural means and the resulting loss of innocence. Religion itself, and in particular the monastic vow of chastity, provides the taboo symbol to be broken. The incest motif is made explicit in the last pages. Ambrosio is revealed as Antonia's brother. He has raped her and murdered his mother. Not surprisingly the mother appears as a warning ghost.

Father/daughter incest which is such a feature of nineteenth-century art and emotional concern is, I believe, a projection of the original son/mother desire. As Sophocles knew, the emotional logical sequel to *Oedipus Tyrannus* is *Oedipus at Colonus*. Inside ourselves we remain the same age. It's only other people whom we observe getting older. The beloved mother ages and disgusts like the crone representation of Morgan la Fee. The hero although he seems no older to himself is aware of his own guilt and lost innocence. He looks for a reincarnation of his mother in something young and desirable. It must be a virgin since what he really wants is his mother before his father anticipated him in conceiving him. The most direct reincarnation of a man's mother is his daughter. There may even be a strong physical resemblance.[6]

This encourages concepts of the submissiveness and purity of girls and the absolute authority of fathers. It also provides ideal conditions for the growth of male homosexuality.[7] Antonia is Lewis's persona; significantly she is said like Lewis to be "below middle size, light and airy as an Hamadryad." Lewis himself retained enough of the earlier rational attitude to sex for his other herone Agnes to be allowed a happy ending, although she has had a child by her lover. She is dreadfully punished by a sadistic prioress while Raymond, the lover, is haunted by a dead nun.[8] The child dies and in her near madness she insists on keeping

[6] This is one form, not the only form, of father/daughter incest. Like jealousy it has several different types, variations of oedipal, narcissistic, homosexual and other situations.

[7] By, for example, the desire on the part of a boy to be father's love object.

[8] Lewis's parallel construction suggests that Raymond was freeing himself from his mother as Antonia from her father. Father is the more persistent. Lewis was torn between his own separated parents. He was only twenty when he wrote the book and deep in his family problem. The dead bastard and Agnes's reaction to it are from Goethe.

its corpse with her where she is chained in her underground cell. Even so she hasn't committed incest and is therefore capable of being restored to her lover and society.

The succubus has modified vampire characteristics like some kinds of fairy. She sucks the poison from Ambrosio's veins when he has been stung by a serpent among the roses. We are made to feel that this is a spine-chilling rather than a beneficient act. But this isn't the only point at which there is a fairy counterpart. Raymond is taken on a wild ride carrying the ghost of the nun in his ams, a phenomenon familiar since William of Newburgh. The first spirit, apart from the succubus, which appears to Ambrosio is a beautiful youth.

> He was perfectly naked; a bright star sparkled upon his forehead, two crimson wings extended themselves from his shoulders, and his silken locks were confined by a band of many-coloured fires . . . Circlets of diamonds were fastened round his arms and ankles, and in his right hand he bore a silver branch imitating myrtle. His form shone with dazzling glory: he was surrounded by clouds of rose-colored light.

Sweet music and perfume also accompany him. He's called a demon but he could equally well be a fairy prince or at least an elemental.

In a long passage in which Raymond's page is trying to charm his way into the convent he gives a dissertation on the four kings of the Oak, the Water, the Fire and the Cloud where will-o'-the-wisps, water sprites, elves, fairies and goblins are all called demons. In a footnote Lewis says he has invented the last three kings by analogy with Goethe's Erl or Oak King, and instances two Scottish ballads, *May Colvin* and *Clerk Colvil,* which tell of human affairs with water sprites. It should be remembered that it was Lewis who befriended the young[9] Scott by including some of his poems in *Tales of Wonder* published in 1801

---

[9] He was four years Lewis's senior but unknown, whereas the younger man was already "Monk" Lewis. Scott told Moore in 1825 that it was Lewis who first set him on to trying his talent at poetry.

"a collection of all the marvellous ballads I can lay my hands upon." Byron's comment on the collection is worth recording:

> Lo! wreaths of yew, not laurel, bind thy brow
> Thy muse a sprite, Apollo's sexton thou!
> . . . Even Satan's self with thee might dread to dwell
> And in thy skull discern a deeper hell.

There is then no distinction to be made at this period between the seemingly different forms of the supernatural, and none was made. As the fairies had always been set back in an earlier period for reasons I've discussed, so at this time they were set first in the Renaissance and then in the Pre-Raphaelite Middle Ages. The obsession with parents, more particularly with father, leads to a visual and emotional projection into an ancestral period which will then be backed up by the rationalizing factors of taste and scholarship. Nowhere is this clearer than in the Gothick revival in architecture and the authoritarian revival of the Church.[10] Ghosts, the stock-in-trade of the genre, are themselves ancestors, therefore parents, come back to warn and accuse, projections of our guilt and desire, and as much fairies as Sir Orfeo's wife and her companions spirited away by sudden death, and the familiars described as fairies who were the dead servants of witches accused in the sixteenth and seventeenth-century trials.

Scott himself, leaving out Lewis's lurid and vital pornographic element, was to go on to exploit the historical background with supernatural accessories in many of his novels, the historical accuracy being another aspect of credibility, while he collected stories and ballads in Scotland which he began publishing in 1802 as *Minstrelsy of*

---

[10] The two forms of nineteenth-century Christian revival would make interesting research: Evangelical and Catholic. They seem to me to embody two different psychological variations on the paternal theme, the first by identification, the second as the beloved object. Newman himself attributes his first acquaintance with Catholic symbols to the reading of Mrs. Radcliffe or Miss Porter (one of two sisters, friends of Scott and novelists; *Dom Sebastian*, 1809?) when he was about ten, but it could have been the breaking rosary sequence in *The Monk* where Ambrosio's beads scatter like sperm among his female flock. If so he would have suppressed the memory.

the Scottish Border. At Lewis's suggestion he wrote a ballad on the Fire King for the *Tales of Wonder*.

Writing his preface to the work of the fictitious monk Onuphrio Muralto, Walpole had said self-betrayingly: "I could wish he had grounded his plan on a more useful moral than this; that the sins of fathers are visited on their children to the third and fourth generation." He had by an almost accident lit upon the text which best embodies the whole Gothick genre however obliquely. Fathers and children, inheritance, sin and guilt, incest, are the themes round which the diabolic lightning continues to play since the patriarchal and authoritarian system is still with us, although possibly in a diluted form, and most of all in family relationships.

CHAPTER XIV

The Magic Carpet

Still eyes look coldly upon me,
Cold voices whisper and say,
"He is crazed with the spell of far Arabia;
They have stolen his wits away."
                        Walter De La Mare

Since the Crusades the East has been enchanted for Western Christendom, an enchantment that cast its last spell with Valentino, T. E. Lawrence and *The Desert Song* and was washed away in a gush of sparkling black oil. Its charm was a combination of sensuality and sexuality, of sophistication and violence, of sherbet drinks and the harem. Whether the picture bore any relationship to reality is irrelevant. What was important was that it supplied a whole new setting for the imagination to work in while purporting to give factual information. When local fairy tales were discredited as impossible, Arabian nights could be enjoyed as a facet of orientalism. One could cry, "How quaint," while indulging. It has never been necessary to believe in fairies to employ them, or allow them to work on us, except while under their spell.

To ignore Anglo-oriental magic on the grounds that it isn't native is merely chauvinist. Sindbad and Aladdin have been naturalized by public consent. The country of faery is just over there and, as more and more of the visible countryside is taken up by man, leaving the supernaturals no place of their own, it becomes necessary to go farther afield to find them, to Arabia or to Andromeda.

The earliest Eastern stories had no need of superficial magic. By the very nature of the setting the taboo-breaking was in-built. The greatest fascination was exercised by the idea of the harem. To the monogamous Western Christian this was both shocking and alluring. In contact with their enemies Christians learnt that the paynim were extremely civilized, cultured people. "Of this lady," says the twelfth-century lay *A Story of Beyond the Sea*, "was born the mother of that courteous Turk, the Sultan Saladin, an honorable, a wise, and a conquering lord."[1] The most common stories are those in which for one reason or another the heroine is carried away by the saracens to become the bride of the sultan. Sometimes she is rescued in the nick of time, sometimes she has to escape later leaving her saracen husband.

To the ladies left at home while the men went on crusade this basic plot had great fantasy attractions. They were able to toy deliciously with the idea of being "carried away"; with forced extra-marital sexual experience for which they as heroines could be in no way blamed. In *A Story of Beyond the Sea* the lady is given by merchants who have rescued her, to the Soudan, who loves her and by whom she has two children. Eventually her former husband, and her father and brother arrive at the court as prisoners. She is able to rescue them and escape, taking her son but leaving a broken-hearted Soudan and her daughter. An interesting part of the story is the reason for her arrival with the merchants. She was given in marriage by her father to one of his friends with her own consent but the couple had no children. Going on pilgrimage to pray for children they were attacked by robbers, her husband bound and herself raped by the band and left. So shamed was she that instead of cutting her husband free she tried to kill him, only severing the cords by accident. He didn't reproach her but was very courteous and kind except that he wouldn't sleep with her. When they reached home her father forced her husband to tell the story and was so horrified that he shut his daughter up in a barrel and set her adrift, from which state the merchants rescued her.

The husband makes it quite clear that he doesn't blame her for the rape for which she was obviously not responsible but the pattern of the story suggests that she herself had felt a certain guilty pleasure in it, both by her violent reaction and by the speed with which she accepts the Soudan and becomes pregnant by him. When she eventually returns home she is able to conceive by her first husband. It's the rape and the element of force in her relationship with the Soudan that breaks her barrenness.

[1] *Lays of Marie de France.* This isn't by Marie but by an anonymous contemporary.

The return of wings in an Inigo Jones design for the *Lord's Maske* by Thomas Campion, 1613.

Winged fays (?) for
Oberon, 1609, by Inigo
Jones.

Winged spirits for Pope's
Rape of the Lock, 1804,
by Thomas Stothard.

The first science fiction painting, by Tintoretto, showing how the Milky Way was born.

Fuseli's fairy paintings were to have a great effect on nineteenth-century fairy painters. Notice the sinister eroticism of the female attendants.

The grotesque, the sentimental and the sadistic are combined in Doyle (*above and opposite*). Notice the elf's phallic nose and the rosebud femaleness of the fairy.

The immensely popular paintings of Huskisson were bought for their veiled eroticism.

The duplication of curves for erotic effect begins with the phallic mushroom.

The immensely popular paintings of Huskisson were bought for their veiled eroticism.

The duplication of curves for erotic effect begins with the phallic
mushroom.

One of the most macabre imaginations of the nineteenth century
belongs to J. A. Fitzgerald.

Fairy paintings were often the cloak for painting the female nude.

Titania, nineteenth-century version, an excuse for refined
pornography in 1867.

Perhaps the most popular of the Eastern stories and forerunner of two famous operas, Mozart's *Die Entführung Aus Dem Serail* and Weber's *Oberon*, is the romance of *Floriz and Blauncheflur*, translated into English in the thirteenth century, known all over Western Europe and surviving in two French versions. The basic plot is of two young lovers of whom the girl is carried away, either by capture or sale, to the harem of the emir or caliph. The boy follows her and they plot their escape but are discovered. The emir threatens them with death but is persuaded to relent.

The central character is the caliph, sultan or emir, cultured, passionate, usually already possessed of wife or wives, with power of life and death, and black. He is a combination of loving loved father and the devil who is himself black father. The rescue of the heroine is the taking of her from dependence on her father who must, if possible, be persuaded by reason to give her up although if necessary the hero will slay him. The blackness is a rationalized symbol of his ambiguous relationship to the lovers.

> Then the Admiral,[2] though he wroth were,
> There he changed his cheer.
> For either would for other die,
> And for he saw many weeping eye,
> And for he loved so muche that maid,
> All weeping he turned away.

The exotic setting, with its fully exploited otherness of fairy tale architecture and forbidden religion, is enough for the usual purposes of fairyland without any other form of magic and this was how the eighteenth century used it. But it is also intensely susceptible to the introduction of overt supernaturalism because of its otherness and because Eastern literature had its own fairy conventions which could so easily be drawn into Western versions.

To Western eyes it has the amorality of fairyland and the allure. Harem girls in diaphanous trousers' with bare

---

[2] English form of Emir. The lines are from the end of *Floriz and Blauncheflur*. The lovers are called the "faire children."

midriffs kept in luxurious idleness just for sex, guarded like virgins but enjoyed like whores, positively encouraged to display active charms at the command of their lord, titillated the imaginations of both men and women.[3] The first oriental fairy tales were written for adults, not for children even in Christendom. Their great exponent in France was Voltaire. It is his tone of voice which is responsible for a particular tone in many English fairy stories for children: that combination of extreme rationality with the incredible which consciously exploits the bizarreness of situation while pretending not to notice it. It is the voice of Alice remarking how the creatures do order one about and of many nineteenth-century fairy writers including Thackeray.[4] It is an authentic dream voice which we all recognize, particularly adapted to narration and dialogue and for a certain kind of satire because it unobtrusively maintains the tension between illusion and reality. Its effect is that of wit. Voltaire brilliantly uses it against superstition and illusion in *Zadig* and *The Princess of Babylon* which he sets in a mythical orient of unicorns, griffins and a talking phoenix.

Johnson used it for *Rasselas, Prince of Ethiopia*, and the contemporary translators of Voltaire caught it admirably. In his introduction to *Zadig* Voltaire specifically mentions the *Arabian Nights' Tales*. Of his story he says: "It was afterwards translated into the Arabic to amuse the famous sultan Oulong-beg much about the time that the Arabians and the Persians began to write the *Thousand and One Nights*, the *Thousand and One Days*, etc. Oulong was fond of reading about Zadig, but the sultanas were fonder of the *Thousand and One*."

In *Vathek*, written in French by William Beckford, translated into English and published by Samuel Henley in 1786, before Beckford could publish his original French version, and with notes of learned oriental scholarship by

---

[3] See, for example, Lady Mary Wortley Montagu's accounts of the harem in her letters from Constantinople, and the paintings of Delacroix and Ingres.

[4] See G. Avery, *Nineteenth Century Children* (Hodder and Stoughton, 1965), pp. 125 and 126, for the self-conscious use of fairy story in later writers. Voltaire's tone of voice is derived, but elaborated, from Perrault.

the translator, the voice sounds again but allied to the decadent exoticism of Araby, the mauve tone which was to supply the other strand in high camp. *Vathek* is the oriental *Monk*, the first expression in English literature of the passion for little Arab boys like flowers rediscovered gratefully by English homosexuals at the end of the nineteenth century on trips to Cairo.

> Both had the same tastes and amusements; the same long, languishing looks, the same tresses, the same fair complexions; and when Gulchenrouz appeared in the dress of his cousin, he seemed to be more feminine than even herself. If at any time he left the harem to visit Fakreddin, it was with all the bashfulness of a fawn that consciously ventures from the lair of its dam; he was, however, wanton enough to mock the solemn old grey-beards, though sure to be rated without mercy in return.

This diaphanous creature is betrothed to his cousin Nouronihar but she is overcome by the fierce passion of Vathek, the caliph who is an oriental Faust in search of eternal wisdom, power and riches. Like Faust and Ambrosio he is deceived by the devil, in this case called the Giaour, into sensuality and violence so that finally he loses all happiness and burns in everlasting torment. So like *The Monk* is it in structure and in the delineation of "unrestrained passions and atrocious deeds" that I am inclined to think Lewis had read it before writing his own book. Only the idiom is different. Both religious and oriental strands are to be found in high flower in the novels of Ronald Firbank but with the sensationalism muted to a skilful frisson which embodies the unconscious motifs in subtle images without needing to carve them out of human flesh.

Gulchenrouz is the only one to escape, saved by a kind old genie who installs him in a roc's nest with lots of little friends and gives him perpetual childhood while his companions "vied with each other in kissing his serene forehead and beautiful eyelids. Remote from the inquietudes of the world, the impertinence of harems, the brutality of eunuchs, and the inconstancy of women, there he found a place truly congenial to the delights of his soul." It is the hoped-for reward of Cherïf in Firbank's *Santal*.

Vathek is supernatural from beginning to end. It never touches reality. All the trappings of Eastern mythology are used except the magic carpet and that's hardly necessary when you have a djinnee to carry you on its back. It is a sophisticate's *Aladdin* with heavy doses of contemporary near-pornography. Some of its elements like Vathek's terrible eye which has the power of striking dead can be found in native British myths like that of the Irish chief of the Fomors, Balor.

The *Arabian Nights' Tales* as they are usually known in English, or more properly the *Thousand and One Nights*, were first translated into French for the court of Louis XIV by Antoine Galland between 1704 and 1717. Later the translation was continued as part of the enormous series of the Cabinet des Fées and was constantly reprinted and reissued throughout the nineteenth century. The tales were translated into English in the 1790s from Galland's version, which is described by the editors of the complete French edition of 1908 as "émasculée de toute hardiesse et filtrée de tout le sel premier." Many versions appeared in English too and in 1898 they were listed as number ten in the *Pall Mall Gazette* poll of the best books for a ten-year-old.[5] This was of course in a bowdlerized version. Sir Richard Burton's unexpurgated translation of the full text had been published in Benares between 1885 and 1888 but by then Ali Baba, Sindbad the sailor and Aladdin had passed into pantomime currency along with the other foreigners, Mother Goose, Cinderella and Little Red Riding Hood.[6]

K.M. Briggs has suggested[7] that the "djinns and afrits and peris of the Arabian tales had no influence on the English fairies, and in no way modified them as the French fairies had done; the tradition was too alien." I find this a rather surprising conclusion. What impresses on reading the stories again as an adult is how like they are to already

[5] There was a chapbook version of Aladdin as early as 1708.
[6] Unbelievable as it seems these are all French imports from Perrault's *Histoires et Contes du Temps Passé* published like the *Arabian Nights* to please the court in 1697.
[7] *The Fairies in Tradition and Literature*, ed. cit., Chapter 20.

existing British traditions, under the superficial difference of names and settings, and how easy it was for them to modify these so subtly that their influence has gone unnoticed by a dedicated folklorist.

This assimilation into the theater proves their general acceptability. The first *Aladdin* was a melodrama-romance of as early as 1788. By 1813 it was, although not pantomime, produced at Covent Garden with Mrs. C. Kemble as Aladdin. With *Sindbad* and *Ali Baba and the Forty Thieves* it has become one of the small number of stock fairy tale pantomimes.

The Arabian supernaturals themselves as they passed into Western literature all have their existing parallels. The peri is quite simply a female fairy. From being originally a rather malevolent, although always beautiful, creature between man and angel it had become more specifically feminine and soft as in the story of *Prince Ahmed and the Peri Banou*. This story itself is an oriental version of Marie de France's *Launfal* or *Thomas the Rhymer* in which a fairy lady takes an earthly lover, provides him with everything but stipulates that he mustn't reveal their relationship. Peris became very popular in the nineteenth century. Stories and poems were written about them. The softening and feminizing process continued and thus they helped to contribute to that gauzy-winged butterfly of the late Victorian and Edwardian period.

An afrit is simply a branch of the djinn, singular form djinnee or genie. Some djinn were made tutelary spirits as slaves of lamp, ring, cave and so on. In function they are no different from a localized brownie. They performed commissions for humans. Kipling's concept of Puck in *Puck of Pook's Hill* as attached to a locality and able to transport the children to any period or rather bring it to them embodied in a character is genie-like magic. The wish-fulfilling fairies either in story or as pantomime Fairy Queen are variations of the genie but also as old as *Huon of Bordeaux*'s Oberon, revived at this time, first in Germany in Wieland's version of the story with a strong oriental favor, then in an English translation by Sotheby and finally and gloriously in Weber's opera *Oberon* with libretto by the English pantomimist Planché in 1826.[8]

Sotheby was a friend of Scott. It's almost possible at this time to speak of another fairy takeover.

The other two important figures in the tales are the sorcerers, familiar as Merlin, and the evil demons, at home as goblins and devils who gave an added strand to the century's passion for the grotesque. None of this seems to me alien, far from it, and its exotic dress simply provided the sensual trappings necessary for both indulgence and credibility.

Wish-fulfillment is the basis of the stories as it is of all magic. In the *Arabian Nights' Tales* this is particularly so. The hero, sometimes beginning as the son of a poor man, sometimes as a prince, gets the lady and the treasure. *Aladdin* is the most unequivocal of the fables. Like the English Jack of the beanstalk he is an idle boy with a widowed mother. The cave with halls and gardens where he finds the lamp is a fairyland exactly like those inside British hills and repeated in the fairyland home of Peri Banou, which is entered through an iron door in the rock face.

That Aladdin has to *rub* the lamp and ring for the djinn to appear is an unconscious revelation of the roots of the wish-fulfilment story in masturbation fantasy. It is this that explains the emotional objectivity in the telling of the story and in its tone, both familiar to the reader of Western romance. In both East and West the complications of the narrative, the trials of the hero, are there to delay the climax as in the masturbation fantasy. The tonal objectivity can also be observed in children's make-believe games whether of the domestic or the cops-and-robbers variety. Time and place are as relative as in any other kind of dream sequence which progresses in a series of highlights, big scenes of transformation, recognition, abasement and triumph ending in happy ever after.

Shape-changing is common and so is flying although the means may be carpet instead of broomstick. Giants are

[8] It was a visit to a concert performance of Weber's *Oberon* in 1970 that was the genesis of this book. Weber had already given the world his version of Gothick magic in *Der Freischutz*. Weber's other oriental opera *Abu Hassan* was first produced in Munich in 1811 and in London in 1825.

frequent. There is a great deal of cannibalism, as in the English giant legends and Arthurian romance. Sindbad has a Polyphemus episode so similar to the Greek that one wonders if the *Odyssey* was part of Scheherazade's "wisdom of the poets." Chaucer retells the story of the enchanted horse, even to the peg which you turn to work it, in *The Squire's Tale*. Ruskin's black stone brothers are there.

Above the stories looms Haroun Al Raschid himself, the oriental Arthur or Charlemagne, with his consort Zobeide and his favorites and concubines. Under his aegis the tales take place sometimes, as in the case of Arthur, simply so that he may be amused. He is the prototype of all the father caliphs, urbane and sensual, terrible yet just. Baghdad is his Camelot. For the convention of knights errant who may roam the known world in search of adventures there are the travelling merchants who may be princes in disguise. The geographical range of the stories includes India and China, which allowed the original tellers greater possibility for the marvellous, as well as Persia, Egypt and Araby.

The format of the Sindbad stories lies behind that of Gulliver. Swift had probably read the tales in French. Voltaire in his turn was indebted to Swift. The correspondences and influences are endless. Finally the relationship of the Bible, which worked upon native fairy traditions, to the other religious texts and tales of the Near East is so close and complex that we must reckon on Pre-Christian oriental elements in our ideas of devil, fairy and sorcerer.

The phallic manifestations are the wonder-working all-powerful djinn themselves, who start up straight and tall before the hero to give him his heart's desire. In *Prince Ahmed and the Peri Banou* the fairy has a goblin brother, one and a half feet high with a beard thirty feet long, who kills Ahmed's father when he discovers the secret of his son's liaison and grows afraid of his son. The doubling of roles is used as in *Sir Gawain and The Green Knight*. A sorceress advises Ahmed's father: "For my part, I shudder when I consider the misfortunes which may happen to you, as the fairy, by her attractions and caresses, may inspire your son with the unnatural design of dethroning his father, and of seizing the crown of the Indias." This is the aboriginal Oedipus myth in Arabian dress. The sorceress is black mother; the fairy is desired mother. Ahmed is ousting his father. Kings are wedded to their countries by putting their heads in the circle of the crown, an enlarged metaphor of the ring on the finger, itself a metaphor for coition. To dethrone a king is to take over the motherland.

Roles are doubled too in *Aladdin*. The princess is carried off by a moor and her father threatens Aladdin with execution. The moor and the father are different aspects of the same character and the same emotional situation. Aladdin has already caused his own father's death from heartache because of his son's wilful ways. In the end Aladdin becomes a hero of every possible kind. He is rich, has the princess, is beloved of the people, wise, a champion in war, puts the sultan father in his place and kills the moor. No wonder Julian Wylie, the successful impresario of pantomime in the 1930s, called it the best part for principal boys.[9]

Yet all these similarities shouldn't cause us to fall into the diffusionist error that has led to so much waste of valuable effort while critics of various disciplines attempted to trace the routes by which certain similar tales spread. Like the myth of degeneration referred to in an earlier chapter this is another by-product of an evolutionary view derived from the Christian myth of first parents. It has caused anthropologists to look for one site for the original evolution of upstanding first man and pre-historians to derive all culture from some Near Eastern original: the Nile valley, the land of the two rivers and so on. Now it seems as if there were very early cultural developments in the hitherto barbarous West, as if megaliths may antedate pyramids and ziggurats, and the smelting of bronze itself have been discovered earlier in Europe than in the East, as if indeed a discovery or a cultural manifestation might have been produced spontaneously in different parts of the world instead of being disseminated from one center.[10]

[9] A. E. Wilson, *Christmas Pantomime* (Allen & Unwin, 1934), Chapter 20.

[10] See the recent work of Professor Alexander Thom on megaliths and two articles by Colin Renfrew, *The Listener*, January 1st and 7th, 1971.

Similarly from a basic human emotional pattern of father, mother, child, siblings and lovers arise the same desires and frustrations which find imaginative expression in similar narratives and symbols. Instead of being alien they are as familiar as our own fantasies. Newman in his *Apologia Pro Vita Sua*[11] listed the oriental stories with Mrs. Radcliffe as one strand in the youthful apprehensions of the numinous that eventually led to his conversion. "I used to wish the Arabian Tales were true: my imagination ran on unknown influences, on magical powers, and talismans . . . I thought life might be a dream, or I an angel, and all this world a deception, my fellow angels by a playful device concealing themselves from me, and deceiving me with the semblance of a material world." Perhaps he had read *Vathek* and yearned for Gulchenrouz's happy fate of eternal childhood in the roc's nest with the kind genie and his little friends. It is the lost voice of Cherry of Zennor locked out of her master's beautiful enchanted garden or of the knight-at-arms palely loitering on the cold hillside deserted by his fairy mistress, the still small voice of the dream that speaks all languages.

[11] J. Newman, *Apologia Pro Vita Sua* (Longmans, Green & Co., 1890), Chapter One.

CHAPTER XV

Lamia

The queen o'Fairies she caught me,
    In yon green hill to dwell,
And pleasant is the fairy-bed;
    But an eerie tale to tell.
        Thomas the Rhymer, Anon.

The most common form of black mother is the witch. In her we gather up all our resentments, fears and guilts against our own mothers and, by displacing them onto some real old crone or onto the fictionalized symbol of fairy story and pantomime, attempt to make them harmless or rather guiltless. Mother is black[1] for many reasons. First she betrayed us in conceiving us and then she is unfaithful to us. She pushes us away by weaning us. However perfect she is, she is bound to fail us in some way and even if in fact she doesn't we will nevertheless think she has for the demands of a baby are limitless. We may be unaware of any element of resentment but it will nevertheless be there. It cannot be otherwise. The basis of the resentment is that she is the object that from the first moment of breath we love and want and cannot have and indeed must learn to do without.

The symbolic personification of the traditional witch shows her origins in her attributes. Some of them are clearly later accretions. The steeple-hat can't, I think, be earlier than the sixteenth century by association with the Quakers who were often popularly accused of witchcraft[2] yet it's psychologically so right that it has become part of the standard kit. Like the mermaid's tail it's a phallus, father's, but perched forbiddingly on the top of the head. Her clothes are black and she is old and bent. This emphasis on age is very important as it marks her off as an earlier

[1] No doubt in a dark-skinned race she would be white. White is the color for funerals in India and the fairies of the Polynesain islands are white-skinned and fair-haired. It's the principle of inversion that matters, not which color.

[2] Keith Thomas, *Religion and the Decline of Magic* (Weidenfeld & Nicolson, 1971), p. 487.

generation and introduces the idea of death underlined by her black clothes. The death is multiple, ours and hers. It is death to us to desire her, and she is already approaching death. The death of a parent is always a traumatic experience. It removes a loved object eternally from our reach, threatens our security and foreshadows our own death. As long as our parents live who give us birth we can't die but as soon as they are dead no one stands between us and death and we become the expendable shields for our own children. The aged female figure also brings home to us our own aging and so is hateful. Our mother who gave us birth and played with us as a young girl is now old and by so much we too must be old. Finally the bent figure, with its half-hidden features in the disguise of old age, hides from us the recognizable face of a parent that we don't wish to acknowledge.

Like other parent figures, she can work magic since she has always had the power of life and death and of fulfilling or frustrating our desires. She may have a wand, rationalized as a stick to lean on. She is a healer by analogy with a mother's power to "kiss it better" and put everything right, and her healing will be done by charms, touching and simple homely remedies. She is also a destroyer by analogy with the awfulness of "a mother's curse."[3] No one can destroy a child more quickly than its own mother who has it totally in her power to starve, beat, mutilate and forbid, and has too the seemingly uncanny faculty of knowing what is in its mind. Her embargo on childish sexuality may make it impotent, now or later, and this impotence can be transferred to cattle, crops or business in the form of bad luck or illness. Mercifully it's rarely so now but until thirty years ago it was commonplace for mothers to threaten their children that if they told lies their tongues would swell or shrivel up and if they stole or played with themselves their fingers or their genitals would drop off or rot.

---

[3] In the ballad of *The Wife of Usher's Well* the mother has power to curse her sons back from the grave.

> I wish the wind may never cease
> Nor fishes in the flood,
> Till my three sons come home to me
> In earthly flesh and blood.

In England the witch was often invested with a familiar in the shape of an animal. In the *Malleus Maleficarum* the way is open for this development on the continent. However, it would have been a very foolish old woman indeed who allowed herself to be on intimate terms with a small animal in sixteenth-century Germany.[4] The familiar was her own household spirit or minor devil which she might commune with or use to make her magic. Hardly surprisingly its connotations are phallic, the usual creatures being the mouse, cat, commonly black, or toad. The mother's penis seems to be embodied in these creatures. Perhaps out of a desire to be born only of a mother, so by-passing the father's rivalry, the mother may be childishly thought at some stage of sexual ignorance, to have a penis of her own. The toad is particularly suitable as a little man able to leap up, the cat by its devilishness, malice and sexuality and the mouse as a very old penis symbol because of its shape and its habit of popping into holes.

All or some of these details might be present in the witch of the trials or the village crone or the witch of fiction. The traditional broomstick on which she flies is the devil's phallus, the sabbat the child's black view of parents observed in the sex act that shuts him out. From us she flies away to pleasure with black father and the detail of kissing the devil's arse and the beastliness of it all betray the child's envy and misunderstanding of what his parents do in bed, the taboos against masturbation, the parental "ugh, that's dirty," the ambiguity of parental sex.

Behind the observed phenomena of witchcraft accusa-

[4] See for example *Malleus Maleficarum*, ed. cit., p. 128 for the cat "an appropriate symbol of the perfidious," p. 190 the instrument of witchcraft, "a piece of wood or a mouse or some serpent," p. 145 "Then she summons her familiar who always works with her in everything and tells him she wishes to milk a certain cow." On this last hedgehogs and fairies were both thought to suckle cows and both called urchins or ouphs in England. For further mention of serpent and toad in magic in the *Malleus* see pp. 116 and 118. Also p. 128 "For the devil receives blows in the form of an animal and transfers them to one who is bound to him by a pact, when it is with such an one's consent that he acts in this manner in such a shape." Keith Thomas, *Religion and the Decline of Magic* (Weidenfeld & Nicolson, 1971), p. 290, calls the animal familiar a "peculiarly English notion."

tions lie these emotions to give them their energy. No doubt most of us can supply from our own acquaintance enough eccentrics of either sex to be the focus of such accusations in a sociological and historical climate where the theoretical context and legal machinery existed to translate them into action and where there was no scientific explanation for misfortune.[5]

Not all witches are old and ugly. The term "bewitched" has a second but closely related popular meaning in sexual enchantment and then the witch is young and beautiful. I have already mentioned Medea as a prototype of this kind. The line between the young white witch and the Fairy Queen is one of wavering mortality. Both may possess a person body and soul. This possession is the "inordinate love" of the *Malleus Maleficarum* from which men pine away and die. "And I have found a woman more bitter than death, who is the hunter's snare, and her heart is a net, and her hands are bands." It is also the irresistible passion of the Romantics, the sorrow of young Werther, incarnate in England in the life and works of Keats.

For if ever a personality may be said to have been bewitched it was his and yet to read his letters gives very little hint of this. He has two quite distinct modes, both literary: the prose and the poetic. So different are they that they amount almost to a kind of verbal schizophrenia. In his prose he is vigorous and rational except in his letters to Fanny Brawne in his illness and even then there is no hint of the enchantment, the uncanny idealization of the poetry, simply the outbursts of someone very much in love, afraid that illness and death will separate him from the girl he wishes to marry. However impassioned the language it remains human and rational. His poetic language is quite different, not simply in its organization which could be said to be the result of the rules of meter and rhyme, but in its vocabulary which is idealized and enchanted. The prose is his mode for the conscious; his poetry for his unconscious.

This dichotomy arose from his almost total suppression of his childhood. His closest friends knew nothing about his early life and were surprised to learn about it after his

[5] See particularly "The Making of a Witch," Thomas, op. cit. The devil often promised food and wealth to the witches as the Fairy Queen does to her lovers, making him an alternative father to God.

death. He hardly ever spoke of it. In a strange comment to Severn who nursed him through his dying he said that his "greatest misfortune" was that "he had no mother" since childhood. Elsewhere he says, "My love for my Brothers from the early loss of our parents and even for earlier Misfortunes has grown into a(n) affection 'passing the Love of Women'—"[6] These are strange remarks. His father it's true died when Keats was eight, but his mother not until he was fourteen and a half. She had married again, like Hamlet's mother two months after her first husband's death, but left her new husband by 1806 and seems to have disappeared for a few years, leaving the children to be brought up by their "Granny good."[7] She returned before 1809 already ill, to die in March 1810 after being devotedly nursed by Keats in his school holidays. So sharp was his grief that back at school he had to hide behind the master's desk to try to control himself while the lesson went on.

The "earlier Misfortunes" must refer to the time after his father's death since before then there were none, apart from the death of a third brother in infancy when Keats was five, an event so commonplace in those days that it's unlikely to rank as "Misfortunes." According to George Keats John was his mother's favorite and she doted on him. In the second remark, for plural "parents" one must understand "mother" and this seems to be borne out by his comment to Severn. If he felt her loss as "early" either he was thinking of her as dying when his father died, in which case the "earlier Misfortunes" are meaningless, or his remark to Severn suggests that he would have liked her alive through his adolescence which suggests that he thought this would have affected his attitude to women which had suffered by her loss or desertion.

"When I am among Women I have evil thoughts, malice spleen . . . I am full of Suspicions and therefore listen to nothing—I am in a hurry to be gone—

[6] Letter 69 to Benjamin Bailey, June 10th, 1818. *Letters of John Keats*, ed. Page (O.U.P., 1954).
[7] There is certain disagreement over these facts. I have given a blanket version without going into the question of whether the children were removed from her and when.

> You must be charitable and put all this perversity to my being disappointed since Boyhood . . . I must absolutely get over this—but how? The only way is to find the root of evil, and so cure it "with backward mutters of dissevering Power"—that is a difficult thing; for an obstinate Prejudice can seldom be produced but from a gordian complication of feelings . . ."[8]

Earlier in the same letter he speaks of women falling "so far beneath my Boyish imagination? When I was a Schoolboy I though(t) a fair Woman a pure Goddess, my mind was a soft nest in which some one of them slept, though she knew it not . . ."

From this idealization he had passed to suspicion, "women have Cancers," they are all "inadequate," they must "want imagination" to be able to "feel happy without any sense of crime." Too often they were "flippant, vain, inconstant, childish, proud and full of fancies," too like his mother when young, of whom his guardian alleged she was so passionate it wasn't safe to be alone in a room with her, and who had deserted him. He liked them best when they were "meek, kind, and tender," "a milk-white lamb that bleats For man's protection" as she must have been when she lay in bed while he nursed her. Then "I hotly burn—to be a Calidore—/A very Red Cross Knight." The image is out of Spenser's *Faerie Queene*, the second work of poetry we're told by his friend and headmaster's son, Cowden-Clarke, who had lent it to him, to make any real impression on him. But the image is earlier in Keats's life. When he was about four or five there was an incident involving his mother and a drawn sword in which he seems to have kept her prisoner. Already he was in a sense a knight-at-arms.

From his letters to Bailey it seems that in the summer of 1817 he caught some form of venereal disease. His difficulties with women only applied to those of his own class and above. Milkmaids and servants, working-class girls in general gave him a necessary sexual outlet.

---

[8] Letter 79 to Benjamin Bailey, July 1818, Page, ed. cit.

> Where be ye going, you Devon maid
> And what have ye there in the basket?
> Ye tight little fairy, just fresh from the dairy,
> Will ye give me some cream if I ask it?

He had the example of Burns[9] both for the activity and the ballad on it but comments from other letters, Keats making feet for little stockings[10] for example, and the poem "Unfelt, unheard, unseen," make it clear that this wasn't just a literary convention. One of his biographers, Aileen Ward, suggests this was common Regency behavior but this isn't quite enough to account for it. It's true that in an age without contraception it was difficult for a middle-class girl to have extra-marital sex without endangering her position, prospects and possibly life. It accounts for a great deal of the girls' teasing behavior that Keats found so irritating. They were forced to deploy their sexual counters to attract a mate but then to play him like a hooked fish to a safe matrimonial bank while the men, excited and then denied, were allowed temporary satisfaction with prostitutes and lower-class girls. Yet this wasn't the only possible answer. Middle-class people often married very young. Shelley and George Keats had both done so and Jane Austen's novels give a fair picture of the matrimonial market. There was also the established convention, under royal patronage, of the mistress. Keats seems to have been presented with at least one opportunity for such a relationship with a lady called Isabella Jones and there was another woman, Jane Cox, "Charmian," who excited him briefly. He made a shot at it, taking Isabella copies of his poems, and visiting her alone in her apartments, but he was unable to fall in love with her although his letters suggest that he tried.

Instead, when one brother was dying, the other newly married and gone to America, he fell in love at first sight

---

[9] There are constant references to Burns in the letters. For another bawdy Devon ballad and the local girls see "Over the hill and over the dale" in the letter from Teignmouth, March 24th, 1818, to James Rice. It seems as if he had read Burns's *Merry Muses of Caledonia*.

[10] An interpolation by Brown in a letter from Keats to Dilke, July 1819.

with a girl who had his mother's, and sister's, name.[11] One of his rare references to his mother is in a letter to Fanny Brawne. She had enquired about his seal. "My seal is marked like a family table cloth with my Mother's initial F for Fanny: put between my Father's initials." Until his brother Tom was dead he was unable to be sure of his own feelings. The letter that gives that news to his other brother George speaks of Fanny as "graceful, silly, fashionable and strange." They were having little tiffs and once he called her "Minx." For some time he struggled against his passion, afraid that it would burn him up, but by the summer of 1819 he had become completely absorbed by it and remained so until his death, his greatest regret in dying being: "I should have had her when I was in health." No doubt the authors of the *Malleus Maleficarum* would have said he was bewitched.

In a sense they would be right. His imagination as projected in his poems was informed by a beautiful fairy shape, by the promise of enchantment and fairyland. Closely linked to it was the longing for death. Unconsciously he knew that what he longed for was among the dead and wasn't to be found in life. His attempt to do so was his falling in love with Fanny, initially as a substitute for the dead, as the means by which he could hold on to life. Even so the attempt was ambiguous. He believed, in common with his time, that passion in itself was a killing thing likely to bring on consumption. In surrendering to it he was killing himself. His letters to her and to his friend Brown emphasize this and his unconscious must have endorsed it. Passion had killed his mother. In clutching at life with the living substitute Fanny he was being unfaithful to her dead image. His greatest wish became to die in the act of possessing her. That way he would have both of them.

With Keats faery isn't simply a convenient idiom, the conscious mediaeval incrustation of the later Pre-Raphaelites; it is a mode of the imagination so natural to him that he can't write poetry in any other way. Spenser was the first poet who penetrated his imagination precisely because

---

[11] "The very first week I knew you I wrote myself your vassal," etc. Letter 139. An earlier Fanny had been offered but she had "a hard brown fist."

it is his native speech too. To him Keats added two other
fairy poets: Shakespeare and Milton. He had no choice,
for the image that he had to come to terms with was that
of his dead mother, the Fairy Queen in her various manifestations.

She appears at once in the earliest poems, in the 1817
volume. The disguise is familiar. It is Cynthia.

> Queen of the wide air; thou most lovely queen
> Of all the brightness that mine eyes have seen.

Already his mind is playing on the Endimion legend of the
beautiful young man chosen to be the goddess's lover.[12]

> Came chaste Diana from her shady bower,
> Just as the sun was from the east uprising;
> And, as for him some gift she was devising,
> Beheld thee, pluck'd thee, cast thee in the stream
> To meet her glorious brother's greeting beam.

This is the first of Keats's meditations on a favorite theme:
the making of a poet. Addressed to his aspiring poet-friend
George Mathew, it visualizes the poet as created by Diana
and Apollo in a fantasy of natural intercourse and birth.
Diana is of course another form of Cynthia, as Keats
knew.

> How, from a flower, into a fish of gold
> I marvel much that thou hast never told
> Apollo chang'd thee; how thou next didst seem
> A black-eyed swan upon the widening stream
> And when thou first didst in that mirror trace
> The placid features of a human face

Keats's unconscious has thrown up an exact parallel to the
process of gestation. The human face in the water is from
the first poem that moved Keats, Spenser's *Epithalamion*,
as is the image of Cynthia. The swan is a Spenserian bor-

---

[12] R. Gittings in *John Keats* (Heinemann, 1968), p. 76 suggests that
Keats got the idea from Wordsworth's sonnet of the Shepherd and
the Moon but this would simply have recalled the image in *Epithalamion* which he already knew.

rowing which Keats used in his first poem and also to metaphor himself as aspiring poet in his epistle to Cowden-Clarke.[13]

The young knight is present in this volume too, *Sir Calidore*, himself one of Keats's favorite identifications, like Hyperion, hero of a poem he was never able to finish, and, I believe, for the same reason which I shall discuss later. Already his vocabulary is elf shot. This might not be surprising in a poet just beginning but for Keats it was not simply a youthful phase he had to go through but the warp of his poetic diction. The fay, elf and magic that are sprinkled through these first poems are still there in his last, notably in the *Ode to a Nightingale* written at the height of his poetic ability. Keats didn't believe in these images literally; he was against all superstition to the point where he could be accused of only the faintest Deism. Even when he most wished to believe in some form of immortality to compensate for intolerable suffering, he found it against reason and supported only by his own desires, some words of Tom Keats and Fanny Brawne and a desperate sense of justice. Without his literal belief enchantment nevertheless provided a consistently valid image for psychological phenomena which he couldn't embody otherwise, partly because he didn't consciously understand the "gordian knot" and partly because the fairy imagery is itself already a projection of such unconscious states.

The themes and corresponding images of his first book were those he was to explore again and again with deepening precision. *Endymion* itself was his next and longest poem, written in a race with Shelley to a theme of his own choosing, more than four thousand lines in just over seven months from April to November 1817. It was his second attempt at this theme. The first *Endymion* is now generally known as "I stood tiptoe upon a little hill." So important was it to him that he renamed the earlier poem and decided to rework the material.

Despising what he called "consequitive thought" he began, allowing himself to be led along in the person of

[13] I am aware that the exact borrowing is from Milton but it's upon an earlier Spenserian experience. The poet as bird appears in the letters too where at one point he describes himself as "moulting" and in later poems.

Endymion in search of Cynthia by "a regular stepping of
the Imagination towards a Truth."[14] Endymion himself is
young but "like Ganymede to manhood grown"; Keats's
own age when he began writing *Endymion* was twenty.
The poem opens as a pastoral like *Acis and Galatea*. Spenser hovers behind it with Sir Calidore among the shepherds and Colin Clout. Amid all the Spring rejoicing when
the elder shepherds tell of their hopes of seeing children,
loves, friends in Elysium, Endymion sits in a trance. His
sister takes him to her favorite island where he falls into a
restful sleep. When he wakes she sings to him and then
asks him what his sadness is. Has he seen Diana's naked
limbs "among the alders green;/ And that, alas! is death.?"
He says that one day he fell into an enchanted sleep and
seemed to soar up towards the stars. Suddenly he saw the
moon "passionately bright," and then a beautiful "bright
something" coming down to him "her hovering feet/ . . .
more whitely sweet/ Than those of sea born Venus." He
faints at her touch and is carried away in her "wooing
arms" through the sky to the top of a mountain. After a
little he falls asleep in the middle of bliss and when he
wakes the vision is gone.

His sister is distressed that he should be so changed by a
dream. Where is his ambition? Endymion answers that
"earthly love has power to make/ Men's being mortal,
immortal," that it may be the source of nature's strength
and that in any case he has seen the divine face again in a
well and heard her voice in a cave. He tells his sister that
he will struggle against his passion and try to be calm.

In the necessary process of artistic rationalization Cynthia appears as a young woman. This is no barrier to her
being a mother symbol, particularly in Keats's experience.
His mother was only twenty when he was born and in her
mid-thirties when she died. Even in dying she would appear young. The image of the pale moon waxing and waning is particularly appropriate for a consumptive. The description of Cynthia has a tell-tale word which links her
with Keats's prose writings about women: "gordian'd" to
describe her hair like the "gordian complication" of his

---

[14] To John Taylor, Letter 42, January 1818, with a correction to
the proof of *Endymion*.

feelings. He is carried away passive in her arms like a child. Kissing her he gives his eyes to death and it is the reflections on happy life after death by the old shepherds that induce his trance. Already love and death co-exist. Perhaps after his mother's death Keats lay in bed at night looking up at the sky and moon and longing for her to return or even saw her in the whitely smiling face.[15]

The face he sees in the mirror of the well should of course be his own as it was Narcissus's. Has this image been suggested by the unconscious as a family likeness but female?[16] The cave of his last vision he thinks at first "The grot/ Of Proserpine" when she returns from the dead. This myth was also one of his favorites and it's not difficult to suggest why. Given Keats's stated method of working, led on by the imagination, that is by an artistic projection from some powerful unconscious source, the images which he throws up will be reflections of deep emotional preoccupations disguised even from the poet himself.

Finally there is the sister figure, Peona. When he had begun on Part III of *Endymion* Keats wrote to his sister Fanny, then fourteen, and told her the story. He wasn't in the habit of writing to her since his letter indicates that he feels he hardly knows her. Something has suggested that he should change this so that they can become dearest friends and he can confide in her, as Endymion does. He is projecting the poem onto an existing relationship and making life mirror art but perhaps because the germ of his relationship with his sister had been the starting point for the fiction. This would make it even more a family poem.

His "fairy journey" continues in Book II in pursuit of his love. As yet he doesn't know it is Cynthia he is in love with and he invokes her in a swooning prayer. The influence of Spenser is very strong in this book. He meets a naiad rising breast-high from the stream, who pities him. She is like an incarnation of a river in *The Faerie Queene* or Milton's saving nymph Sabrina in *Comus*. When he was

---

[15] Of Jane Cox he wrote to George Keats: "I don't cry to take the moon home with me in my pocket not (nor) do I fret to leave her behind me."

[16] George Keats thought John resembled his mother facially although otherwise he was like his father.

dying in Rome Keats's last thoughts on poetry were of writing on Sabrina. Led into an underground cavern Endymion invokes Diana who answers his prayer with a burst of magic foliage through the paving which leads him to a further Spenserian scene, parallel to the main story, of the sleeping Adonis surrounded by cupids. He meets Venus and then dark Cybele, the earth mother, and falls into a dream in which at last the loved figure comes to him, the "Known, Unknown," his "Enchantress" whose breasts are "tenderest milky sovereignties." He swoons with pleasure. Cynthia, afraid to let him know who she is as yet, promises him eventual bliss. He is her "dear youth." She leaves him and he wakes calmed. Again there is a child and mother image.

> O he had swoon'd
> Drunken from pleasure's nipple

Endymion meets two more lovers, the river creatures Alpheus the god and Arethusa the nymph who, being vowed to Diana, must refuse him. Endymion asks his unknown goddess to make them happy and finds himself translated from underground to the sea bed and Book III.

> What is there in thee, Moon! that thou shouldst move
> My heart so potently . . .
> No tumbling water ever spake romance
> But when my eyes with thine thereon could dance
> No woods were green enough, no bower divine
> Until thou liftedst up thine eyelids fine . . .
> Yes in my boyhood, every joy and pain
> By thee were fashion'd to the self-same end;
> And as I grew in years, still didst thou blend
> With all my ardours . . .
> Thou wast the charm of women lovely Moon . . .

Endymion's passion for the moon began in childhood. Now he has his "strange love" and he begs the Moon to forgive him for his unfaithfulness to it. At this point he sees an old man who hails the young man as the one who shall release him from a spell and tells Endymion his story with an Ancient Mariner's compulsion. His name is Glaucus. He fell in love with Scylla who fled from him and so he rose from the sea to ask Circe to help him. Instead she seduced him so that he forgot Scylla. Circe, like Medea, is a prototype of the vamp witch. To love is to be bewitched into bestiality. She betrays her real self in Glaucus's words:

> She took me like a child of suckling time,
> And cradled me in roses.

One morning, waking and missing her, he is led by "an agony of sound" and a blue flame "like the eye of gordian snake" and finds her in an arbor queening it over the monstrous shapes of her lovers and throwing them grapes which they guzzle down. With a charm she first bloats and then banishes them with a nod. This marvellous and terrifying passage owes something to *Comus*'s rout and to *The Odyssey* but most to Keats's own imaginative energy and fascination with the grotesque.

Glaucus tries to flee in horror but Circe stands before him accusing him of unfaithfulness and of finding her too harsh.

> So, fairy-thing, it shall have lullabies
> Unheard of yet: and it shall still its cries
> Upon some breast more lily-feminine.

She condemns him to a thousand years of old age and kills Scylla in her jealous anger. Eventually he is given the task of assembling the bodies of all drowned lovers in the crystal hall, where he has laid the body of Scylla, and awaiting the arrival of Endymion. The spell is broken, Glaucus restored to youth and all the drowned lovers to life. There is revelry in Neptune's palace and again Venus promises Endymion he shall soon be happy but, overcome with the greatness of the old sea gods and the whirl of feasting, he sinks down in a slumber to wake in Book IV to the earth again and the lament of the Indian maid.

At once Endymion falls in love with her, causing subsequent critics a great deal of trouble. He is caught by a double love. In loving the Indian he loses the "wings wherewith/ I was to top the heavens." She is his executioner.

> Be thou my nurse; and let me understand
> How dying I shall kiss that lily hand.[17]

These words might almost be a quotation from Keats's letters to Fanny Brawne of nearly two years later.[18] Love and death are already bound up together. They were not, as has been suggested, first linked after his brother Tom's death but were always part of Keats's unconscious based on the experience of the double loss of his mother. With the Indian Endymion feels guilty and believes he must die.

Together they fly on two black winged horses up to heaven where they are overcome by a sleep in which Endymion dreams he is at last to be united to Cynthia. Waking he finds it is no dream but as he turns towards the Indian at his side he is afraid again of his own "heart treachery" and of Cynthia's revenge. He feels his identity slipping away in the conflict.[19] As the moon rises and pours full on them the Indian herself grows "gaunt and spare" to dissolve away completely. Endymion falls into a healing trance in which he hears the wedding song for Diana like that *Epithalamion* that first awakened him to poetry.

Restored to earth he finds the Indian again and proposes a life of rustic simplicity. "Gone and past / Are cloudy phantasms." He has loved a nothing. "On earth I may not love thee" he says to Cynthia. Perhaps they may meet in Elysium. The Indian says that she is forbidden to be his love by "gorgon wrath." She longs to embrace and die: "perverse deliciousness," an idea Keats used again in his "Bright Star" sonnet.

Peona, his sister, reappears, happy to find him with such

[17] This is an image from Scott's *Thomas the Rhymer* Part III, see below. It suggests that Keats had read this fairy queen poem early, perhaps even when he was at school.

[18] Particularly the letter of Sunday, July 25th, 1819. "I have two luxuries to brood over in my walks, your Loveliness and the hour of my death. O that I could have possession of them both in the same minute."

[19] Compare his letter to Fanny Brawne, October 13th, 1819: "You have absorb'd me. I have a sensation at the present moment as though I was dissolving." This sensation which is based on a fear of castration and of going back through the womb to nothing pre-birth is already present in *Endymion*.

a beautiful partner but he tells her that he will live as a hermit and the Indian says that she will be a votaress of Diana. They part, promising to meet later at the grove. Endymion is alternately manic and depressive in his renunciation. The Indian and Peona arrive for the final farewell but as it is spoken the Indian is transformed into Phoebe/Cynthia and she and Endymion go away together.

This ending of happy ever after has seemed to some people lame, but the myth makes it certain that it must end happily and Keats surely intended that the Indian maid and Cynthia should fuse in one from the beginning of the book. In Lemprière, which he reputedly knew almost by heart he would have read that Titania was another name for Diana. Shakespeare says in *A Midsummer Night's Dream* that both Oberon and Titania are from India and the votaress of Titania's order, mother of the changeling, is an Indian. This, I believe, is the origin of Endymion's Indian maid. From the first she is an aspect of Diana, Queen of Earth and Heaven and Hell, as he called her in a sonnet.

Endymion's problem is how to have both earthly and idealized love without being unfaithful to either; a reflection of Keats's own problem. *Endymion* solves it by fusing both in one; Keats tried to solve his by fusing the two Fannies and in the *Ode to Fanny* she becomes his "silver moon." Such a problem can be solved artistically by symbolizing it with enchantment and myth. Endymion's journey in search of his love is an emotional progress. Cynthia says that he had to be spiritualized and that she has been kept from him by "foolish fear" and "the decrees of fate." These remarks seem to me the least satisfactory part of the mythological machinery. What works is the attempt to explore the "gordian complication of feelings." The magic enables him to embody them in characters and happenings that have the eerie force of dreams.

The erotic passages in *Endymion* shocked some contemporary reviewers. Others, taking Keats at his own word in his angry preface,[20] found it in youthful pretentiousness and inadequacy. They also found echoes of Leigh Hunt

---

[20] He was disappointed with the poem as all artists are in their post-natal depression and when they have become involved with another work. At such times their self-criticism isn't to be relied on.

and examples of the "bardling's" vulgar origins. Critics are still inclined to be apologetic and not to realize that it is the key work to an understanding of Keats's enchanted personality and its themes and images appear all through his later work. The central problem in *Endymion* is unfaithfulness, and there are half a dozen versions of the mother goddess.

Although he had already begun thinking about *Hyperion*, his next completed long poem was *Isabella*, the story suggested to him by the woman of the same name. This and *The Eve of St. Agnes* are his two poems about a pair of young human lovers. Both are influenced by the vogue of mediaeval romance, "fine Mother Radcliffe names"[21] as he called them. It seems that Isabella Jones suggested the theme for the second one too. Between the two poems Tom had died and John had fallen in love with Fanny.

The first story, from Boccaccio, has a revenant element found in many folk songs. Murdered by her brothers who want her to marry a rich man, young Lorenzo returns to tell Isabella where she can find his body. She goes to the forest, digs it up, cuts off the head and buries it in a pot under a sprig of basil which she waters with her tears until it grows thick and green. Suspicious of her constant attendance on it, the brothers steal the pot and find the head. They flee the country; Isabella goes mad and dies.

Not in love with the real Isabella, Keats was prepared to indulge the masochistic fantasy of his death and her weeping over his head. *The Eve of St. Agnes* however is the most sustainedly hopeful of all his poems. Its powerful magic is of a fulfilled eroticism. On St. Agnes Eve, January 20th, as on Hallowe'en, a girl who performs the right ceremonies can conjure up the face of her future husband. While the rest of the castle is revelling, Madeline[22] goes up

[21] They are actually more fine father Scott names. *The Eve of St. John* was published in Lewis's *Tales of Wonder*. It's an amalgam of *St. Agnes* with a revenant lover murdered by the husband, a castle and a bringing of the lover by invocational magic on St. John's Eve. Perhaps Tom Keats's love of Scott had caused Keats to suppress the real origin of the names.

[22] "(beautiful name that Magdalen)" Keats wrote in a letter to Reynolds in March 1818 calling her the "reputed Magdalen." The idea lurks behind Madeline herself and Porphyro's desire to seduce her.

to her room. Porphyro has crossed the moors and found his way into the castle. Like Montagues and Capulets the families are at feud. He is let in by the old nurse whom he begs to take him up to Madeline's room. He will only look at her not touch and leave a feast beside her bed to show he has been.

The old nurse hides him in the room before Madeline arrives. At the door her taper is blown out, she enters by moonlight through the stained-glass window and the colors are thrown on her skin like jewels. Her purity almost causes Porphyro to faint.

> Anon his heart revives: her vespers done,
> Of all its wreathed pearls her hair she frees;
> Unclasps her warmed jewels one by one;
> Loosens her fragrant bodice; by degrees
> Her rich attire creeps rustling to her knees
> Half hidden, like a mermaid in sea-weed,
> Pensive awhile she dreams awake, and sees,
> In fancy, fair St. Agnes in her bed,
> But dares not look behind, or all the charm is fled.
>
> Soon, trembling in her soft and chilly nest,
> In sort of wakeful swoon, perplex'd she lay

It is a scene of purest voyeurism. In imagination Keats has crossed the miles between Chichester and Hampstead to where Fanny is going to bed. Possibly it owes something to the mirror scene in *The Monk* where Ambrosio sees Antonia naked for the bath with the tame linnet between her breasts, and almost certainly to Coleridge's *Christabel*.

At this point the living Fanny has subsumed into her all the dead Fanny and Keats is able to enjoy her in every sense. The dead Fanny is present in the moonlight and the mermaid. There was no need for Keats to use this second image. It gives a half rhyme, which the period disliked and heavily criticized, to two full rhymes and must therefore be there because Keats wanted it. It expressed a moment of taboo, broken when the girl undresses completely and becomes the ideal of his boyhood sleeping in "the soft nest" of his mind. The slight trembling expresses together the cold and the girl's virginity, both to be broken by the entry of the lover in a permitted rape.

Porphyro spreads the table with delicacies[23] and then tries to waken her but she is fast asleep. To lengthen the fantasy he falls asleep himself on her pillow; the verse employing faery terms, "midnight charm," "stedfast spell," "woofed phantasies," to express this moment. Waking he takes her lute and plays the song *La Belle Dame Sans Merci* on it. Madeline opens her eyes and seeing him in the moonlight takes him for his ghost. Quickly he reassures her and in lines which the publishers insisted must be toned down makes love to her while "an elfin storm from faery land" flings ice impotently against the windows.

> See while she speaks his arms encroaching slow
> Have zon'd her, heart to heart . . .
> With her wild dream he mingled as a rose
> Marryeth its odour to a violet.[24]

The Elfin storm "of haggard seeming" Porphyro says will cover their love-making and their escape. Emotionally it can only be taken as a complaint from the other world against this warm human love and the half line: "St. Agnes' moon hath set" bears this out. Keats has found the "solution sweet" which is psychologically right; the physical consummation casts off the dead and the faery hold, as it does in *Tam Lin* when the girl holds on to her lover who has been taken by the Fairy Queen, while he becomes a snake, a fox, a lion and so on and finally a naked man.

> And they are gone: ay ages long ago
> These lovers fled away into the storm.

Their elopement is Keats's wish-fulfilment for himself and Fanny. "I should have had her when I was in health and I

[23] See A. Ward, *John Keats* (Secker & Warburg, 1963), p. 309 for Keats and food.

[24] For the background to this see R. Gittings, *John Keats*, ed. cit., pp. 340, 366–7. It was Keats's revision of the verses to make the climax unambiguous that Taylor objected to, whether from motives of expediency or prudency hardly matters. However, it might be pointed out that people have always made a distinction between what they are prepared to do and what they are prepared to read or print.

should have remained well." They leave behind them the dead nurse and old Beadsman, childhood and religion, fallen grotesque or into the irrelevance of cold ash.

Before, between and after these two poems he continued his struggle with *Hyperion*, even attempting to revise it completely as *The Fall of Hyperion*. He didn't succeed; he couldn't. The emotional material was too inflammatory; it burned him up and itself out. Naturally he rationalized his difficulty. "I have given up *Hyperion*, there are too many Miltonic inversions in it—Miltonic verse cannot be written but in an artful, or rather artist's humor."

The story of *Hyperion* is the making of a poet. The Titans, led by old Saturn, are being dethroned by the new gods, Jove, Neptune and Apollo. Hyperion is the old sun god. In the first book there is a mighty picture of Saturn bowed in misery. Then, Hyperion's wife tries to comfort him. Meanwhile Hyperion himself is the only one of the old gods still in power and he vows to avenge and restore Saturn. In the second book there is a council of the fallen when Oceanus tells how Neptune deposed him by his sheer beauty and rightness. Clymene tells the same story of Apollo but Enceladus protests and tries to rouse them to fight back. At this Hyperion himself arrives. The third book tells of the young Apollo. He is restless and frustrated and wanders through his island birthplace until he meets the goddess Mnemosyne and tells her his sadness. Looking into her face he feels the power of a poet overcoming him like a birth and the poem breaks off with his shriek.

To understand why Keats was unable to go on we should look as well at the second version. It begins this time with the poet himself tasting a divine feast he finds and then going to the foot of an altar where a female figure is ministering under a huge statue of Saturn. It is the veiled and terrible Moneta who tells him to climb the steps or rot below and be forgotten. Struck numb and chill he manages to climb. Eventually she removes her veils and he sees her face "bright-blanch'd by an immortal sickness." She promises to show him a vision of the fall of the Titans. This leads into the beginning of *Hyperion I*. In the second canto Hyperion himself is introduced and then the poem stops.

Both versions were intended to go on with Apollo causing the fall of Hyperion. The title of the second shows this.

The basic myth is of sons replacing fathers. Keats had already tried to tackle this theme in the early, also unfinished, *Sir Calidore*. There the young knight finds himself in the company of two older knights and two ladies whose hands he kisses passionately. Suddenly the poem stops. It can only go on by Calidore ousting a knight and taking a lady. The subject is too dangerous.

Names were always important to Keats and this included their literary forerunners. Hyperion is in *Hamlet*. It's Hamlet's name for his father in comparison with his uncle stepfather. "Hyperion to a satyr." He's asking his mother how she could bear to replace one with the other. Keats's *Hamlet* references are worth considering here. At the height of his jealousy about Fanny he writes to her in Hamlet's words to Ophelia, "Get thee to a nunnery." In another letter to his friend Reynolds he says that now he will relish *Hamlet* more than he has ever done[25] and to Miss Jeffreys that Shakespeare's "days were not more happy than Hamlet's who is perhaps more like Shakespeare himself in his common every day Life than any other of his Characters." He knew the play extremely well and I have no doubt identified deeply with Hamlet as he did with Apollo as god of poetry. His mother too had transferred from Hyperion to a satyr in two months. Now her son was destroying Hyperion.

Many artists in their lives have made themselves imaginary fathers from the past masters in their own medium and Keats is not an exception. His first was Spenser, with Shakespeare, Milton and Wordsworth in rapid follow-up. He would have liked Wordsworth's to be a more living relationship but the older poet wasn't prepared for this. For a time Leigh Hunt filled this role but his own talents and character weren't big enough to sustain it. Hyperion stands

[25] Much as I would like to I can't accept R. Gittings's suggestion (op. cit., p. 209) that this is necessarily a reference to Keats's mother's remarriage. An earlier reference in the same letter is to "the death of a friend and the ill 'that flesh is heir to.'" Reynolds had said that he feared there was "little chance of anything else in this life" except, I take it, ills and poetry. Keats's understanding of *Hamlet* is of the "To be or not to be" speech. See the letter to Miss Jeffreys and the several references to his speech in the letters. A further Hamlet borrowing is his use of *Caviare* as a pseudonym in Hunt's magazine.

for all these glorious dead, rolled into one and speaking in Milton's literary voice. In the course of writing the poem Keats became disillusioned with this too. Yet to pull down the artistic father-figure as Keats was doing in the character of Apollo, is a dangerous enterprise. *Hyperion* has begun as an expression of Keats's aspirations to poethood but it could only be carried through by the destruction of this figure. It required him to affirm that he was greater than Shakespeare or Spenser. By denigrating Milton's language in its Latinity, and his insight into humanity and philosophy, he destroyed Hyperion in his letters, an opinion he later completely revised.[26]

This destruction is, as many of Keats's explanations are, a rationalization of an emotional situation which he didn't fully understand. Behind the dethroning of a literary father lies the dethroning of a real one which he couldn't face. The very size of the Titans, when we remember giants, suggests parents seen through a child's eyes. The mother herself, I believe,[27] is behind the veiled figure of Moneta, memory, and also Mnemosyne. The initial M is no accident.

> As near as an immortal's sphered words
> Could to a mother's soften, were these last:
> And yet I had a terror of her robes,
> And chiefly of the veils, that from her brow
> Hung pale and curtain'd her in mysteries
> That made my heart too small to hold its blood.[28]

She is also I believe in the veil'd Melancholy of the ode, and Maia, mother of Hermes and still youthful, to whom he addressed one invocational stanza.

Hyperion is a charioteer on his winged orb. Thomas Keats was particularly remembered as a horseman and was, in fact, killed by being flung from his horse. Did Keats's imagination intend that Hyperion should be flung from the chariot by Apollo and balk at this hindsight of intended murder? Once he compared himself to Phaeton

---

[26] Letter to Bailey, August 14th, 1819.
[27] As does Ward, op. cit.
[28] *The Fall of Hyperion*, I, 249.

who was killed trying to drive his father Apollo's chariot. If Hyperion is the horseman, Apollo is the poet, the creator. The very act of being a poet for Keats is a vying with a father in relationship with the muse mother.

> During the pain Mnemosyne upheld
> Her arms as one who prophesied.—At length
> Apollo shriek'd;—and lo! from all his limbs
> Celestial . . .

These are the last words of the poem. He dared go no further.

With *Lamia* itself and *La Belle Dame Sans Merci* Keats's fairy allegiance breaks through all disguises. The plot of *Lamia*, as found in Burton's *Anatomie of Melancholy*, a book Keats read with deep attention constantly underlining and annotating significant passages, reads like something from Walter Map's *De Nugis Curialium*. Keats expanded and embellished it, but left it essentially unaltered. Hermes in love with a beautiful nymph goes to Crete to find her. A serpent tells him that she has made the nymph invisible to protect her from the satyrs but will show her to him if he in return will restore the serpent to her former woman's shape. This he does. The lamia is in love with a beautiful youth Lycius whom she has seen in wandering dreams. She asks Hermes to put her down near him which he also does. Lycius, having just landed after a voyage, decides to walk home across the hills to Corinth like any farmer pixilated on his way home by night from market in an English story. Lamia waylays him. He falls in love with her and she takes him to her luxurious palace in Corinth where they live happily secluded for some time while Lycius makes the mistake of wishing to marry her. His old philosopher-teacher forces his way into the wedding feast and fixes the bride with his "demon eyes." She begins to wither. Lycius begs him to stop but he reveals that Lamia is a serpent, she vanishes with a shriek and Lycius falls dead.

Lamia is another face of the Fairy Queen. She seduces Lycius and provides him with all delicious luxury. What is interesting in Keats's view is that she is nowhere blamed. Lycius is blamed for his desire to show off the sadistic pleasure he takes in forcing Lamia to his will. Apollonius, the philosopher, is blamed for destroying Lamia. "Do not all charms fly / At the mere touch of cold philosophy?" But Lamia herself is a creature of passion and enchantment and is never blamed. This is a quite different emphasis from say the story of Henno cum Dentibus in Walter Map where the woman was a dragon who, when sprinkled with holy water, bounded through the roof with a shriek. There Henno was felt to have had a lucky escape. Keats has turned the story into a pro-love, anti-marriage one.

> O senseless Lycius! Madman! wherefore flout
> The silent blessing fate, warm cloister'd hours,
> And show to common eyes these secret bowers?

Perhaps he had been influenced by the story of Peri Banou. He had certainly read the *Arabian Nights' Tales* and mentions peris in the poem with fairies and goddesses.[29] This Eastern aspect could have been further underlined by the recent gossip about a "fair Circassian" brought over by the Persian ambassador.[30]

The anti-marriage twist, very much his own, ties in with remarks in his letters and his comments on that ripe misogynist Burton. Keats both felt marriage a tie and was increasingly anti-clerical. Brown, with whom he was staying for much of this time, was also against marriage and against Fanny Brawne, so much so that he admitted later to putting indecent verses among Keats's papers to dissuade her from reading them. Brown's idea was of the "bachelor gay," taking sexual satisfaction when and where he wanted it but not becoming involved. Emotionally Keats would have liked to elope with Fanny, to simply run away to some idealized "purple-lined palace of sweet sin." Instead he couldn't sleep with her, any engagement was likely to be a long one, he was short on money and health. Yet in her situation at that time it must be marriage or nothing. This on one level is the philosophy, coupled with Brown's and Burton's misogyny, which wasn't seen as such but as the commonsense manly attitude to women, that will "clip the Angel's wing."

> Love in a hut with water and a crust,
> Is—Love forgive us—cinders, ashes, dust;
> Love in a palace is perhaps at last
> More grievous torment than a hermit's fast.

In the original account in Burton there is no suggestion that Lamia was against marriage or that it was Lycius's idea alone or further that she was against Apollonius being invited to the wedding feast. These are Keats's additions. If the plot refers particularly, as has sometimes been suggested, to the triangle of himself, Brown and Fanny it has become inverted. Fanny wished to marry him.[31] He wished to possess her.

Once again, I believe, the real Fanny has been superseded by the dead one in the unconscious. She cannot marry him because she is already married. The moon image hovers behind her when Lycius calls her "My silver planet." At first she woos him as a goddess and only changes to a woman's pleading when she realizes he can't love her while he is "in half a fright." Apollonius's accusing stare is another of Keats's additions. It causes her to melt like the Indian maid in *Endymion*. She becomes a "deadly white," "an aching ghost" like so many of the fairy and mythological women in Keats, deeply affected by the image of his dying mother which had been reinforced in his mind by the dying face of his brother Tom and by his sister Fanny of whom he said at last, "[she] walks about my imagination like a ghost—she is so like Tom." Both of them, and George Keats too, were said to be like their mother. In a further comment from a letter a few days earlier he says of Fanny Brawne and his sister, "The one seems to absorb the other to a degree incredible."[32]

Apollonius's age is stressed in the poem. In his denunciation of Lamia he calls her a "foul dream." In Lycius's eyes he becomes a demon and Lycius curses him with blindness. The original says that Apollonius discovers Lamia's secret

---

[31] This is clear from her letters to Fanny Keats after death.
[32] Lamia too is a "gordian shape" of his tangled emotions.

"by some probable conjectures." There is none of this in Keats. The philosopher forces his way into the wedding already determined. Lamia is pierced with his stare. His words "A serpent!" cause her to vanish. He is pointing out the tail that marks her as already married. In the triangle he takes a father's place.

Far from fading out as he and his work matured, Keats's fairy imagery grows stronger and more precise. It is everywhere in his two most accomplished poems *The Eve of St. Agnes* and *Lamia*. He adopts Burton's theory to give it a logical background.

> Upon a time, before the faery broods
> Drove Nymph and Satyr from the prosperous woods,
> Before King Oberon's bright diadem,
> Sceptre, and mantle, clasp'd with dewy gem,
> Frighted away the Dryads and the Fauns . . .

There are two faery powers: love and imagination or "heart's affections" and "fancy." The faery world is a combination of the two, at once most dangerous and most alluring.

> Real are the dreams of Gods, and smoothly pass
> Their pleasures in a long immortal dream.

Madeline asleep in his imagination, lies:

> While legion'd fairies pac'd the coverlet
> And pale enchantment held her sleepy-eyed.

Overshadowed by death and the dead, by "the family disease" and his dead family, by the sexual frustration of his love, both love and the imagination are shot through with an elfin malevolence. The immortality which he hungered for as poet and lover constantly eludes and mocks. Only the gods, inventions of the imagination, and the lovers stilled on a work of art cannot fade. His hope to be among the English poets after his death is a lust for immortality, to defeat that death which had constantly robbed him and which he himself had courted, since it held what he had loved most and to live was to be unfaithful to the loved dead.

La Belle Dame Sans Merci is the culmination of all this. Another Launfal story, it nevertheless has an unhappy ending. It returns to Keats's earliest literary master and earliest romance symbols of the knight and the Fairy Queen. Phaedria from Spenser's *Faerie Queene* has influenced it and so has a minor Jacobean, William Browne, supplying the near echo "Let no bird sing." A third literary influence shouldn't be missed: Scott's version of the ballad of *Thomas the Rhymer* published in *Minstrelsy of the Scottish Border*, 1802–3.

An autobiographical incident sparked off the poem. Keats had been going through his dead brother's papers, including his own letters to Tom from his Scottish tour. Among them were the letters purporting to be from a girl in love with Tom, Amena, which Keats realized were nothing but a cruel joke written by Tom's schoolfriend Charles Wells and even containing Spenserian echoes from Keats's own early poems. Yet Tom had languished and pined during his illness for this fictitious girl and had even gone to look for her. Tom was addressed as a knight in the letters. Keats wrote angrily to his remaining brother George about his discovery.

Tom had been a devoted reader of Scott. Just before Keats's transcript of *La Belle Dame* in the same letter to George in which he tells the story of the Amena joke, he says he has been to see a new opera called "the heart of Midlothian." The combination of circumstances had reminded Keats of the ballad *Thomas the Rhymer* which gave him the form of the poem and the plot.[33] The name had itself pressed a spring, for Keats was susceptible to the power of names. He had underlined *Poor Tom* in his copy of *King Lear* when Tom was very ill.

Scott's version of the ballad is in three parts: the original story as taken down from "a lady residing not far from Ercildoune," a second part by Scott on Thomas's prophecies and a third, also by Scott, telling how the Rhymer

[33] His mind was also running on mock ballads because of Reynolds's parody of *Peter Bell* which he discusses in this letter too. There's possibly an influence from *Tam Lin* itself which Keats may have known through his love of Burns.

returned to fairyland. Thomas is lying on Huntlie bank when a beautiful lady comes riding by. She is the Queen of fair Elfland. If he will kiss her rosy lips she will have his body to serve her. Undaunted he does so and she takes him up on her horse. She shows him the roads to heaven, hell and elfland and warns him that if he speaks a word there he will never return to his own land. They ride on in their magic journey that is a going back through birth.

> On they rode on, and farther on,
> And they waded through rivers aboon the knee,
> And they saw neither sun nor moon,
> But they heard the roaring of the sea.
> It was mirk, mirk night, and there was no stern[34]
>   light,
> And they waded through red blood to the knee . . .

At last they come to a garden green and she gives him an apple. In fairy queen convention she clothes him in beautiful clothes. He isn't allowed to return to earth for seven years.

The ballad is one of the finest in English. Scott's additions can only fall sadly short but they contain one or two interesting parallels for Keats's poem. The pale kings and princes are from Part II which foretells the dooms of various Scottish kings; Part III supplies the time of year, autumn, when Thomas is finally called away, the fairy song, the warrior of the lake and Tristram on his sickbed with Isolde's lily hand to nurse him.

> And, while she o'er his sickbed hung,
> He paid her with his heart.
>
> O fatal was the gift . . .

This last is particularly important for *La Belle Dame Sans Merci*. Isolde was of course La Belle Iseult and I have already discussed her meaning as an incest figure. The sickbed is not only Tristram's but Tom's and by imaginative extension Keats's own. The love of Tristram and

---

[34] stern-star.

Isolde is like that of Paolo and Francesca, incestuous by the laws of the Church. It betrays its secondary meaning by the fact that it is always the woman who is already married.

The letter to George contains other hints about the poem. A piece of extempore verse pictures Keats as a dwarf, George as an ape and Tom as a fool, Tom-fool as Robert Gittings notes, trying to persuade a princess, George's wife Georgiana,[35] not to enter the faery court without being invited. The dwarf rhymes of himself.

> I was a Prince—a baby prince—my doom
> You see I made a whipstock of a wand
> My top has henceforth slept in faery land.

This piece of half-conscious autobiography explaining Keats's shortness which worried him particularly in relation to women[36] seems to refer to some incident in his childhood like his threatening his mother with the naked sword. The "baby prince" is an exact anticipation of Freud's "His Majesty the ego" in its childhood form and a reminder of George's comment about John's mother making him her favorite. The lines betray guilt, a fear of impotence and that his imagination has been with the idealized dead since childhood.

Keats had been reading with Fanny Brawne the stanzas in the *Inferno* about the fatal love of Paolo and Francesca which he took to themselves. Under its influence he had a dream which he retells in the letter. As the sonnet "As Hermes once" he copied it for George and into the volume of Dante which he was reading with Fanny. "I floated about the whirling atmosphere as it is described with a beautiful figure to whose lips mine were joined at(s) it seemed for an age—and in the midst of all this cold and darkness I was warm . . ."

[35] I believe her name helped Keats to accept her as his sister-in-law. He sent her an acrostic on it in which he says of their family name "(enchanted) has it been the Lord knows where."

[36] See in the 1817 volume the sonnet "Had I a man's fair form" and the bitter comment on womankind and "Mister John Keats five feet high" in the letter to Bailey, July 1818.

> ... Pale were the sweet lips I saw
> Pale were the lips I kissed and fair the form
> I floated with about that melancholy storm

Some of this has crept into *La Belle Dame*. The "starved lips in the gloom" are from Dante's hell, as well as from Scott, and the parade of ghostly Scottish kings in *Macbeth* from Keats's schoolboy reading. The dream has been reversed to one of terror, "Ah woe betide!/ The latest dream I ever dreamed."

The rhymer deceived by the fairy isn't Tom but John. This is what has been suppressed in the poem to be replaced by the knight, his familiar disguise. He wished to believe that the beautiful figure met in hell was a Francesca and so it was but a composite of the two, his mother and Fanny Brawne, and it suggested to him that she would deceive and leave him as she had already done. The story of Paolo and Francesca had been known to Keats for a long time. Leigh Hunt had made it the basis of his poem *The Story of Rimini* under whose inspiration Keats had begun an Induction "Lo I must tell" which tells of a knight riding by a lake. The choice of the Dantesque subject was, I think, an element in Keats's early enthusiasm for Hunt.[37]

The dead kings and princes who warn him about *La Belle Dame* are also the dead male members of his family. It's interesting here to notice that Spence in his *British Fairy Origins* records the belief that consumption was itself a fairy disease, the fairies being supposed to drain the victim's strength to replenish their own.[38] The resulting languor Keats mentions earlier in the same letter provided an image of two women and a man that formed the starting point for his *Ode on Indolence*. This image leads straight to a comment that he has just heard from his friend Haslam that his father is dying "—his mother bears up he says very well—" which leads him to speak about the uncertainty of happiness in the world and his identification with

---

[37] The story probably also influenced the choice of names in *The Eve of St. Agnes*: Porphyro Paolo. In the original manuscript he swears by St. Paul. No one could understand why and it was changed.

[38] Spence, op. cit., p. 92.

Haslam's misfortune. The origin of the image is himself and the two Fannies, rationalized as ambition, love and his demon poetry, three curiously disguised shadows with joined hands, the male figure in the middle.

The gift of poetry was made by the Fairy Queen to Thomas the Rhymer. Keats too inherited a faery song. Sir Calidore wins the lady only to find that she is like the nightmare life-in-death of Coleridge's *Ancient Mariner*.[39] Porphyro had wakened Madeline to love with the song of *La Belle Dame Sans Merci* who had been mortal, cruel in the conventional Romance sense, but the lady of the ballad is Lamia, the veiled Moneta, melancholy, Cynthia, his aspiration and despair. It was said that those whom the Fairy Queen carried away faded and pined without her unless they were rescued by a human love. Undoubtedly Fanny Brawne tried as fair Janet did to rescue Tam Lin but time and the social conventions were against her. She loaded Keats with talismans against his journey, a white stone to cool his hands, a lock of hair, a silk lining to his cap, a paper knife and committed him to "perilous seas, in faery lands forlorn." By then he believed his passion for her was so great that it would have killed him anyway. The silk lining of his cap burned into his brain. Did she ever realize who her deathly rival was? He links them with the same phrase "in thrall."[40] Unlike Thomas the Rhymer he was never allowed to return.

---

[39] I accept that the conversation with Coleridge retailed in this same letter was an element in the making of *La Belle Dame*.

[40] *La Belle Dame* and the sonnet "I cry your mercy."

CHAPTER XVI

The Brothers Grimm and Sister Andersen

Am I in earnest? Oh, dear no. Don't you know that this is a fairy tale, and all fun and pretence; and that you are not to believe one word of it, even if it is true?

The Water Babies, Charles Kingsley

Fairy stories weren't originally composed for children. No doubt children eavesdropped on them as they were told round the fire at night or as the women worked at the more communal jobs of net-making, laundering, sewing, in kitchen and dairy or the fields or at the larger social gatherings where there would be singing, dancing and storytelling, and undoubtedly they bullied their nurses and mothers for stories, but these were passed down to them not fabricated to suit the child mind any more than *Gulliver's Travels, Robinson Crusoe, Ivanhoe* or *David Copperfield* which are now standard children's classics. The idea that there should be separate imaginative food for children is a relatively late one in Britain.[1] Literature for them began as part of their education or moral training. The fairy story was sold in cheap chapbooks comparable to broadside ballads in sheets, but to many adults it was highly suspect as both escapist and immoral.

The growth of a sense of adult guilt with the nineteenth century and the emphasis on lost innocence helped to let back the fairy story. Children become the receptacles for adult fantasies about the Golden Age, itself a symbol of sexual innocence. This was coupled with another fantasy about the simple peasant who was a child at heart. It was industry, the dark satanic mill, which brutalized him and encouraged him in the sophisticated vices of drunkenness and lechery hitherto reserved for the upper classes who could temper them with refinement and education.

—But there's a Tree, of many one,
A single Field which I have looked upon,

[1] See Avery, *Nineteenth Century Children*, ed. cit., who sets 1780 as the beginning of children's literature, but also see Percy Muir for the pre-nineteenth-century children's books, *English Children's Books* (Batsford, 1954).

Both of them speak of something that is gone;
    The Pansy at my feet
    Doth the same tale repeat
Whither is fled the visionary gleam?
Where is it now the glory and the dream?[2]

Nature and childhood were joined in what was thought
of as the rustic childhood of nations. Folk literature became by definition the most innocent and was given even
greater respectability by the backing of scholars and the
wave of Teutonism which, beginning as an aspect of German patriotism exploited by princelings anxious to underline their own independence and power, swept over northern Europe like a new migration, bringing with it concepts
that were to be expressed in international politics and art
with ultimately terrifying consequences.

Italy and the South were labelled degenerate. The North
was the home of manliness, the domestic virtues for
women, an uncontaminated culture which had preserved
the peasant and was now yielding a mythology to rival that
of Greece while being at the same time apparently less
erotic in content and therefore more suitable for children
and less offensive to Christianity. The fairy story was not
true but because it was initially a folk tale collected by a
scholar it wasn't quite a lie. Some editions, including those
of the *Arabian Nights' Tales*, added notes on customs and
geography which emphasized this or an apologetic fore-
word. Retelling the legend of the Neck, a water spirit that
wanted to be saved, a translator of Andersen's tales says:
"Who shall call a legend like this profane? Is it not rather
the popular expression of the truth that 'the whole creation
groaneth, and travaileth together in pain until now.' " Even
so such things weren't to be read on Sunday.

There had always of course been British fairy stories.
Folklorists are inclined to play down their popularity and
suggest that the foreign ones were and are better liked but
there seem to me a few which are as well known as Little
Red Riding Hood or Cinderella: Jack and the Beanstalk,
Dick Whittington, The Three Bears, the Three Little Pigs,
and Tom Thumb. Many of the less popular have their

[2] *Ode on the Intimations of Immortality*, Wordsworth.

counterparts in Grimm or Andersen. Of those I've listed at least three are known from the Middle Ages and 'appeared in popular chapbooks. Perhaps the illusion of their lesser popularity is fostered by their not having appeared suddenly and under one aegis. Certainly most children's fairy primers have them and there are pantomimes based on all of them, a reasonable test of at least commercial favor. However, it is true that they had to wait till the 1890s for the dignity of an unbowdlerized collection by the folklorist Joseph Jacobs. Perhaps it was this lack that has left an unfavorable impression. This doesn't take account of Celtic folk tales which must of course be included in any study of British fairy stories but their appeal has been more to adults than to children and by oral rather than written transmission.

The first foreign collection to be translated was Perrault's, as *The Tales of Mother Goose* in 1729.[3] This includes the Sleeping Beauty, Little Red Riding Hood, Bluebeard, Puss in Boots, Cinderella and Hop o' my Thumb. I realize that in attempting to analyze the psychological appeal of such stories the least I shall be accused of is swatting a dragonfly with a steam hammer. Our fundamental resistance to knowing what goes on in our heads is so strong that we employ any form of rationalization to avoid understanding. This is particularly true in relation to childhood, partly because the myth of innocence is still very powerful, partly because to do so is to look at our own preoccupations and guilts which we have spent a lifetime covering up. If we read James Joyce's *Ulysses* we are consciously on guard, accepting and rejecting as we explore the Bloom's erotic fantasy life. We can shrug off Molly as a nymphomaniac, Leopold as a masturbating voyeur and withhold identification. We can admire the skill and scope of a work of art and so maintain our poise between involvement and intellectual distancing. But to be told that as children we sank ourselves without intellectual reservation in a story which presented perhaps an incest theme under the innocuous and charming exterior of the Sleeping Beauty is to be made to feel that we have been both seduced and caught masturbating. This is why we resist with disbelief any suggestion of psychological content and insist that we read only a harmless childlike narrative.

Why then did it appeal to us? Why do children react so strongly, sometimes with nightmares and tears, to what is seemingly a piece of light nonsense? It is, I believe, because the mythological symbols externalize conflicts and situations which they can't yet understand or explain and yet must express in order to be able to cope with them. They express them by emotional participation. They will also act them out in unsupervised play.

A story may work on several levels and contain more than one suppressed theme. No story if it is to be successful even with children can be entirely without artifice, which will attempt to conceal the crude emotional material that gives it its drive. At the same time there may well be a tendency to postpone the climax of the story by various methods, repetition being the most common as in masochistic masturbation fantasies.[4] Often a number of people must go through the same situations before the hero who will succeed, or a number of things must be done as in the labors of Hercules, or a number of people encountered, or wishes fulfilled. This prolongs the suspense, building up the energy to be released by the denouement.[5]

The first of Perrault's stories, *The Sleeping Beauty*, has two parts in his version. The princess, promised all beauty at birth, is also cursed by death from a spindle. This is commuted to a hundred-year sleep. The king forbids all spinning but one day the princess comes upon a little old woman who doesn't know of the order and she pricks herself. She falls asleep and a protective hedge grows up all round her through which only the hero prince can force his way, a theme familiar to Wagnerites. She is wakened by the prince and marries him.

This first part is a father/daughter incest myth like the opera story of Brynhilda and Wotan. She is so beautiful that her father will desire her. Mother's spindle, that is

[4] See Theodor Reik, *Masochism in Modern Man* (Grove Press, New York), Chapter IV.

[5] Compare the masochist fantasy cited in Reik of the series of young men to be sacrificed to Moloch of which the fantasist was to be the last.

father's penis belonging to her, will cause her death. She is cast into sleep and surrounded by a hedge to protect her from him until the prince shall come and break the taboo. Correctly in Perrault the king and queen go away once she has fallen asleep. The old woman in the tower is mother in disguise.

The second part continues the story with the prince's mother who is a cannibal ogre. She tries to eat Sleeping Beauty and their two children while the prince is away but is foiled by the good-hearted cook. The prince returns in the nick of time and the wicked old queen jumps to her death in a vat of venomous reptiles.

Here the object of hatred and guilt suppressed from the first part comes through. It is the mother again who will punish the daughter for her desire for and attractiveness to the father and the hero and must be made to be monstrous so that she can be legitimately hated and disposed of. Another version of the story makes the prince a king already married and his first wife the ogre. Perrault carefully mentions that the prince belongs to a different family from the sleeping princess. Logically one would expect it to be the same family. The terror that Sleeping Beauty suffers when her children are seemingly killed and when she herself is to die is a guilt payment. After this she is entitled to her happy ending.[6]

Little Red Riding Hood is doted on by her mother and her grandmother who makes her famous hat. English has linked it unequivocally with gnomes' redcaps emphasizing its phallicness. The French version suggested a kind of bonnet, according to one writer,[7] with a red ribbon. On her way through the wood to visit her sick grandmother she meets the wolf. They take separate paths to grandmother's. The wolf arrives first, gobbles up the old lady and gets into her bed. Red Riding Hood arrives and after the ritual repetition is eaten too.

[6] One of Perrault's rhymed stories *Donkey Skin* is a stated father/daughter incest. This is an open situation because the princess repulses her father. The Grimms' version is *The Many Furred Creature* where the incest theme is consciously suppressed by the king marrying the princess to an elderly councillor. *Cap o' Rushes* is the English version.

[7] See Brereton's introduction to the Penguin edition of Perrault.

Red Riding Hood is being punished and we are driven to wonder what for. On the face of it it's a very nasty story that has a little girl eaten while on an errand of mercy, and her poor sick old grandmother too. What have they done? It's no good Perrault saying that the moral is never trust a stranger. What they have done is make a matriarchy of grandmother, mother and daughter. There are no men in the Perrault version. The Grimms have a woodcutter who warns the child and then comes to slit open the wolf's belly and lets them out conveniently undigested. Red Riding Hood has been made too phallic by her mother and grandmother. Her independence and brightness are spoken much of in the story which in Perrault is designed to cut her down to size. It's a story of female castration.

The wolf is the aggressive male, possibly her own father. The popularity of the story suggests an appeal to childish masochism, that the little girl, or boy (for boys enjoy the story too), wants to be dominated in this way, plus a confusion about sexuality, who has the baby and how, apparent in the alternative ending of Red Riding Hood and her grandmother alive in the wolf's belly and the mock birth.

Another story which duplicates parent figures in this volume is *Hop o' my Thumb*. The children's parents who have abandoned them in the wood are doubled in the giant and his wife who wish to eat them. This is a playing with the fear many children have that their parents will leave them. The hero, who is a little penis figure like Tom Thumb, has the phallic characteristics of brightness in every sense and saves his brothers by a brutal murder of the ogres' girl children, a murder which disguises the real wish by exactly mirroring it: the death of the other siblings. At the root of the story is sibling jealousy giving rise to the fear of abandonment by the parents. The anxiety and resentment is worked off by supposing an ogre family to be legitimately killed. Since Hop o' my Thumb is so small any ordinary beings will be giant size to him. At the deepest level is the baby, the smallest of the family even without being a midget, and at the mercy of, and in competition with, them all.

The childish ego has taken the part for the whole in picturing itself as simply a little penis. A final piece of wish-fulfillment gives it father's seven-league boots which fit perfectly and enable Hop o' my Thumb to have all the attributes of the giant and make the family's fortune rather like Joseph and his brethren in the Old Testament, a euhemerizing folk tale of a similar kind. The boots are a symbol of power and potency which isn't surprising when we remember that feet have sexual connotations not only for fetishists. The fairies are always tireless dancers. Their ring dances mesmerize the people caught in them and sometimes they are drawn into the dance too.

Cinderella turns on a piece of sexual foot-fantasy. The glass slipper with its matching foot is a symbol of the size of her vagina. A folk joke equates the size of a man's nose with the size of his penis, the size of a woman's mouth with that of the vagina. Cinderella's is the most dainty and delicate, as can be seen through the medium of the glass slipper. A further extension of the joke about the mouth is the story of the girl who being told this piece of lore practiced saying "prunes and prisms" in an attempt to make hers smaller. This is analogous to the ugly sisters cutting off toes and heels to make the slipper fit them. To have a small vagina is the sign of virginity and delicacy: the opposite suggests a coarse and loose woman.

The story is about female purity. However poor, ill-treated and shabby, a girl still has her jewel which she can exchange for riches and a handsome husband. She mustn't be out after twelve for that would endanger her reputation and also her one asset since she might be seduced or raped. The stated time is a taboo on pre-marital sex. The trying-on of the slipper is a virginity test similar to the Andersen story of *The Real Princess* who was tested by the groom's mother with a pea under twenty mattresses. She was a real princess because she could feel it hard and bruising while she tried to sleep. The Scottish ballad *Gil Brenton* also has a virginity test, this time undisguised, by the groom's mother. To be a princess is itself a metaphor for virginity. Cinderella is contrasted with her ugly sisters; ugliness and coarseness, like dirtiness, are synonymous with sexual laxity. Her fairy godmother is her dead mother;[8] the sisters

---

[8] In *Ashputtel*, the Grimms' version, it's indeed the dead mother who gives her the three dresses she wears to the ball through a hazel tree planted on her grave. The slipper is golden but small and dainty. The ugly sisters' mutilations are bloodily done in this version. The blood that gives them away is hymenal blood, cf. *Bluebeard*.

are daughters of a stepmother, herself impure because she has been married before.

Another virginity story is *Toads and Jewels*. Here there are two sisters, one good-tempered and beautiful, the other peevish and proud. The first is rewarded with the faculty of letting jewels fall from her mouth when she speaks because she gives a poor woman a drink at a fountain. The other is punished with uttering toads because she refused a drink to the same fairy but now disguised in rich clothes. The bejewelled daughter marries a king's son while the other is driven out by her mother to die in the wood.

Even on the narrative level this is a nasty story though artistically beautifully balanced and economic, and rich with the startling images of the falling jewels and toads. The mouths are again vagina symbols. The gentle softspoken one is suitably, that is sexually, rewarded with a prince who sees the jewels and thinks, in Perrault, that they are worth more than a dowry. The rude aggressive mouth spawns reptiles associated with witches as if it had coupled with the devil. The message of female virtues and their reward is unmistakable.

In this case the fairy is the kind often associated with blessing or punishing. K. M. Briggs says that this is unusual in native English tradition but although not worked out it's there in germ in the fairies who came to Arthur's christening and the old woman who directs the girl to the Well of the World's End. It was an idea that fitted nineteenth-century morality and finds its fullest English expression in Kingsley's Mrs. Doasyouwouldbedoneby and Bedonebyasyoudid of *The Water Babies*. Quite rightly they are seen in the end as two aspects of the same figure like the poor and the rich fairy in *Toads and Jewels*. Both are extensions of mother, as we would expect, in her punishing and rewarding capacities.

Bluebeard has certain similarities with the opening of the *Arabian Nights' Tales* in a husband who, having killed off a succession of wives, marries one who gets the better of him. This basic plot is also known in ballad form as *The Outlandish Knight*. Usually the girl defeats him by her cleverness but in *Bluebeard* it is her brothers who arrive to kill him. The *Arabian Nights'* version has the wives punished in turn for the adultery of the first. In *Bluebeard* it's merely curiosity that seems to be her undoing. However it is curiosity as a form of disobedience. A like story by the Grimms has a girl punished by the Virgin for curiosity leading to disobedience in refusing to confess. Each of the stories has a masochistic sequence. In *Bluebeard* and the *Arabian Nights' Tales* it is formed by the procession of dead wives. The Virgin has a sequence of punishments, three for the Trinity the girl sees behind the forbidden door.

The parallel with the more outspoken Eastern story gives a clue to the kind of curiosity. When the sultan goes away his first wife indulges in an orgy. The curiosity is sexual. This leads us to ask why Bluebeard's first wife was killed. Unlike her successors, she couldn't have discovered him by unlocking the door on his guilty secret since it didn't yet exist. The secret is therefore a concealing device for the original crime. Bluebeard simply murders his wives. He cuts their throats with his big sword. Much is made of the blood, some of which sticks to the little key which opens the door and reveals that the wife has been into the forbidden room.

A much more elaborate theme is concealed here than at first appears. Another story by the Grimms, *Fichter's Bird*, tells of three sisters captured by a wizard. Each is given the keys to the house, including a forbidden little key, and an egg. The first two enter the room and see a basin of blood and dismembered bodies. They let their eggs slip in and can't wash off the blood, with the usual deadly results. The third sister hides her egg safely first. This again looks like a virginity test. The first two sisters have already been deflowered. Their eggs are bloody. The third keeps hers carefully. The little key in the lock of the forbidden room provides a penetration symbol.

The blood in Bluebeard is also defloration blood. The wives are killed by a cut throat which symbolizes the breaking of the hymen. This legal rape is what frightens the heroine wife. She opens the door with the little key and it becomes bloody. She fears she has broken her own hymen with masturbation and will be punished for her sexual curiosity since this will be discovered. Even this won't free her from the rape of the big sword. The final episode with the famous "Sister Anne, Sister Anne what do you see?" is a masochistic prolongation of the ordeal comparable to a rape fantasy of pursuit, familiar in the story of Daphne and Apollo. Murder, as so often, is a symbol of sexual violence.

The story of the Virgin collected by the Grimms also has sexual curiosity as its centre. What the child finds, translated into religious terminology as the Holy Trinity, is the tripartite male sex organ, the father's. Like Noah's sons she has committed the unforgivable sin of uncovering her father's nakedness. The Virgin is a barely concealed mother, hence the punishment and the guilt.

Removed into the safety of fantasy the unconscious is able to play with the unthinkable, to express a forbidden desire or deal with an inexpressible terror. *Bluebeard* is particularly complicated because the wished for is also the feared. The dreamer wants the rape. Bluebeard himself becomes "quite an agreeable man." He has riches and several houses. There is only one thing wrong with him which is the enormity of his blue beard, the visible counterpart of his pubic hair. The marriage is celebrated in the story and a month passes but time in faery is relative. The month elapses before bedtime. The discovery which is the equivalent of wedding night fears takes place while waiting for him to come to bed. Like Scheherezade the wife has her sister with her to delay the dreadful moment. Her brothers come to her rescue and she is returned unharmed to her family. The whole thing has been a masturbation fantasy of a kind common to many adolescent girls but with a heavily masochistic slant.

For the male reader or listener the story offers either the opposite side of the coin, the satisfaction of deflowering a succession of girls and of being the dominating and potent Bluebeard, or a chance for a feminine identification.[9] The end punishment simply makes it permissible to have enjoyed the rest, a common fiction formula particularly in thrillers which *Bluebeard* closely resembles. Scheherezade's

---

[9] Reik suggests, op. cit., that in a sado-masochist fantasy the subject may simultaneously act out both roles. This is probably true of all bipartite fantasies, except where a specific identification is chosen to the suppression of the other, since both parts are created by the same mind. If *Little Red Riding Hood* is narrated to a group some will identify with the child, some with the wolf and some alternately with both.

husband has a passion for virgins. Once broken they no longer interest him. The queen's job is to maintain his interest which she does by providing him imaginatively with all the sexual variety he needs. The literary device of *The Thousand and One Nights* is a conscious structural parallel to the unconscious function of fairy stories, a piece of delicate Eastern baroque sophistication.

The ballad form, which has two French versions in which the Outlandish Knight is replaced by the Devil or Renand, is a masturbation fantasy too. The girl is made to ritually undress verse by verse but when naked or nearly so asks the knight to turn his back and then pushes him into the water and leaves him to drown. The previous wives provide the male figure with the necessary attributes of potency and ruthlessness which cause the lady to elope with him. He is obviously irresistible until the last minute. No blame attaches to the heroine because of this. If there is any it's purged by her fear and she returns home unsullied. As I've already said, in his outlandish or diabolic form the male figure is a fantasy father.

Perrault's tale of *Puss in Boots* introduces another genre of fairy story, that concerned with magic animals who usually have the gift of speech. This idea is common to many literatures including all the fairy story collections, classical Greek where it's moralized as Aesop, Eastern tales, Apuleius's *Golden Ass*, the Old Testament, Ancient Egyptian, stretching the idea back five or six thousand years, and the latest television commercial by way of Disney and Kenneth Grahame.

Puss himself is a simple phallic projection[10] from the youngest son who has nothing else to gain a fortune and win the girl. *Puss in Boots* is the male counterpart of *Cinderella*. His English version is Dick Whittington's cat.

[10] Cf. the youngest son helped by the fox in the Grimms' *The Golden Bird*. At the end the fox asks the prince to chop off his head and feet which he eventually does, whereupon the fox is seen as the princess's brother, either a rationalization on lines parallel to other stories or a suggestion of brother/sister incest atoned for by loving and helping the young prince. The close relationship between the fox and the prince may be a homosexual one for which the rest of the story is an elaborate justification. There's no reason why there shouldn't be elements of all three: human relationships are complex enough.

Like Reynard he has the phallic cunning and bravado and the pubic furriness. His boots are a sly touch of visual symbolism by the unconscious. They should really be in the bag which is his other trademark.

He makes his master strip naked before the king and his daughter, by having him rescued from a fake drowning, and the princess falls madly in love with him. Finally the cat gains a castle for his master by tricking the ogre who owns it into turning himself into a mouse which the cat swallows, a defeat of one phallic symbol by another quite breathtaking in its consistency and wit.[11]

Animals are an alternative projection to fairies when made to behave in a humanoid way. In the Grimms' story of *The Three Feathers* the toads are fairies. Often they're endowed with magic powers apart from speech. The two kinds overlap most clearly in the beast creations of science fiction where different forms of sentient being are imagined for other parts of the universe. The *Three Little Pigs* is an English story of the defeat of the wolf, mainly by the youngest pig, which surely needs little explanation as a Uranos myth translated into nursery animal symbols.[12] Under the disguise of animal behavior human emotions can be acted out. The animal disguise covers the taboo situation as do the animal disguises of folk rituals.

One of the Grimms' Hansel and Grettel stories is of brother/sister incest with an animal hide. The two children decide to run away from their wicked stepmother. As they go the brother becomes thirsty. At the first river his sister hears a voice saying if he drinks he will become a tiger and

[11] An interesting parallel is the continual feud between Brer Rabbit and Brer Fox in the Uncle Remus stories, the re-creation of a folk myth by a people in an alien continent out of the materials to hand, geographical and cultural. The stories were retold by Joel Chandler Harris in the well-known form. "Cunning Rabbit" occurs in *West African Folk Tales* collected in 1903 by Cronise and Ward (London Swan, Sonnenschein and Co.). There is also a Mr. Turtle, a possible forerunner of Brer Terrapin.

[12] So too also the Grimms' *The Wolf and the Seven Little Kids* where the mother is constantly impersonated by the wolf. Eventually she fills the wolf's belly with stones instead of her children and sews it up, this is the myth of Rhea whose children were devoured by Cronus their father until she brought forth Zeus when she gave him a stone instead of the child, wrapped in swaddling clothes, which he swallowed.

tear her to pieces; at the second a wolf and devour her. At the third, unable to resist any longer, he becomes a roebuck. They live together in a hut in the forest until the king comes hunting and the roebuck is driven to run by the sound of the horns. Eventually the king marries the sister and they have a son. The stepmother murders the queen and substitutes her own daughter. All comes right in the end, the queen is restored to life, and the roebuck to his human form when the stepmother is burnt.

What the sister fears is sexual assault from her brother. He is the only one with the raging thirst. As a roebuck he is gentle but the sound of her husband-to-be's horn makes him run away. After the marriage the queen has to be punished because she has emotionally aquiesced in the incestuous relationship. The husband breaks the enchantment. The restoration of the brother's human shape marks the release of them both from the incest situation.

Stepmothers in fairy stories are often real mothers disguised.[13] The disliked aspect of the mother is displaced onto the stepmother, allowing her to be hated and so removing the guilt of hating one's own mother. In this story it is all the mother's fault since it's she who makes them brother and sister and therefore taboo for each other. The brother's enchanted animal shape symbolizes this taboo.

Often the animal shape is straightforwardly phallic. The frog in the Grimms' *Frog Prince* and the English *Well at the World's End* is the disgusting penis the girl must encounter on her wedding night. Both stories have a chastity opening. The English girl has been sent to fill a sieve with water, the means by which Tuccia proved her chastity in Petrarch; the German princess is playing with her golden ball which implies childhood, purity in the gold and masturbation in the play. In both stories a parent insists the frog shall be let in (the girl must keep her promise), fed

---

[13] The most famous is the wicked queen in *Snow White and the Seven Dwarfs* who is jealous of the rivalry of the girl's beauty. Father has been completely suppressed from this story. He must be understood like a missing part of speech. Snow White has seven phalluses, brothers, to guard her. She is put into a taboo sleep to keep her from the father. The wicked queen is sexually punished by the red-hot shoes. This is an anti-mother story with the girl replacing her mother and eventually destroying her, but made, for the comfort of the ego, to seem as if it is the persecuted one.

and eventually taken into bed. Then in the morning the frog begs the girl to cut off its head, a graphic representation of detumescence, and is revealed as a handsome prince. The story is teaching that there is nothing to be frightened of even if the marriage is an arranged one.

Another marriage fear story is part of *The Many Furred Creature*. The heroine has been turned against marriage by her father's desire for her so she alternately makes symbolic feminine presents to the king and then hides from him under a furry cloak. *The Goose Girl* has a similar pubic hair symbol in the princess sitting and combing her hair while the herd boy chases his hat and the king watches. The clue is that the herd boy tries to steal some of her hair and the combing is related to the alluring occupation of mermaids.

Repeatedly the hero is the youngest son or a simpleton. We are all at some point youngest sons even when we are the first born and this position is the favorite one for the childish ego with the rest of the family to idolize it. If the youngest son is shown being despised or ill-treated by the family this simply underlines his own merit and the unfairness of everybody else. He is the hero because he has the audience's sympathy and is the focus of each member's feelings of having been unloved or underestimated. His eventual success is a promise to each of us that we too will succeed, get the girl, the money and the esteem. The simpleton too carries our hopes. We are few of us as wise, handsome or strong as we would like. We all fear for our potency and attractiveness. Yet the simpleton is worse off than any of us and he succeeds. There's also an element of the natural unthinking phallus behind the idea of the fool who beats everyone. He recurs as a common type of the folk hero, Beowulf in his youth or Siegfried.

Many of the Grimms' stories have English counterparts or ones in Perrault, indeed the brothers withdrew some of their originally published tales thinking that they were too close to the French versions and possibly derived from them. There are some cautionary peasant tales of the Aesop type among them but the major part of the collection shows great complexity and therefore sophistication. The brothers were concerned to deduce a German mythology and the collection of tales was part of this attempt.

Jacob Grimm in his introduction to *Deutsche Mythologie* states as one of the proofs of the antiquity, originality and affinity of the German and Norse mythologies "The evident deposit of god-myths, which is found to this day in various folk tales, nursery tales . . ."

They were also concerned to prove its superiority: "as the Gothic, Anglo-Saxon and Old High German dialects have their several points of superiority over the Old Norse, so may the faith of inland Germany have in many points its claims to distinction and individuality." Some of this attitude rubbed off on the English and not only on William Morris. "I think Scandinavian Paganism, to us here, is more interesting than any other . . . It is interesting also as the creed of our fathers; the men whose blood still runs in our veins," wrote Carlyle in *Hero-Worship*. True he was writing specifically of Norse mythology and the Grimms were concerned to go one better than that but it was all part of the Teutonic front.

This concern has obscured the universality, the artistry and the psychology of the stories. Perrault in his dedicatory letter says that his are stories told by the lower classes but doesn't say that they are for children nor does he mention them in his retelling.[15] The Grimms' are *Kinder und Hausmärchen*. One wonders what audience they were intended for. If it was for children it must have been in the sense in which Reginald Scot mentions "our mother's maids" terrifying children with tales of Robin Goodfellow and so on. This doesn't mean that the stories are composed for them. Indeed the content shows plainly that they weren't in that it's the same content as the *Odyssey*, Ovid's *Metamorphoses* or the British ballads.

There is no reason why the person telling the story at the end of the eighteenth century should have given it literal belief or that it should ever have been so believed. I may invent a fantasy that my head is full of cotton wool which spills out of my ears and blows away as thistledown, to explain a sinus condition. I don't believe it literally yet it

[14] Translated Stallybrass, 1882 (Bell & Sons). The first English edition of the stories was published 1823–26.
[15] Although the frontispiece to the original edition does show a governess relating them to children.

may seem a valuable image to carry my feelings on the subject and in this sense it is true. The folk tales collected in Germany by the brothers are literary inventions by and initially for adults. A literal-minded industrially expanding culture with its adult fantasy in orthodox religion appropriated them for children.

The symbols were released to work unconsciously, exerting a fascination that can only have a psychological basis and by which the unconscious minds of thousands of children could consider problems which they would never have been allowed to discuss or even to acknowledge. They could even laugh at them. *The Golden Goose* is the story of a boy who finds such a potent penis substitute that everyone runs after him. The princess, whose sexual anxiety is so great that she has never laughed, has her fears allayed by the comedy in an explosion of laughter and marries Dummling. A silhouette of the goose under the boy's arm with its long neck and head jutting out in front shows why she laughed. Like the introduction to Scheherazade's tales this particular story is a metaphor of how folk tales work.

Although there are parallel British stories our folklorists have never found as fertile a crop as the Grimms did. However, this shouldn't be a cause for too much regret. It seems to me that the arts of story and song are unlikely to co-exist in equal strength. The extreme wealth of British folk song and ballad has probably absorbed most of the available narrative and symbol. Certainly the materials of the two forms are very often interchangeable. Probably social conditions decide which shall flourish in a given area or time though this is in no way to suggest that the two media are mutually exclusive. There are German ballads as there are British stories.

Both deal with the royal family, king/father, queen/mother, prince and princess. This royalty makes them universals and a fit accompaniment for "His Majesty, the ego." It would be foolish I believe to think of the tales as unaffected by external influence. In the same way that ballads travelled so did stories. As ballads were influenced by the invention of cheap printing so must tales have been. They are clearly related to short story lays like those of Marie de France and in the original are probably individual in phrasing and dialect within the limits of the idiom and the artistic ability of the teller. Each teller becomes in turn author-adaptor. The very complex story of *Seven in One Blow* has elements of the Polyphemus story, the sowing of the dragon's teeth, a mediaeval unicorn story, a comic Adonis and the boar passage and the cunning character of Ulysses. It's probably impossible to be certain of the origin of these themes but they could have had a literary origin before they went through the folk mill rather as Tom D'Urfey's songs can be heard modified but still recognizable from a traditional singer.

Translated into English the stories took on ever greater verbal homogeneity so that it was possible for Ruskin to write his story in convincing parody and Thackeray to poke gentle fun by imitation in *The Rose and the Ring*. However, what these literary stories gain on the conscious level, particularly in humor, they lose in unconscious depth. Gluck in *The King of the Golden River* is a youngest son. The dwarf king owes a lot to Huon's Oberon and is a suitably fierce little phallus. The elder brothers are properly punished by transformation and there's no sympathy for them but there's no underlying taboo situation either. The story is about greed, which is only occasionally a theme in the folk tales and then usually as a symbol of something else, as in *The Golden Goose*. Published in 1851 Ruskin's story was written for the twelve-year-old girl whom he later married although the marriage was never consummated. He seems to have lacked just that element that the story lacked. It was illustrated by one of the most famous of contemporary fairy painters, Richard Doyle, and was very popular. The highlights are the king himself and the trial on the mountain although this is given an aggressively Christian cast which its prototypes, *Fritz and His Friends*, *The Hut in the Forest*, from Grimm, don't have.

Andersen's stories are also thoroughly Christianized. No one goes to bed without saying his prayers and there is a great deal about goodness and innocence. With a few exceptions his tales are literary creations written with children particularly in mind. Some of them have a folk basis, *The Tinder Box* for example which is a Western Aladdin story with the three dogs as djinn of the tinder box itself. If this is an uninfluenced traditional tale the similarities are remarkable and a testimony to the likeness of human psychology which can throw up two such parallel stories so far apart.

The Garden of Paradise is another traditionally based story in which Andersen explicitly brings out the taboo nature of the fairy of the garden:

> . . . a song floated over him sweet and gentle as his mother's voice; it seemed as though she sang, "My child; my dear, dear child."
>   Then the Fairy beckoned gracefully, saying, "Come with me, come with me!" and he rushed to her.

He kisses her eyes where she lies sleeping and the garden sinks from sight with a clap of thunder. It's impossible to decide whether Andersen had made a conscious equation or quite what he expected his audience to infer from the juxtaposition of mother and fairy. If it isn't there in the original, which seems likely given the traditional idiom which prefers to express things through symbols, it reads like a suggestion thrown up by Andersen's unconscious as things often are in the course of a work of art.

The Snow Queen is another story that deals with this particular relationship from which Kay is rescued like Tam Lin by the human love of Gerda. A curious episode which once again seems to give away more than his conscious mind intended is the quasi-homosexual relationship of Gerda and the tomboy robber maid who sleeps with one arm round Gerda's neck and a dagger in the other hand. Nothing like her appeared in English children's literature for a long time. She must have been a great comfort to many girls who weren't of a patient Griselda nature or of Alice's cool demureness.

Many of the protagonists in Andersen's tales are girls. His most famous is of course *The Little Mermaid*, a castration story. The mermaid wishes to lose her tail so that she can become an ordinary girl and marry the prince. The usual folk meaning of the mermaid has been totally disregarded. This is no alluring siren irresistible to mortals nor even one of the kinder ones who occasionally occur saving the drowned or fulfilling wishes. She is a gentle loving creature who wants, as real mermaids never do, to leave the water. Her character indicates that she is a made-up figure yet the significance of the tail remains the same, except that it's her own.

Her hidden longing is symbolized by a desire for an immortal soul. Humans achieve immortality by reproducing themselves. Andersen was unmarried and apparently childless. He couldn't have a child himself because he was a man; he had a tail. The mermaid is willing to give up her tail but in return she must also lose her tongue, become dumb, and at every step she will feel that she is treading on knives. Added to this, unless she can make the prince marry her she will die. She becomes dumb after a secondary castration of the tongue which symbolizes the writer's fear of the loss of words. It would be worth it in return for the physical immortality of marriage and children. But the mermaid can't be sure of this. Indeed the prince is already in love with a very beautiful girl, human although a princess. Andersen's unconscious seems to be acting out a fantasy in which he gives up his tail (has it cut off hence the image of the knives) and his career as a writer to become a wife and mother. His conscious mind rejects this as a possibility and so the mermaid fails. The climax of the story is her attempt to murder the prince who has rejected her. With his death she can get back her tail. She must castrate him. This is an elaborate narrative of a male homosexual fear, recognized by psychiatrists, that the two partners castrate each other. One can only get back his tail at the other's expense, that is by forcing him to play a passive role.

However, this is only the more particular version of a general fear. Both men and women may be afraid of castration through intercourse, the woman by being reduced to passivity, the man by losing his penis in the woman. The universality of this fear gives *The Little Mermaid* its wide appeal whatever may have been the precise nature of its origin.

Andersen's version puts the blame firmly on the mother, the sea witch, for it's she who determines the child's sex in folk belief, either by her will or by what she eats or does during pregnancy. The sea witch also symbolically castrates the little mermaid's sisters by cutting off their hair in return for the dagger. Hair-cutting as in the story of Samson and Delilah induces impotence because head hair and pubic hair are interchangeable.

The Little Mermaid becomes an image of all our fears of castration in a sexual relationship, fears that must be overcome before we can happily go to bed even with someone we love. She doesn't resolve them except by sacrificing herself, but this is because the prince doesn't love her. Had he done so, Andersen suggests, all might have ended happily. As it is she gains a kind of immortality by a device that echoes the nature of the author's own, by becoming a singing airy spirit and visiting children as he did by writing stories for them.

A story with an authenticated autobiographical element is *The Red Shoes*. Karen, a poor child, is given a pair of red felt shoes which she wears to her mother's funeral. An old lady sees her and, taking pity on her, has the child to live with her. Karen believes she has done this because of her red shoes but the old lady has them burned. Again she gets a pair of red shoes which she wears unsuitably to her confirmation. The old lady is angry and the shoes are put away but the child gets them out and wears them to church, where an old soldier bewitches them. Her protectress falls ill and Karen must nurse her but there is a ball which she is unable to resist and she puts on the shoes and goes off to dance. She finds that she can't stop. The old woman dies. In desperation Karen dances up to the headsman's door and makes him cut off her feet which go dancing away before her. Eventually she is able to repent her vanity and goes to heaven.

Children in the nineteenth century had strong stomachs and heads. The gruesomeness of *The Red Shoes* would make it be regarded very askance if it were put forward as suitable television material for children's viewing. Such material was however common in the period particularly in a context of punishment for sin.[16] What it betrays again is Andersen's castration fantasy. I have already discussed the phallicness of feet and similarly of the magic color red.

[16] See Avery, op. cit., for a discussion and documentation of this point.

Here they are combined. The punishment of dancing for ever is an old one[17] and Andersen probably knew of it. The autobiographical element he records in his account of his life is the pair of new boots that distracted him during his confirmation. A further incident is his emotional adoption by the Conference-Councillor Collin who became a second father to him.

What he expresses through his identification with Karen is first his guilt at having left his parents and his poor background to go to Copenhagen and become a writer. Karen is punished on one level for pursuing vanity at the expense of God and the people who have been good to her. It is the obverse of the Ugly Duckling whose early sufferings and slights are rewarded when he becomes a swan, a happy image of Andersen's own career and one of the few in a collection where the overruling tone is sad, with the only happiness to be found in an eventual heaven. Even the happy endings come only after almost overwhelming misfortune and are often ambiguous.

Karen's punishment is too hideous however for simple vanity and ingratitude and it is self-chosen. She elects in effect for castration rather than pleasure. Through indulgence she causes the death of her benefactor. Once she has begun she can't stop. It's better to have the instrument of her destructive pleasure cut off. The symbols show that the pleasure she must renounce is sexual. I read it as an image of Andersen's own renunciation.

As a rough guide the more traditional the story the more likely it is to have a happy ending: *Great Claus and Little Claus, The Tinder Box, The Wild Swans, The Real Princess* and *The Fellow Travellers*. This last has a theme well known in England, for example in Peele's *Old Wives' Tale*, of a hero who gives money to bury a dead man and is helped by his ghost. It has the highest concentration of fairy lore. There are trolls, flower elves, nisses —a sort of Danish brownie with a red cap; fernseed for making people invisible and magic ointment. The story turns on a love test by a princess enchanted by a monstrous troll king who demands the sacrifice of all her would-be lovers, a plot we

[17] For example the dancers of Colbeck in *Handlying Synne* by Robert Manning, begun 1303.

have already met in several lands and periods. Although rich in allusions it lacks the urgency of other stories, except perhaps in the devotion of the ghostly friend who acts as a counter-magician to win the princess for the hero.

The literary fairy tale, like the traditional, works best when it has a solid psychosymbolic core. Without this it's inclined to be thin and hollow. No amount of overwriting however beautiful can compensate for the structural weakness that comes from not having used the machinery of enchantment with meaning rather than as ornament. Some of our most praised science fiction suffers from this but it's a tendency which can already be detected in Andersen's descriptive passages which foreshadow the nostalgic lushness of Ray Bradbury.

Much of the increased sentimentality of the Andersen stories, which is there particularly in the presentation and the endings, must be attributed to the greater infusion of nineteenth-century Christianity. The Grimms' collection, taken down at the end of the eighteenth century, knows no more of this than *Gulliver's Travels*. Christianity in Andersen is itself treated as part of supernatural myth but the part that is unreservedly believed. From the rationalism of the Deists religious belief had entered a new mystical phase. The fairy story as children's novel was seized on as a way of putting over Christianity to children but in the course of doing so writers unwittingly worked out their own emotional concerns. The idiom they had chosen imposed its own conventions on them. If they allowed their imaginations to work through the conventions the result could be artistic success; otherwise it was merely another tract.

In spite of its unappetizing combination of muscular Christianity and patriotism, Kingsley's *The Water Babies* does work simply because of its imaginative power. It was published in 1863 and addressed to Kingsley's youngest son Grenville Arthur to whom it's dedicated and who is apostrophized throughout as "my little man." Kingsley continues and expands the element of scientific credibility introduced by Voltaire in stories like *Micromégas*, an element that was to become the dominant in science fiction, obscuring for many people its true nature as a branch of the faery genre.

Nothing but its imaginative power could account for the long popularity of *The Water Babies*. The idea of the little chimney sweep who becomes a gilled elf only four inches long owes something obviously to Tom Thumb, something to Kingsley's interest in evolution and something to a pre-birth fantasy about the little boy it's addressed to. Tom is at one and the same time the questing penis and the unborn foetus in its amniotic fluid. Grimes the sweep is his wicked black father; his fairy mother I have already mentioned. The book's ethic is concerned with how a boy may resist temptation and grow up pure to marry. "And what was the song which she sang? Oh, my little man, I am too old to sing that song, and you too young to understand it. But have patience, and keep your eye single, and your hands clean, and you will learn some day to sing it yourself, without needing any man to teach you."

Whether he realized it or not Kingsley's main aim was to try to stop the little boy masturbating. The obsession with washing in cold water, with Tom's and other people's dirtiness, and the tell-tale "keep your hands clean" if you wish to grow up and gain the beautiful She, Ellie, which is the book's climax, pinpoint this. Those who have followed the symbols of the folk tales will recognize the otter which wants to eat Tom, the truncheon which beats Mr. Grimes stuck in a chimney with a pipe that won't draw, Tom's crimes of popping stones into sea anemones' mouths and stealing lollipops.

Tom forgives Mr. Grimes as Ellie forgives Tom for appearing all black and ugly in her clean pretty bedchamber, frightening her with attempted rape in the metaphor of coming down her chimney while she is asleep. Like the traditional tales the book amazes by its psychological consistency and the appropriateness of its detail. To those looking for conscious consistency in the working out of a scheme of ideal education, of punishment and crime, *The Water Babies* is bound to appear an "inchoate mass"[18] but when we remember that the result of masturbation was generally thought at this time to be impotence and madness, while sexual laxity was thought to be inevitably followed by venereal disease then "the very saddest part of all

[18] Avery, op. cit., p. 48.

my story," Tom's obsession with the hidden sweets, his stealing and sickening himself and growing prickles all over, make sense. It is arguable that if you truly although mistakenly believe that if he masturbates your child will go mad by simple process of nature, then you are as bound to be worried and try to stop him as you would from burning himself with a hot poker.

Whether Kingsley knew consciously what his concern was I can't say but it is stamped all over the story which no doubt mirrors his own fears about masturbation. "Those that will be foul, foul they will be," the Irishwoman warns Grimes when he tries to stop Tom washing. Without external evidence from the author's letters or notes there's no way of being sure how far the precise meaning of this was clear to him any more than we can know whether Perrault understood Puss's boots or a Black Forest peasant the Goose Girl's secret as he told it to the brothers Grimm.

CHAPTER XVII

Goblin Market

Must your light like mine be hidden,
Your young life like mine be wasted,
Undone in mine undoing
And ruined in my ruin,
Thirsty, cankered, goblin-ridden?

Christina Rossetti

The vogue for fairy painting may be said to have really got under way with Blake and Fuseli, though Reynolds and Romney both produced versions of Puck but more as an outcropping of interest in the theater and portraiture. Blake studies are already so numerous that there's little point in even commenting in a book of this length and in any case he lies, as so often, rather outside the mainstream. Nor do I want to enter that chicken and egg controversy on Blake and Fuseli and who cribbed from whom. For the purposes of fairy development however the prize for sheer weight of contribution must go to Fuseli.

Perhaps an element of chauvinism in that he was English by adoption, Swiss by birth has made him less well known in this country than he deserves. Undoubtedly he set the tone and the subject-matter for the fantastic for a hundred years at least. The themes which he illustrates and the grotesque mannerist style can be seen again in the work of Beardsley a century later. Above all it is the grotesquerie of the erotic which is his specific contribution to the art of the nineteenth century, the alternative tradition to the pop idealization of the Pre-Raphaelites who deal in the same subject-matter but with a high blush of naturalistic Romanticism.

His themes are from Shakespeare, Spenser, Milton, the *Niebelungenlied* and *Parsifal*, strongly influenced by the German and Swiss Romantic movement derived from English eighteenth–century Gothick. It was no accident that Fuseli chose to settle in this country for his early intellectual development in Zurich had been thoroughly anglicised.[1] His most complete fairy paintings are those which

[1] See F. Antal, *Fuseli Studies* (Routledge and Kegan Paul, 1956), I, Early Years.

he did for Boydell's Shakespeare Gallery 1789-1804, but there are many others including drawings, some of which were done for his own abortive Milton Gallery.

The mingling of the grotesque and the erotic is particularly clear in the two paintings at present in the Tate Gallery, "Titania and Bottom" and "The Peasant's Dream from Paradise Lost."[2] The Titania picture is one of several on this subject. Bottom sits with his ass's head and his peasant's bare muscular legs and feet while Titania caresses him and her fairies are grouped about. Fuseli has a series of courtesan drawings, unequivocally labelled, and from these his .women, slyly provocative and unmistakably as sexually bizarre as the ladies of Longhi or Beardsley, are derived. These appear as Titania's ladies-in-waiting while she herself is simply the most lustrously desirable of them. Around gambol or crouch miniscules and goblins with animal attributes. A further painting in the series includes Oberon, a mannerist baroque figure emotionally the male counterpart of Titania but curiously without genitals. The belly narrows to a smooth neck between the thighs causing one to wonder whether this is a personal preference or a bow to contemporary morality. The conventional wisp of cloud or leaf would be less disturbing than this obvious castration. The same crowd appears with mutations in the "Peasant's Dream" which corresponds to lines 781-88 in Book I of *Paradise Lost* and is a simile for the shrinking of Satan's legions to elf size before entering Pandemonium.

This subject is itself used in a painting by John Martin, the visionary painter of the grandiose who took England and Europe by storm later in the century. The fallen angels are shown shrunk to winged midgets, very like the fairy figures in Turner's "Queen Mab's Cave," and backed by lowering Dantesque landscape.

A further development of this Fuseli painting is the dream picture, particularly by J.A. Fitzgerald, who specialized in sleeping figures surrounded by demon goblins of a Bosch-like intensity. Fuseli has another favorite theme

---

[2] The drawing for this second is wrongly labelled in Antal, op. cit., as "Guyon's Dream from The Faerie Queen." I take it the responsibility for the attribution is that of the Albertina Gallery where it hangs in Vienna, not the author's. The moon in the drawing is specifically referred to in Milton's lines.

akin to this: the nightmare. Sometimes it crouches, a cross between ape and demon, on the chest of a contorted sleeper, sometimes it plunges in horse shape in or out of the bedroom window. At least three of Fitzgerald's dream pictures show the shadowy desire figures of a man and woman beyond the sleeper who is attended by goblins.

The most illuminating literary commentary on this fascination with the grotesque is Christina Rossetti's *Goblin Market*. It contains another favorite Victorian pair, the sisters who appear repeatedly in paintings and drawings from Millais to Sargent. This double female image is an interesting component of the period's eroticism akin to the heterosexual male desire to see blue films about lesbians or for similar themes in the work of Courbet, Lautrec or Schiele. Ostensibly the kinship and innocence of the girls deprives it of eroticism but in fact it merely represses it. Two girls entwined

> Cheek to cheek and breast to breast
> Locked together in one nest

are no longer individuals but duplicate feminine images ripe for polygamy. Laura in the poem tastes the goblin fruits and pines. Lizzie

> Longed to buy fruit to comfort her,
> But feared to pay too dear.
> She thought of Jeanie in her grave,
> Who should have been a bride;
> But who for joys brides hope to have
> Fell sick and died
> In her gay prime

Jeanie like Laura had eaten goblin fruit. Unable to hold out Lizzie goes to the goblins and tries to buy from them. They try in turn to push the fruits into her mouth. She runs home with the juice dripping down her face and begs her sister

> Did you miss me?
> Come and kiss me.
> Never mind my bruises

> Hug me, kiss me, suck my juices
> Squeezed from goblin fruits for you
> Goblin pulp and goblin dew.
> Eat me, drink me, love me;
> Laura make much of me

The "fruit forbidden" is sexual experience before marriage but the emotion between the sisters is hardly less strong than what the goblins offer, indeed in the poem ultimately stronger, and the dedication to Christina's elder sister Maria Francesca, and the knowledge that she refused marriage on religious grounds, fit the poem perfectly.

Throughout her life Christina Rossetti was obsessed with an advancing apprehension of evil. "How dreadful to be eternally wicked," she is reported to have said once, "for in hell you must be eternally so." This is already apparent in *Goblin Market*, yet it's difficult to be precise about the nature of it although at first glance it seems easy. Sex is equated with eating forbidden fruit, both traditionally and psychologically a common equation. But the second sister's redemption of the first is more difficult to interpret. It suggests the assuaging of Laura's thirst by non-sexual affection. What then is her traffic with the goblins and indeed what precisely has Laura done? Who are the goblins? In the case of the ill-fated Jeanie she was to have been a bride so the goblins for her may have been intercourse with her husband-to-be. Laura is in no such position.

From their description the goblins represent animal instincts. They coo like doves. Laura has no money. She pays them with a curl. By the usual transposition we know it is pubic hair. The image of her eating the fruit is a powerful masturbatory fantasy of feeding at the breast. She "sucked their fruit globes fair and red."

> She sucked and sucked and sucked the more
> Fruits which that unknown orchard bore;
> She sucked until her lips were sore

The result is the contemporary classic description of the habitual masturbator.

The pale complexion, the emaciated form, the slouching gait, the clammy palm, the glassy or leaden eye, and the averted gaze, indicate the lunatic victim to this vice.

Apathy, loss of memory, abeyance of concentration power and manifestation of mind generally, combined with loss of self-reliance, and indisposition for or impulsiveness of action, irritability of temper, and incoherence of language, are the most characteristic mental phenomena of chronic dementia resulting from masturbation . . .

writes an eminent surgeon and physician.[3]

Laura sits up in bed

in a passionate yearning
And gnashed her teeth for baulked desire, and wept.

"Her hair grew thin and grey," "she dwindled," "she no more swept the house" or did any of her other tasks but "sat down listless in a chimney nook/ And would not eat," until she seems "knocking at death's door."

When Lizzie goes in her turn to the goblins they are mostly in phallic bird and fish forms. The temptation for her seems closer to fellatio.

Bob at our cherries
Bite at our peaches.

The goblins "stretch up" to her and, thwarted, claw at her and pull her hair, hold her hands and squeeze the fruit against her mouth. The assault is a little equivocal. The girl "Would not open lip from lip/ Lest they should cram a mouthful in" which suggests attempted rape. Laura's reaction as she kisses and kisses her sister is a violent image of spontaneous orgasm while she "gorged on bitterness without a name" and finally fell down in a swoon. For the two sisters the goblins aren't real but fantasy sex and the temptation for each is therefore subtly different. Contemplating

[3] William Acton, *The Functions and Disorders of the Reproductive Organs*, 1857.

her sister's aroused eroticism (since they shared the same bed she could hardly avoid it), rouses Lizzie's sexual curiosity but she resists. Laura is able to slake hers on her sister and her affection for her, not surprisingly since Lizzie will be the image of her mother, and so fulfill her homosexual fantasy. Appropriately Laura has the last word, telling their children of the episode and that "there is no friend like a sister."

Often in fairy paintings the subject simply provides an excuse for painting the naked female form but these are some of the least interesting among the pictures although possibly more remunerative than the goblin ones. Strands of rather pale nymphs whirl through the sky or along "these yellow sands" in compositions derived from apotheoses via Fuseli and Blake. The courtesan element in Fuseli's fairies touches both a traditional element in the stories of fairy mistresses and a contemporary one in the idea that nice women don't enjoy sex.

> As a general rule, a modest woman seldom desires any sexual gratification for herself. She submits to her husband, but only to please him; and, but for the desire for maternity, would far rather be relieved from his attentions. No nervous or feeble young man need, therefore, be deterred from marriage by any exaggerated notion of the duties required from him. The married woman has no wish to be treated on the footing of a mistress.[4]

The mistresses and prostitutes, "loose and vulgar women," where drawn from the lower classes. The combination of the ideal and the forbidden in the fairy female therefore fulfilled a specific need alongside the classical nymphs and Venuses. Etty's "The Fairy of the Fountain" shows a nude girl with dove and small naked putto. Unless somewhere along the line the picture has been wrongly catalogued this is a Venus bathing with Cupid under another guise. Yet the classical doesn't as a rule spill into the goblin.

Goblins themselves are evil thoughts, and this remains

---

[4] William Acton, op. cit.

their meaning in George MacDonald's famous novel for children *The Princess and the Goblin* published in 1872. Although it is a thoroughly worked out allegory it nevertheless seems impossible that children could have read it as such and in the one case where I have been able to check a child's response to it at the beginning of this century the answer has been, even from a strict religious upbringing, no. The adult reading it is first gently aware of the allegory and then relieved that it is never made specific. It's quite possible to read the whole book without any idea that the fairy woman who changes shape so often is divine grace or faith or that the goblins are powers of evil in a rather precise sense. It's not so easy in its sequel, *The Princess and Curdie*, 1883, where the allegory is much more intrusive. Here the evils are people who have the souls and sometimes the bodies of animals. The goblins' lowness is expressed by their living in the mines. They are specifically identified with the Cornish buccas[5] but are also from the underground of the spirit.

Grotesquerie runs through many of the illustrations to children's books. Both Tenniel and Cruikshank have it. The original frontispiece illustration to *Through the Looking Glass* of the Jabberwock had to be displaced to the appropriate place in the text because it was so terrifying. The drawing has, I believe, influenced the beasts in *The Princess and Curdie* and Beardsley's Questing Beast in the *Le Morte D'Arthur* illustrations.

Richard Doyle, illustrator of *Punch* and twenty odd books for children apart from those for adults, shows an interesting dichotomy in his treatment of fairies. His most famous fairy book is *In Fairyland*, 1870, with text by Rossetti's Irish friend, William Allingham. Critical opinion differs sharply about these famous illustrations. Jeremy Maas in his excellent chapter on fairy painting in *Victorian Painters* says: "There is no hint of mawkishness, a common pitfall in fairy painting, although there is a faint hint of cruelty." Yet K.M. Briggs in *The Fairies in Tradition and Literature* finds the opposite. I don't dispute the cruelty; there's often cruelty in Victorian fairy painting of

---

[5] Called by the German form for goblin of the mine "cobbold" in the book.

the little-boys-pulling-wings-off-flies kind with creatures being taunted by fairies, robbed or attacking in their turn. *In Fairyland* has a lot of this but there is mawkishness as well, particularly in the sequence of the courtship of a fairy by an elf round a large toadstool. This is kitsch unalloyed, the first real appearance of the garden gnome and toadstool, of Blyton and Fyleman, the brass piskey and wishing well for tourists.

The first actual appearance of the toadstool I have come across is in an illustration to Cholmondley-Pennell's *Puck on Pegasus* of 1861, a book of largely facetious poems, one in the metre of *Hiawatha*, which was reissued several times during the century with illustrations by Cruikshank, Tenniel, Doyle and others and which gave its name to a Beardsley design for the cover of *The Savoy* in 1896. The pointed-eared Puck is sitting on a toadstool thumbing his nose. A drawing to another contribution *Song of In-The-Water* has goblins, wingless but flying, with a toadstool. The fairy ring is traditionally the dark circle made by a fungus, Shakespeare's "green-sour ringlets,/ whereof the ewe not bites," but the toadstool in fairy iconography seems a late-comer although an appropriate one. I wonder if it was introduced into England, certainly it was underlined, by William Allingham, as are the red caps and green jackets of the elves. From now on Ireland was to have an increasingly strong influence on the common fairy tradition. Allingham may also have been responsible for *Goblin Market*. His poem *The Fairies*, "Up the airy mountain," remarkably anticipates, in 1855, the plot of the goblins of the later poem. Christina Rossetti must have known it through his friendship with her brother.

The elves *In Fairyland* display the phallic redcaps but their bodies and faces are those of children, soft and smooth. Elves are boys, fairies are girls; a new mythology has been established. The childlikeness can't be laid exclusively to Doyle. Two paintings of Ariel by Joseph Severn dated 1826 show the process in action with Ariel a smooth pre-adolescent, a slim cupid, on the bat's back or sucking flowers. The childish love element is Doyle's however, an attempt to desexualize a relationship the Victorians found difficult to handle. By putting it in these terms it was seemingly rendered innocent. To other, later eyes it appears coy and disingenuous. The symbols of red-capped elf and winged female which I've already discussed keep their meaning, the kiss is over the gigantic phallus toadstool, but the displacement onto children is either to deny the sexuality or unacknowledgedly kinky with the Victorian leaning towards suppressed paederasty. To turn back suddenly to the passion of Oberon and Titania or Launfal and his Fairy Queen is to suffer an emotional redshift. The Elfin Dance picture shows a child king and queen having quarrelled. The boy, wearing a little crown, sulks on a toadstool with his back turned.

This isn't to say that the image Doyle presents in this series is invalid. For its period it is perfectly valid and one remembers the comment of one countryman to a collecting folklorist that the fairies dress according to the time and place in which they are.

On the other hand many of Doyle's illustrations belong to the grotesque tradition. Here the cruelty is apparent too, supposedly with its edge laughed away, but to some tastes only enhanced by the distortion of the figures. "The Fairy Tree" has no real structure as a painting. It's simply an excuse to cram in dozens of tiny mutated figures.[6] The temptation of the Bosch-crowd seems to have been one of the strongest in fairy painting even when, as in the work of Sir Joseph Noel Paton, the figures are of a marshmallow softness. The same lusts and cruelties go on round the margins of his "The Reconciliation of Oberon and Titania" but Fairy King and Queen have become almost unrecognizably romanticised, robbing the composition of any impact. The cruelty needs some comment. The favorite object for this in Doyle's pictures is a bird, or birds. He is unconsciously following traditional symbolism in pitting one phallic symbol against another. At least it seems unconscious but Beardsley's use of the word "cockstand" and his comment, in a letter to Leonard Smithers of December 1896, "Yes *every*thing is phallic shaped . . . ," on his drawing of

[6] Most crowded of all is Richard Dodd's *The Fairy Fella's Master Stroke* where creatures of every kind gather round to watch the fairy split a nut with a tiny axe. Dodd was an inmate of the Bethlehem Royal Hospital after killing his father and took nine years over this picture. There is a similarity between this kind of picture and illuminated manuscripts crowded with grotesques.

an extracted tooth with three-pronged root, should perhaps alert us to nineteenth-century consciousness of sexual symbolism behind the drapes. The bird crushed underfoot in the "Lysistrata" drawing of women masturbating suggests that Beardsley was fully aware of the "bird in the bush."

The ambiguity of contemporary feelings towards women expresses itself most horrifically in a small painting by J. A. Fitzgerald called "The Fairy's Lake," with a goblin twisted into the form of a real knight, lance held in two-clawed paw, charging, on a bat-bird, a female fairy floundering with huge wings and submerged clothing in a cramped lake. Another tell-tale in Fuseli's "Titania and Bottom" is the courtesan Nimue with tiny tempters at her ears leading the aged, and subdued to one-fifth size, Merlin on a string. This theme of the wise old man enslaved by his passion for a young woman, known as well to mediaeval times in the story of Aristotle allowing Herpillis to side-saddle and ride him, was also painted by Burne-Jones in 1873 and later illustrated by Beardsley as an imperative in his Arthurian sequence.[7]

In this situation of unrelation between the sexes it's hard to decide who came off worst: Sir Launcelot or the Lady of Shalott, bound by a spell that forbade her to look on the real world. The poem was a favorite for illustration, particularly among the Pre-Raphaelites. Correctly magic is used for taboo sex but by this time it's quite simply any sex that has become forbidden for the nice woman. She's allowed her dreams, what she sees reflected in the idealizing mirror of art, novels, poems, paintings. Characteristically the shadows in the mirror are in terms of contemporary pictures, all of harmless subjects.

> Sometimes a troop of damsels glad,
> An abbot on an ambling pad,
> Sometimes a curly shepherd-lad,
> Or long-hair'd page in crimson clad

Then comes Sir Launcelot, a strident male figure, "flaming" and "bold" with "coal black curls," singing as he rides:

[7] The theme of mixed ages in an erotic context is common in Beardsley's work.

> And from his blazon'd baldric slung
> A mighty silver bugle hung

She leaves her magic loom and does the forbidden thing, looking down in desire on the real world and Launcelot's plumed helmet, again the working of unconscious symbol like the great plumed helmet of Otranto.

> Out flew the web and floated wide;
> The mirror crack'd from side to side

She suffers at once a metaphorical rape and the ideal is shattered. Her only course is repentance and death. The inhabitants are terrified by her gleaming form as respectable society was by any woman who broke the embargo even emotionally. Only Launcelot is left to make what could be thought a characteristic male comment that "She has a lovely face" and ask for God to be merciful to her.

> See him in the House of Commons
> Making laws to put down crime,
> While the victim of his pleasures
> Trails her way through mud and slime.[8]

Another inversion of the traditional view that nevertheless works emotionally for the period is Matthew Arnold's *The Forsaken Merman* which could chronologically have had some effect on Kingsley's *The Water Babies*.[9] This too is a story against a woman stepping off the straight and narrow, this time by becoming the mistress of a sea king. I say mistress although this is never mentioned in the poem but then, conspicuously, neither is wife. She is "mother," "dear heart" and "loved one." The merworld is without religion, therefore without marriage.

> She said: "I must go, for my kinsfolk pray
> In the little grey church on the shore today
> Twill be Easter-time in the world—ah me!
> And I lose my poor soul, Merman! here with thee."

[8] Anonymous ballad, "She was Poor but She was Honest."
[9] 1849 and 1863 respectively.

It is the fear of Hind Etin's wife. But Margaret, unlike her forerunner, leaves her children behind. She is that least to be forgiven of Victorian women, the heartless mother. Even the comforts of the church won't make her forget "the strange cold eyes of a little Mermaiden/ And the gleam of her golden hair." The merking rubs in both this and his own loneliness. But beneath this surface of Victorian pathos, which is all of a piece with *East Lynne*, are two other layers: the traditional one in which the merman is Margaret's father and the story is an oedipal fantasy, and the underlying contemporary morality which said that nice women didn't enjoy sex. What was Margaret doing under the sea having children by a man, even if he was half fish, to whom she wasn't married? Clearly it was his tail she was drawn to and this is why it's quite all right for her to repent and leave him and sing "most joyfully" while she spins.

There's also something of the period's penchant for the dead mother[10] in the final picture of the merman and his children returning on fine moonlight nights to gaze at the town,

> Singing: There dwells a loved one,
> But cruel is she!
> She left lonely for ever
> The kings of the sea.

Obviously too the merman wants her back but all he offers is sex and money in the form of the sea treasures, amber, pearl and redgold, while she is deprived of human society and the comforts of religion as a kept woman. One thinks of Gladstone wandering the streets at night attempting the rescue of fallen women. Because the story is told by the forsaken merman, readers today may miss the very real equivocalness which made it so popular although the volume in which it originally appeared was unsuccessful and soon withdrawn. It too has become a children's poem.

At either end of the century like two terminal gods stand the masters of fantasy, Fuseli and Beardsley. I'm unable to

---

[10] See Avery, op. cit., for children and death in the literature of the nineteenth century.

find any circumstantial evidence that Beardsley knew Fuseli's work except for two oblique comments in Robert Ross's memoir, that he did know the British Museum thoroughly, where he might have studied Fuseli's Roman notebook, and that for his illustrations to *The Rape of the Lock* he turned to eighteenth century painters including Pietro Longhi, who has affinities in emotional tone and treatment with both Fuseli and Beardsley. Once again it's a question of diffusionism or spontaneous creation by a like imagination, and as so often the answer is likely to be a combination of both.

This is not the book in which to make an elaborate survey of all the points of similarity between Fuseli and Beardsley in subject-matter and in treatment, visual and emotional, but one or two likenesses can be indicated. The first is in the treatment of young women: Fuseli's courtesan-fairies; Beardsley's Arthurian fairies, women of the *Lysistrata* and miscellaneous females. They have in common the erotic delineation of clothing and built up hair-styles[11] and the sly, cool expressions. Another similarity is in the clothing of fairy figures in human flesh and period costume. Beardsley's Ariel is an eighteenth-century beau without wings, with nothing of the obviously supernatural about him as he whispers through the bed-curtains. The Titania of Fuseli's "Titania's Dream"[12] sleeps propped on one elbow, an open book fallen from her hand, like a Jane Austen heroine on a window seat. Two other pictures by Beardsley strongly recall Fuseli: "The Murders in the Rue Morgue" where the dangling girl is strongly reminiscent of the curious drawing "Die Fee"[13] and "The Black Cat" which suggests Fuseli's demon nightmares. These are random choices from many possible comparisons.

I have mentioned the similarity of subject-matter which a simple rundown of contents would confirm. But Beards-

[11] Cf. Fuseli's "Woman seen from the Back," plate 62 in Antal, op. cit., with Beardsley's "Rape of the Lock, The Toilet" in particular, but the treatment of hair and hats in general in both. Also compare for clothes Beardsley's "Katherine Klavinsky" and Fuseli's "Woman in front of a Fireplace," Antal, 32.

[12] Plate 61, Powell, *The Drawings of Henry Fuseli* (Faber and Faber, 1951).

[13] Plate 100, Ganz, *Die Zeichnungen Hans Heinrich Füselis* (Bern, 1947).

ley's oeuvre is the culmination of all that has gone on in the preceding century added to Fuseli's vision of the erotic and the macabre. At the same time it is a denial of those who would prettify the fantastic. In Beardsley's hands the baby elf becomes foetus or cupid; the grotesques of Cruikshank and Doyle inspire the astounding inventions of the Bon-Mots vignettes, with every mutation of the diabolical; the Pre-Raphaelite illustrations of Walter Crane are caught up into the *Le Morte D'Arthur* series. Picture after picture expresses the magic of taboo, the things that daren't be said, the associations that daren't be made. Satyrs show their hooves in drawing-rooms, clogged pierrots, latterday fools, pale anti-goblins, stroll past the telephone wires: no hallucination seems out of place.

Above all Bearsley time is elsewhere, as time is in the surreal dreamscapes of Spenser and it's partly this that makes all things possible and inevitable. His pictures are stills in the very precise sense that there is no movement towards or away from them. Even the facial expressions are caught and held, transfixed like dead butterflies in the now of the Never-Never Land.

Beardsley seems not to have completed a projected design for *The Rape of the Lock* which would have shown us the sylphs and we can only speculate from Ariel and Umbriel. We can know that they wouldn't have been the naked ladies with butterfly wings of Walter Crane's illustrations to *The First of May*: a fairy masque, but closer to Titania's courtesans by Fuseli. Nowhere has Beardsley given us a simple fairy as such but in an unused poster design for *The Yellow Book* he has two figures I'm tempted to label Fairy Queen and Puck. The queen's head-dress is, as so often in Fuseli, a mothlike creature with spread wings. On her outstretched hand stands a mop-headed dwarf, with pointed ears and satyr horns, in pierrot clothes: perverse madonna and child, Venus and Cupid. The names are interchangeable. Black mother, the witch, is there too in his work, as Messalina, Herodias, *An Evil Motherhood*, Erda. The credibility factor which Burne-Jones and Watts attempted to supply by historical naturalism he achieves by the authority of his technical mastery and invention. However fantastic we no longer ask if it is true: it quite simply and rightly is.

CHAPTER XVIII

Do You Believe in Fairies?

Can you wonder that People of the Hills don't care
to be confused with that painty-winged, wand-waving,
sugar-and-shake-your-head set of impostors? Butterfly wings indeed! . . . It was Magic—Magic as black
as Merlin could make it . . .

Puck of Pook's Hill, Rudyard Kipling

Nothing is more surprising in the history of faery than the consistency and continuity of the images and their symbolic content. Whatever the medium through which they are projected, they remain recognizably the same though given a new burst of life by a new idiom as if they were their own metaphor of shape-changing. They survive equally in painting, film, poem, tone poem, opera, sculpture and decorative motif.

Relationships between the faery world and orthodox belief have been complex and shifting, from the fulminations of St. Augustine to the exploitations of C. S. Lewis. If it is valid to advance the longevity of belief in a god as evidence for his existence, one might equally advance, as evidence against, the longevity of unbelief in the fairies. The continuity of a system of images unsupported by literal credence and an organized church is itself a comment on the nature of other related image systems. In its occasional attempts to keep the supernatural field open the Church has shown that it understands that it's only too possible that the holy baby will get thrown out with the magic bathwater.

On the other hand those who find the holy baby difficult to take may be anxious to keep some supernatural solution. This was the feeling of many people in the first quarter of this century. Madame Sosostris and the Cottingley Fairies provided a frisson from the numinous for some; theosophy and spiritualism a more inclusive system for others. Black magic had a new vogue with Aleister Crowley; Yeats in a state of mythological DTs saw fairies much as others might see pink rats. Eminent people went nowhere and did nothing without first consulting their favorite soothsayers[1] and packing their talismans.

The renewed Christian fervor of the nineteenth century had spent itself in internecine warfare and the attempt to come to terms with Darwinism. Like any state concerned with internal conflict the Church siphoned off dangerous interest by engaging in external missionary war with heathenism. The rapid development of empire enabled both sons and daughters to escape the heavy paternalism of the earlier period. The fear of Jacobinism began to fade; socialism and unspecific deism became once more tenable alternatives. Yet as the nineteenth century neared its end a new fear was manifested, epitomized in the death of Victoria, the second "faery queen" as Disraeli called her. "One phrase was on my lips—God help us."[2]

The new era brought, it seemed, a new freedom, the blossoming of the gay nineties into the Edwardian era. Inevitably it brought a new hidden fear, the other face of any rebellion against parent figures. Something had to be placated: fate and luck if God was dead. At the same time the greater freedom brought a burgeoning of the imagination. Wilde's doctrine that "Art never expresses anything but itself" was restated by Yeats in defence of the Abbey Theatre's right to put on unpopular plays, and Wilde's statement that "the mythopoeic faculty" was "essential for the imagination" became, however unwittingly, the carte blanche on which Yeats wrote all his works. Similarly Wilde's use of the fairy story, "to mirror modern life in a form remote from reality" and as "a reaction against the purely imitative character of modern art" encouraged the use of the fantastic and the faery as imaginative material.

The fairy story was in Wilde's blood inherited from both his parents who were folklorists. Indeed his mother's book on Irish folklore is still a standard reference work. The Victorian literary forms which he was born into he found unstimulating, possibly because of this early inheritance of the Irish fantastic, and he was driven to re-invent: restoration comedy, Gothick novel, Socratic dialogue, gallows

[1] This had begun by at least the end of the nineteenth century. Both Oscar and Constance Wilde for example consulted the fortune-teller Mrs. Robinson.

[2] E. Longford, *Victoria RI*, Chapter XXXVI.

goodnight and fairy tale. He was equivocal about whether these last were intended for children or not. To excuse the writing of them at all, he said in letters to Gladstone and G. H. Kersley that they were "really meant for children" and "meant partly for children, and partly for those who have kept the childlike faculties of wonder and joy." Later when the second small collection, *The House of Pomegranates*, was criticized by the reviewer of the *Pall Mall Gazette* for being of doubtful suitability for children, Wilde answered: "I had about as much intention of pleasing the British child as I had of pleasing the British public."

Wilde himself acknowledged the note of doom in the stories, particularly in *The Happy Prince* and *The Young King*, recognizing obliquely[3] the autobiographical element in them. As K. M. Briggs has rightly pointed out in *The Fairies in Tradition and Literature* the form and tone of Wilde's stories are derived from Andersen but they may also owe something to the fairy stories for adults, short romances published at the beginning of the nineteenth century in cheap threepenny editions rather like the later twopenny novelettes, and something too to his native tradition. Certainly it was a very easy step for Yeats from Wilde's stories to the full use of Irish legend in plays and poems. The complete study of them belongs more to Wildeana than here, but one or two points can be made.

Hesketh Pearson in his biography of Wilde says:

> Like all who have expressed themselves in stories or plays for children, from Hans Andersen to James Barrie, he was emotionally undeveloped. Even Dean Swift, who must have been revolving in his grave ever since Gulliver became a favourite in the nursery, was strongly immature in that respect . . .[4]

But Swift was not expressing himself for children but for adults as was Wilde, and Dickens, Defoe and Scott have all become nursery fare too. Are they also "immature"? There

[3] In the long letter from prison to Lord Alfred Douglas commonly known as *De Profundis*.

[4] Hesketh Pearson, *The Life Of Oscar Wilde* (Methuen, 1946), p. 137.

really aren't many writers who don't in some way fall into this category.

What is striking in Wilde's stories is the tendency to fantasize about self-immolation and rejection. There's hardly a "happy ever after" among them. Anyone who had read them with any attention need not have been surprised at Wilde's failure to leave the country when he had the opportunity between trials. It's the devoted swallow who dies at the feet of the Happy Prince when winter comes, as Wilde himself longed to die when he was first imprisoned. *The Birthday of The Infanta* is a mirror of that ugliness he must have seen in himself, the too large head inherited from his mother along with the heavy mouth and jaw. Most noticeable in several of the stories is the sense of guilt, the betrayal of the star-child and of the fisherman who falls in love with a mermaid for whom he gives up his own soul, for a creature beautiful, feminine but tailed, only to betray love. This, like *The Picture of Dorian Gray*, is a projection of Wilde's unconscious desire with its attendant guilt: if I do this will I be punished? The fairy story is being used in its customary function to embody a taboo situation.

Yeats himself added nothing new to the faery traditions. He simply took them as they were along with classical mythology, Christian, Catholic and Byzantine, and used them as naturally as Kipling used India as a source of imagery. By rejecting Christianity as a unique spiritual revelation he cut himself off from the roots of Irish faction. The gap was filled by Irish legend and folklore. The rigid Protestant-Catholic cleavage was to Yeats the death of the imagination and of art and he wanted no part of it. Similarly he was forced eventually to reject the simple dualism of the Irish Nationalist struggle. However, these two rejections, rooted in the earlier one of his own impoverished childhood, left an imaginative vacuum to be peopled with the whole of human culture and a guilt to be assuaged by a devotion to Ireland's mythical past that could paper over the torn loyalties of her present. It meant, too, that Yeats lived as much in his imagination as other people do in their present; the "pavements grey" transmute with hardly a tremor to the Lake Isle of Innisfree.

Yeats saw both the consistency and the psychological pattern at the heart of all myth.

> Man, woman, child (a daughter or a son)
> That's how all natural or supernatural stories run.

The myth was more important than the reality; art than truth. Appropriately Yeats brought letters of support for Wilde from Ireland. He took from him a theory of art that supported Yeats for the rest of his life.

At their best Wilde's doctrines lead to surrealist jewelled Byzantium but they could also let in the fey and whimsical.

> One morning the old Water-rat put his head out of his hole. He had bright beady eyes and stiff grey whiskers, and his tail was like a long bit of black indiarubber. The little ducks were swimming about in the pond, looking just like a lot of yellow canaries and their mother, who was pure white with real red legs, was trying to teach them to stand on their heads in the water.

This, that reads like a first draft for *The Wind in the Willows*, is a story by Wilde, *The Devoted Friend*. Animals had already become popular in children's books, particularly through the efforts of Walter Crane beginning with *The Fairy Ship* in 1869, a deliberate attempt to provide something less grotesque in the way of illustration for children. The large clear colorful drawings are still the basis for much of the best work for very young children. In case there should be any doubt about the affinity between the white mice who man the fairy ship and customary fairies, the sailors all wear red elf caps.

Some kind of phallic identification is very important in the development of young children. The penis or its substitute is an extension of themselves which is nevertheless an object with a life of its own which can be addressed and made to respond. As well as the actual organ which little boys have, children of both sexes need symbols, actual in the shape of toys, dolls, soldiers, but also imaginary or fictional, the protagonists of stories. This period provided several of the classics in this field: Peter Pan, Puck, Mowgli, Kim, Rat, Mole, Toad, Mickey Mouse, Peter Rabbit. Where the Victorian emphasis had been on little girls, the Edwardians specialized in boys.

Peter Pan was first produced in 1904, based on games

which Barrie had played with the original Lost Boys, the children of the woman he was in love with. Quite simply it's about sex or more precisely about infantile sexuality and sexual curiosity. The youngest child Michael begins the theme by asking about his own birth. Then Wendy and John play an incestuous game of mothers and fathers in which they have just had a baby. This leads to the question of whether boys or girls are better, John showing a preference for a boy that upsets Wendy. Michael acts out some more of his birth fantasy and Mr. Darling appears to play the father with power of life and death but still his wife's child emotionally.

Into this family group comes Peter Pan, the boy who will never grow up. He lives in the Never Land of complete fantasy. He can fly and he must never be touched. He is the phallus of what psychologists recognize as the latency period when sexuality is expressed in a sublimated form as adventure, aggression and fantasy. This is what he has come to lead the children away to. Rightly Barrie has characterized this period when children are most separate from their parents and absorbed in a world which is quite distinct from the adult, existing within it like one Chinese box within another, later forgotten by most adults. It is the world of secret gangs and schemes. Its sexual curiosity is unconnected with emotion because the emotions in being severed from the parents have to be repressed until puberty when they can find new love objects. Curiosity and fantasy are both at their strongest.

Wendy is already almost too old for the Never Land. She is falling in love with Peter who is also loved by the Indian chief's daughter Tiger Lily and by the fairy Tinker Bell, who resembles Max Beerbohm's Queen of the Fairies being presented to George Moore by W. B. Yeats in the same year. She makes him play the part of father to the family of lost boys but he's only happy in this role as long as he knows it's pretend. The real father of the Never Land is Captain Hook, the natural enemy whom Peter has already tried to castrate by feeding his arm to a crocodile. Wendy however is only too happy in her mother role.

As the play progresses its structure becomes the familiar Oedipus-Uranos situation with the Lost Boys and the Pirates struggling for possession of the mother figure. Eventually Peter defeats Hook and rescues Wendy and the fantasy ends with the Darling children returning to their own home where their father has taken to the dog kennel in his shame. The defeat of Hook is paralleled in this way. Hopefully Wendy tries to persuade Peter to stay and "speak to her mother" but he refuses, preferring to remain a little boy and have adventures.

Much of his phallic character he has in common with Mowgli and Kim who preceded him. Had boys been caught behaving as all three do at this period they would have been punished but they are fantasy heroes not real boys. The exotic backgrounds of Kipling's characters work in the same way as the fantasy world of Barrie. All three are boastful, lying, agile, inventive and aggressive. Peter Pan and Mowgli are, like the traditional brownie, virtually naked; Kim assumes clothes only as disguises. Both Kim and Mowgli are able naturalistically to be brown; Peter Pan is so by virtue of being clothed in "autumn leaves and cobwebs." All of them are unwilling to be caught or confined, symbols of the free masturbatory penis. All are arrogant, unattached, with the overstated masculinity of the latency period when girls are basically "sissy" even though sometimes useful as hostages or objects to be fought over. Walt Disney was to create another version in *Pinocchio*. They aren't simply boys.

> Hook: Boy?
> Peter: Yes.
> Hook: Ordinary boy?
> Peter: No!
> Hook: Wonderful boy?
> Peter (to Wendy's distress): Yes!

Pinocchio is made of wood and trying to become a boy. Kim and Mowgli are both cast out from their human place and are therefore not ordinary boys: Mowgli, the boy forerunner of that other natural phallus hero of the period Tarzan,[5] because he has been brought up by the animals;

---

[5] Tarzan's swinging through the trees, so much a part of his iconography, is the logical equivalent of Peter Pan's flying.

Kim because he is white but has been brought up as a child of the bazaar. They are all threatened by human society and principally by school which stands for discipline, the curtailment of freedom and pleasure. They have no parents.

Their mischief and agility also mark them out as Puck figures with their ability to "get into anything." Gillian Avery in *Nineteenth Century Children* suggests[6] that this is a period attitude, an act of rebellion "by people who remembered the strict upbringing in vogue in the middle years of the [nineteenth] century" and that Kenneth Grahame's *The Golden Age*, 1895 and *Dream Days*, 1898 introduced this theme. *The Jungle Book* and its sequel appeared, however, in 1894 and '95. Mowgli's rebellion isn't just against adults; it's against people and human society, both its unnaturalness and its unimaginativeness.

Tarzan himself didn't appear until 1914. He is the contemporary equivalent of the Wild Man of the Woods and Spenser's Sir Satyrane. His mixed inheritance lets him behave with the freedom of the savage tempered by the supposed good breeding of an English aristocrat. The scene in which he first encounters Jane and wishes to rape her but is stopped by something stirring in his brutish mind lets the reading ego have it both ways; Edgar Rice Burroughs's formula for success.

This desire for greater sexual freedom found overt adult expression in the work of Henry Miller, D. H. Lawrence and James Joyce. Miller and Lawrence particularly wrote in celebration of the penis; a necessary piece of liberation at the end of a long repressive royal matriarchy which, however modified in fact, nevertheless existed to the corporate imagination. But theirs was only the visible tip. Wendy is distressed that the stories that Peter likes best are the ones about himself and "it is the boy's cockiness, which disturbs Hook."[7] Either comment could be made with hardly any change about Miller's tropical zones.

Peter has no wish to become the responsible father. It's Wendy who wants to make him.

---

[6] op. cit., pp. 183–5.

[7] Peter "crows" when he is pleased and at one point is mistaken by Hook for a "cock a doodle doo."

Wendy: Peter, what are you to me?
Peter (through the pipes): Your son, Wendy.
Wendy: Oh, goodbye.

The female wants to catch and tie down the free phallus but it wants only to be her lover, not a parent, and to move on at the end of the play to another younger little girl who would be simply the organic equivalent of his own free symbol-self. Peter's pipes he has from Pan and from Oberon. They are the traditional masturbatory fairy music and he always plays them at moments of deliberate self-absorption when he wants to cut himself off from Wendy's claims.

Least convincing and most sentimental in the play are the fairies and the moment at which Peter makes his appeal to the gods to save Tinker Bell by affirming their belief, a moment when Barrie shamelessly plays on a youthful audience to bolster his ego by demonstrating just how effective his theatrical magic is. The fairy lore is his own mawkish invention. Perhaps this is why it's so unconvincing, whereas with Peter he is drawing on and fusing already existing traditions. Fairies are said to be born every time a baby gives its first laugh and to die with a child's disbelief. Yet later in the play Wendy explains: "Their mothers drop the babies into the Never birds' nests, all mixed up with the eggs, and the mauve fairies are boys and the white ones are girls, and there are some colors who don't know what they are." Peter tells her that they are nearly all dead but she denies this to her mother. Tinker Bell is simply a little flying pudenda of female bitchiness and possessiveness.

The myth of childish innocence had taken a strong knock in 1898 with Henry James's story in *The Two Magics, The Turn of the Screw*. Here again the beautiful and desired object is a boy, Miles; his sister Flora is included for the sake of artistic symmetry and variation and because she was in the original anecdote as told to James by the Archbishop of Canterbury. The two children as their names show are simply male and female, soldier and flower. They have been "corrupted" by two previous servants. The corruption is real: the girl says terrible things to the elderly housekeeper that no nice little girl would know, the boy is sacked from school for saying things to boys he liked. He is in love with the dead servant Quint and longs to get back to the male milieu of school. But the new governess wants him for herself, flirts with him and tries to save him from his homosexuality personified in the ghost of Quint. Her desire under its cloak of puritanism torments him by suggesting that Quint is present in the room although the boy can't see him and the trauma kills him. The servants' influence on the children has been real but it's only the governess who sees the ghosts though the children would like to see them and wander about the house and grounds looking for the loved dead.

The supernatural has been used to embody a triple taboo of sex, age and class. To pretend that paederasty, particularly homosexual, was a subject to be discussed openly in literature at this period is a failure of historical sense. The trial of Oscar Wilde still reverberated. That children of good families might be corrupted by servants to the point of being quite unrepentant and turning their back on the conventional idea of goodness and sin as Miles and Fora do, that beauty and a shining appearance of innocence meant nothing and that the rot could be further spread through the best schools was a lot for society to accept even in literature.

Although the governess is horrified at what she finds in the children, James's telling of the story is equivocal as the many critical attempts to unravel his meaning prove.[8] By its nature, corruption involving the lower classes, the crime smacks of Wildean stableboys. Quint had been the young master's valet and worn his clothes. His relationship with his employer might also have been "too free." James gives the boy Miles great dignity and charm when he admits having said things to boys he liked and a real devotion to Quint which leads him finally to call the governess "you devil" and then to his death. Condemnation comes only from the women. The one man, the absentee master, deliberately doesn't want to know.

[8] For a brief discussion of the various critical viewpoints see Maxwess Geismar, *Henry James and His Cult*, p. 157 on. James himself opted out of the discussion in advance by calling the story "a piece of ingenuity pure and simple, of cold artistic calculation, an *amusette* . . ."

Miles is yet another "wonderful boy" in his "pretty waist-coats" and with "his grand little air, Miles's whole title to independence, the rights of his sex and situation, were so stamped upon him that if he had suddenly struck for freedom I should have had nothing to say."

The Wind in the Willows extended the preponderant maleness to the exclusive club of the river bank. Here are all types of animal symbol to suit a range of reader identifications. The only female figures are those who help Toad to escape from prison and although shrewd they are very much the lower order. I have already discussed the meaning of animal figures in unconscious symbolism and there is no need to repeat. All that applies to "the weary wanton moldiewarp," the witch's toad familiar and the mouse of Apollo applies to Mole, Rat and Toad. In old Badger they have an appropriate father figure but they are all under the aegis of the animal phallus himself as is the whole book, placed there in a chapter which children often find puzzling but which is perfectly understandable to adults. The god of the animals is the satyr, Pan, fitted logically into a post-Christian world as "the Friend and Helper." He is indistinguishable in appearance from the devil or naked hairy lust.

Grahame is trying to fit in some form of convincing religion to his animal world. The episode fails because the symbol he choses pokes through the banality of its function, which is a watered down version of the Christian god caring for the fall of a sparrow like an RSPCA inspector: "Helper and healer, I cheer—Small waifs in the woodland wet—Strays I find in it, wounds I bind in it—Bidding them all forget!"

Curiously this episode has affected a book for adults: E. M. Forster's collection of short stories *The Celestial Omnibus* which contains among others *The Story of A Panic*. The Edwardian desire for male sexual freedom faintly tinged with unconscious homosexuality takes the form of an adolescent boy possessed on holiday in Italy by Pan in a grove who becomes wild, free and filled with animal understanding. Here again are the piping, the hoofmarks, the awe and the prayers. Grahame had used the sentence: "It was no panic terror" which Forster modifies to the title.

The three hero animals of the river bank are three recognizable phallic or fool types; the gentle and rather sad pierrot Mole, the dashing imaginative harlequin Rat and the bouncing, boasting but essentially cowardly and foolish Pickleherring Toad. Their adventures are a species of harlequinade but without the Columbine although Badger provides a sympathetic pantaloon and several of the other stock figures appear in the Toad adventures which recall some of the situations undergone by Mr. Punch.

With his last important books for children Kipling reintroduced Puck himself. He has little of the brownie mischief. Indeed he's rather a sobersides but he has still the power to make wishes come true and to shape-change when he wants. He is "a small, brown, broad-shouldered, pointy-eared person with a snub nose, slanting blue eyes, and a grin," dressed in a dark blue cap, like a big columbine flower, and with "bare hairy feet." His appearance is authentic. What he does is to bring back episodes from the past, creating a device that has become a standard favorite of fantasy series on television and radio. *Dr. Who* stems directly from *Puck of Pook's Hill* by courtesy of Well's Time Machine.

Like James in *The Turn of the Screw*, Kipling has both a boy and a girl, Dan and Una, but there is little to choose between them. If anything Una has slightly the edge in intelligence and sympathetic characterization. The stories are told to the children; they don't become involved in them as in C. S. Lewis's and later fantasy tales. They are transported by the power of narration, not by a complete abdication of reason. Puck re-creates for them an added historical dimension as a conscious extension of Kipling's preoccupation with England, understandable in someone born in a distant part of the empire. The roots he finds in English history are parallel to those Yeats found in Irish myth and in both cases fill a personal gap.

> She is not any common Earth,
> Water or Wood or Air,
> But Merlin's Isle of Gramarye,
> Where you and I will fare.

As he grew older this need for a mother country was fined down to one county, Sussex, with its peculiarly long history and feminine mouldings of treeless downs. It has become a loved body marked like a middle-aged woman with the lines of love-making and children and even more attractive for it.

With the failure of organized religion and the all-absorbing march of industrialization like a galloping consumption, the urge to get away from it all that has manifested itself in different forms, in the twelfth-century passion for Arthurian romance and the late eighteenth century succumbing to romantic scenery for example, probably since the beginnings of civilization with its repressions and demands (the Greeks and Vikings founded colonies, the Romans dallied in the East and with mystery religions), and that is a basic human urge initially to get away from parents, looked for a new dimension to adventure in. Kipling breaks time like Wells. Other writers break credibility.

That "whole sensible appearance of things," which had caused the early Christian fathers such pangs in case it should keep men's minds from the supernatural with its strong magic, had so lost its power that twentieth-century man inverted the problem. Now it was the spell of the supernatural he hankered after to turn his mind from the dreariness of everyday, rushing even into the wholesale death of the First World War out of boredom and because his fantasy life had broken down in the endless laboring of industrial capitalism, backed by technology which ensured that he could go on working even when it grew dark, and all the year round, and that his life would conform as nearly as possible to that of the next man so that they could be satisfied in bulk. Monotheism had led to the monopolizing monolith of uniformity. The eccentricities of the Edwardian period are "the iridescence of decay" before the wasteland.

From now on the concepts of mass and the masses become inescapable and a new art medium sprang up, an overnight fairy ring, to cater for mass fantasy. What was new was that the same work could be presented simultaneously to millions of people. The concept wasn't of course new; it was already contained in the copying of manuscripts in the scriptorium, in copies of a picture by an artist or his studio and in engravings, not to mention performance before an audience, but the scale and the uniformity were new. Even printing isn't as exact as photography. One print of a film could be screened for years.

There was further uniformity in the nature of photography since it reproduced exactly what was put before it as many nineteenth-century painters had mistakenly been trying to do. The release of fantasy had to come from the content, from the covering darkness of the cinema and from the mythology which it immediately began to construct for itself with its own gods and goddesses and its own fairy tales. Not surprisingly it soon took over existing fantasies. Cinderella, which might be a metaphor for the whole industry, was first made in 1907, twice in 1911 and repeated from then on. Rip Van Winkle, Sleeping Beauty, the Goose Girl and Aladdin appeared before 1920 along with more literary fantasies, *The Blue Bird*, *The Wizard of Oz*, *A Princess of Baghdad* and *The Magic Wand*.

With cartoon, film became fantastic in form as well as content. *Gertie, The Trained Dinosaur*, 1909, was quickly followed by *Felix*, *Koco the Clown*, *Krazy Kat* and *Oswald the Lucky Rabbit*. Derived from comic strips (*Krazy Kat* and *Mutt and Jeff* were both strip and film) the cartoon became briefly an art form in its own right under the imaginative overlordship of Walt Disney whose series of full-length films, particularly *Snow White*, *Pinocchio*, *Bambi* and *Dumbo*, was an inspired blend of kitsch and fantasy, as much the product of the years of depression and war as the romances of Chretien de Troyes were of the twelfth-century renaissance. The happy ending of Hollywood tales was demanded by the era, not imposed by the makers.

For as conditions of life worsened for most people, the need for something to believe or at least escape in grew, together with a reverence for what was cozy or hinted at the childhood Never Land that life mostly left unfound. Plaster gnomes in the back garden, wishing wells, lucky horse brasses, a Piskey Present from Cornwall, leprechauns at the end of *Finian's Rainbow*, more fairy prints to hang on the wall and "fairies at the bottom of the garden," seaside fairy glens and Disney comforted and consoled. Highly colored, mass-produced to meet a mass need, the girl figures simpered with a Shirley Temple childlike perversity while the men were old and wise, wrinkled phalluses made impotent by alternate overwork and shuffling in the dole queue.

For intellectuals there was reassurance in the Hobbits of Tolkien with their underground homes like wartime dug-outs and T. H. White's rationalized retelling of Arthur and, for religionists, in the Christian fables of Charles Williams and C. S. Lewis, derived from George Macdonald's nine-teenth-century supernatural parables. Perhaps it was the wish "there must be more to it than this," struggling with the discoveries of cosmology and physics, that led to the taking up of one faintly numinous writer after another, Simone Weil, Kafka, Teilhard de Chardin, and to the recrudescence of Roman Catholicism in the forties touch-ing the wasteland with a weary Greene. Eliot's own Anglo-Catholic pilgrimage perhaps charts it best. It led too to the perversion of the observed, clinical insights of Freud into the neo-mysticism of Jungian pseudo-psychology. Only Dylan Thomas was able to use the parallel symbols of different mythologies as imagery without bolstering them with his own credibility but so much was this outside the desired fashion of the time that he has therefore been misunderstood and a sea of uncritical ink dried in explor-ing him as a Christian writer. Thomas's religious position is nutshelled in the two lines:

> Heaven that never was
> Nor will be ever is always true.

The credibility factor itself now operates best in space.

CHAPTER XIX

And Ever After . . .

"We'll build a new Avalon, you and I. A technical one. A scientific fairyland. We will create a new world."

Kid Stuff, Isaac Asimov

Science fiction is old wine in new bottles: fantasy with technological trappings. Its most precise parallel and direct ancestor is Arthurian romance. Once again the fairies are making a takeover. Even the height of the UFO craze, when flying saucers were spotted every night, was anticipated in the twelfth-century chroniclers' accounts of fairies seen and met with, with names and places to back them up.

The credibility factor is harder at work than ever. To cover fantasy it has invoked science. Where the Middle Ages placed their fantasy period back in time so that anything might have been possible, now science, that is knowledge, insists on a future location where everything may be possible. This is also a trick of the unconscious. Placing in the past was a structural echo of the past, childhood, situation that was being acted out. The future simply mirrors this by a common trick of inversion. As unconscious apprehension of psychological processes grows, so the methods of repression become more devious. Most readers and writers have enough knowledge of psychoanalytic theory to be unconsciously suspicious of their own preoccupations and symbols. So the disguise must be heavier or more subtle. Childhood is projected into the future where babies come from.[1]

This forward projection ensures great freedom. It's technically after our time and therefore we aren't responsible for it. Like fairyland it's beyond our morality. The magic of wish fulfilment and the breaking of taboos are all effected under the mantle of science which makes all things

[1] Compare Maeterlinck's *The Blue Bird* for an unscientific fantasy version.

possible. A great deal of ingenuity is spent on the how. Preferably the magic is worked by the ultra-logical extension of physical laws. The formulae of physics are the spells and the abracadabra of the new enchanters. The mathematical equation is the cabalistic sign of power.

Again this is a parallel to twelfth-century Arthurianism. Then the idiom was Christian, mythical but given a magical twist which made it in reality anti those very ideas which it was exploiting for imagery. Similarly science fiction exploits the technological idiom to produce something which is basically anti-scientific for as soon as anything can be proved or done it ceases to be material for sci-fi. Brian Aldiss recognized this in turning from science fiction to undisguised masturbatory fantasy after the moon landing. The moon is no longer any more than a bus stop from which we can catch the fantasy coach or celestial omnibus. In both Arthurianism and sci-fi the fantasy is against the idiom which it exploits to give it credibility and this itself is an unconscious image of taboo breaking.

This particular brand of fantasy is generally recognized to have got under way in the 1890s with the first real doubts about progress and the benefits of nineteenth-century industrialism and technology, a feeling close to the sudden burst of secularism in the twelfth century. It is hard to realize that *The Time Machine, Tales of Space and Time* and *The War of the Worlds* were all published before 1900. Like twelfth-century Arthurianism too is the proliferation of the genre through dozens of writers in several languages, all recognizably exploiting the same themes through a basic vocabulary with a high level of scientific terms from the less accessible reaches of physics and cosmology, mingled with primary sensual description.

J. G. Ballard himself makes this point about the homogeneity of the species in an article:

> Science fiction has always been very much a corporate activity, its writers sharing a common pool of ideas, and the yardsticks of individual achievement do not measure the worth of the best writers, Ray Bradbury, Asimov, Bernard Wolfe (Limbo 90), and Frederick Pohl. The anonymity of the majority of the twentieth-century writers of science fiction is

the anonymity of modern technology; no more "great names" stand out than do in the design of consumer durables—or for that matter of Rheims Cathedral.[2]

The comment shows some of that illogicality which overtakes writers about science fiction. If the anonymity is essentially that of modern technology what is it doing in Rheims Cathedral? Further, although there is a certain anonymity about the architect of Notre Dame de Rheims it's largely fortuitous. "Le grande architecte" Hugues Libergier built a Benedictine abbey at Rheims at the same time that the nave of the cathedral was being finished. Even if we don't know the name of the cathedral architect after several hundred years it's against the evidence to assume that there wasn't one and that well known. Ballard is wanting to claim an almost folk or craftsman anonymity when he can justifiably claim a community of style and theme similar to Arthurian romance and lay but having some outstanding names within it as Chretien de Troyes was in the romance. His is an attempt to make sci-fi the pop literature and to cut it off from the rest of contemporary literary products.

An emotional tit for tat lies behind this since traditional criticism has ignored or scorned the genre, a fate doled out equally to the thriller and the romantic novel. Yet there is also a real desire by many science fiction writers to be ignored, since this gives them the position of front liners and martyrs, necessary for all revolutionaries. The difference is that science fiction isn't revolutionary.

Isaac Asimov, however, is well aware of its sources.

So success is not a mystery, just brush up on your
    history and borrow day by day.
Take an Empire that was Rome and you'll find it is
    at home in all the starry Milky Way.
With a drive that's hyperspatial, through the parsecs
    you will race, you'll find that plotting is a breeze,

[2] J. G. Ballard, "Fictions of Every Kind," *Books & Bookmen*, March 1971.

> With a tiny bit of cribbin' from the works of Edward
> Gibbon and that Greek, Thucydides.[3]

Many other writers too, particularly those one might call
the Neo-Mediaevals, allow the bones of their ancestors to
poke through.

The Neo-Mediaevals, among them Andre Norton with
her *Witch World* series, Robert Heinlein in *Glory Road*,
Poul Anderson with *Operation Changeling*, use bows and
arrows and ray guns indiscriminately. From some quite
commonplace situation the hero walks in the footsteps of
Gugemar and John Carter, Edgar Rice Burroughs's American gentleman on Mars, through to another world. Simon
Tregarth is translated by the Siege Perilous itself.

> "Your world, Colonel, and I wish you the best of
> it!"
> He nodded absently, no longer interested in the
> little man who called to him. This might be an il-
> lusion, but it drew him as nothing else ever had in
> his life. Without a word of farewell Simon arose
> and strode beneath the arch.[4]

In his case the escape is from immediate danger but
often the rationalizing concept is the escape from modern
life itself.

> I know a place where there is no smog and no park-
> ing problem and no population explosion . . . no
> Cold War and no H-bombs and no television com-
> mercials . . . The land is lovely, the people are
> friendly and hospitable to strangers, the women are
> beautiful and amazingly anxious to please—
> I could go back. I could—[5]

The clue is in the idea of going back; the return is to the
unmechanized irresponsible childhood world of gratifica-

---

[3] "The Foundation of S. F. Success," copyright 1954 by Fantasy
House, Inc., from *Earth is Room Enough* by Isaac Asimov. Reprinted
by permission of Doubleday and Company, Inc.

[4] Andre Norton, *Witch World* (Ace Books Inc., 1963).

[5] Robert Heinlein, *Glory Road* (Avon Books, 1963).

tion. For "people" we should read "adults," for "strangers" (little strangers) "children" and for "women" "mother." "The climate is lovely" he says, as it is in all remembered infant summers.

The anti-mechanization, anti-industrialization of the Neo-Mediaevalists is the expression of a childish memory from when its desires were within its natural grasp. I mean no criticism of such writers when I use the term "childish" and its relatives. All artists explore the buried-in-time, therefore "infant," unconscious. The very real dissatisfaction with the errors and limitations of modern technology and the fear of diminishing individual freedom is energized by an earlier conflict. In the contemporary child's world it's largely father whose image is that of the mechanic, the technocrat, the worker and provider although mother may drive the children to school, run a whole range of domestic appliances and even have a job. Her image, possibly with no relation to the actual domestic situation but as projected by the media and approved by society, is still natural, earthy, intuitive, unmechanized. A child's first apprehension of her is still inevitably in these terms as she baths, cradles, feeds.

Rejection of modern society becomes a metaphor for the rejection of father; return to a primitive naturalism a desire to return to the exclusiveness of the natural mother and baby situation. Repeatedly in these books the mother herself appears to confirm this. Usually older than the hero, often immortal, she is witch or empress. In *Glory Road* she provides everything for the hero in accepted fairy queen style. There too he must defeat a monster, descendant of the father dragon as all male monsters are, in a womb labyrinth. The monster is a phallic shape-changer, once a rat, once "an ugly cocky little man" with "the biggest nose west of Durante." They fence to the death. Often the villain, single or corporate, will wield a more advanced technology than the hero not only making his defeat more heroic but symbolizing both the father's image as technocrat and his more advanced phallic weapon.

The two most appropriate, and therefore common, penis symbols are the raygun and the spaceship. Early science fiction was supposed to be asexual.

> Then eschew all thoughts of passion of a man-and-
>   woman fashion from your hero's thoughtful
>   mind
> He must spend his time on politics, and thinking up
>   his shady tricks, and outside that he's blind
> It's enough he's had a mother, other females are a
>   bother . . .[6]

Asimov himself understands the fallacy in this. In his short story *Dreaming Is A Private Thing* one character says of a dreamie, the fiction of the future: "It has your Freudian symbols. Narrow crevasses between the mountain peaks. I hope that won't bother you." Yet even as sly a writer as Gore Vidal has been misled into writing of imaginary worlds as being "more Adlerian than Freudian: the motor drive is the desire not for sex (other briefer fantasies take care of that) but for power, for the ability to dominate one's environment through physical strength . . ."[7]

The "briefer fantasies" were introduced into the genre according to Sam Moskotz its historiographer by Philip Jose Farmer in *The Lovers*, 1952, though one should perhaps remind him of Orwell's *1984* and Rice Burroughs. As in recognized fairy stories scientific magic enables the incest taboos to be disguisedly broken. The slim rocket of our hero penetrates deep space and nuzzles through the galaxy. Tintoretto's "Origin of The Milky Way" may be the first science fiction painting; Leonardo's the first designs.

We have two mothers: Earth, our first and natural mother, and the galaxy our wet-nurse. Leaving Earth for ever, returning to it after centuries of wandering, are common themes. Sometimes we come as visitors from an alien system before man himself or while he is still in his infancy, a situation reflecting the child's desire to be first, the curiosity about conception or the wish to placate a strange and powerful father. *Encounter in the Dawn* in Arthur C. Clarke's *Expedition to Earth*[8] is an example of the last kind. For this Clarke draws on an existing legend of the

[6] Isaac Asimov, "The Foundation of S.F. Success," op. cit.
[7] Gore Vidal, "The Waking Dream: Tarzan Revisited," *Reflections Upon A Sinking Ship Esquire*, December 1963.
[8] Sidgwick & Jackson, 1954.

Prometheus type. The "gods" come to earth in their shining spaceship and make contact with man still in the neolithic stage. Then they go away, leaving him a knife and a torch, back to their own dying empire among the stars.

Another often repeated theme is the shaming and virtual destruction of Earth as in another story by Clarke in the same collection, *If I Forget Thee, Oh Earth* . . . There a Father (author's capital) takes his son Marvin to look at the planet from the arid darkness of the Colony, sited perhaps on the moon. Still it glows "with an evil phosphorescence," even though Marvin can see its natural beauty of color and form, but one day when the poisons have been scoured away by wind and rain his children's children will return. This is the wicked mother polluted by evil men who have left her disease-ridden so that she would contaminate and kill her children. The emotional power of the story comes from thoughts about mother's adultery, real or imagined, the bad woman of *East Lynne*.

A similar story, *Suicide World*, by Harlan Ellison[9] has atomic waste as the spreading evil which causes the earth to erupt in volcanic boils. The fear is rational. Atomic pollution, environmental pollution, is a very real problem. But the image is the monstrous one of a human body far gone in the suppurations of venereal disease. In the end the earth saves itself by the natural lancing of the volcanic boils. "As time was spent, the Earth licked its wounds. And healed slowly. Far slower than the memory of the men who had wounded it." The image has become that of a hurt animal, still organic though no longer anthropomorphic.

Sometimes earth casts her children out, leaving them to roam space indefinitely. Often our hero saves her from violation by the visiting aliens who are usually more diabolically advanced in their superior weaponry. Politics is a construct from emotional politics. Asimov's line that "It's enough he's had a mother" is more accurate than perhaps he knew.[10] One of the most successful science fiction

[9] *Strange Fantasy* No. 8, Spring 1969.

[10] I've no means of checking whether the half line was there for the rhyme but with such a perceptive writer I'm happy to give the benefit of doubt.

novels, George Stewart's *Earth Abides*, makes the symbol explicit. Ish, having become god-folk hero to a new civilization after the twentieth-century one has perished, is dying beside the Golden Gate Bridge. He looks up at the two pointed peaks on the crest. They are called Twin Breasts and they make him think of his wife Em and his own mother. "The earth and Em and the mother all mingled in his dying mind, and he felt glad to return.[11]

When earth is exhausted there is the great starry body of the galaxy to nourish us where we can drop the seeds of our culture to spring up as new civilizations. The starships come and go, docking at the different planets and unloading their cargoes. Civilizations grow decadent and are destroyed but always the hero figure is left, sometimes mutating through several generations like an extra-terrestrial Forsyte, sometimes attaining individual immortality.

Immortality and potency are closely linked; the search for the elixir of life is the search for the infallible aphrodisiac and continues in science fiction. Both are fairy gifts. *They Shall Have Stars* by James Blish typically combines the two when the young couple, having been made immortal, "eternally young," are sent off together to the stars. Immortality is of course not new. Both Arthur and Merlin have it, as well as the more common fairy denizens even though it's sometimes modified into extreme longevity. Asimov's *Foundation* trilogy has a Merlin figure, Hari Seldon, professor of psychohistory who predicts the future, founds an Arthurian counterpoise to destruction and appears at moments of crisis to exhort and confirm by a species of televisual magic, much as Merlin did for Arthur's empire.[12]

Magic may be euhemerized as advanced technology, travel by solar or advanced nuclear power which may annihilate time and space, straight old-fashioned magic, the forty-minute earth girdle, or the development of extraordinary powers of mind, telepathy, illusionism and materialization, the ability to be there now. This twin conquest has remained vital in all mythologies. Sometimes it's feared

---

[11] George R. Stewart, *Earth Abides* (Gollancz, 1950).
[12] C. S. Lewis in *That Hideous Strength*, 1947, awakened Merlin himself to help his hero Ransom.

as well as desired. A day in fairyland or in the sleep of Rip Van Winkle may be a human century. The spaceship may return by the laws of relativity to find that after eleven years of light-speed travel everyone the voyagers know is long dead.

This fear reflects the guilt of fantasizing. We shouldn't want to get away and if we do we may be punished by never being able to get back. In particular, parents who are necessarily older than we are may be dead or gone away. Who doesn't remember this fear, half guilty wish, when returning from a long day's playing out, forgetful of time and meals, in childhood? All the same, to be able to warp time is to be able to make ourselves the age equal of anyone and never to die. It's also to be undetected in our fantasy if parallel times can exist. Space is time between. Speed can give us all worlds, all variations. Timewarp can let us play out for hours and still be home in time for tea. Ray Bradbury most consciously exploits the childhood experience in *Dandelion Wine* through his twelve-year-old Douglas Spalding's 1928 summer.

To provide the ideal length of fantasy, science fiction has revived the short story, the prose lay. Credibility is difficult to sustain in the longer novel form corresponding to the romance. The invention and literary talent must be greater and the scientific blanket rich and self-consistent. The "hardware" school deals with the credibility factor by heaping up gadgets, technical jargon and descriptions of processes, after the manner of a mediaeval interpolation on correct armor or boar-skinning, to disguise a knight-errant romance.

The dramatis personae of space are drawn from the enormous stock of world mythologies. The hero-knight I have already discussed.[13] All versions of the mother in both black and white aspects appear. J. G. Ballard's *The Day of Forever*[14] for example has a vamp-lamia in the title story, a siren-merrow in *Prisoner of the Coral Deep*,

---

[13] A quick run-through of the exhaustive lists at the back of K. M. Briggs's *The Faires in Tradition and Literature* will reveal a host of space creatures. Particularly important is the brollachan, a shapeless evil forerunner of many variants of evil mind, the blob, the thing, the brain, the master and so on.

[14] Panther Books Ltd., 1967.

the nightmare-life-in-death murdered wife in *Tomorrow is a Million Years*. The theme of several of the stories is wife-murder, a reflection of the current uneasy sexual confrontation of men and women under the unhappy aegis of the consumer society.

For however futurist science fiction appears it is in truth often deeply reactionary, trying to reaffirm in the space age the emotional values of a heroic society where men are men, adventurous, physically aggressive, self-sufficient except for the release of appetite and women are either disguised mother or sexual objects. Currently, for the genre has fashions too, the control of mind over matter is in. This reflects an ancient desire on the part of the individual to be able to create, reproduce, by parthenogenesis as Zeus brought forth Athena, divine wisdom, out of his own head. Although common to men and women, as the number of mythological virgin births testifies, the idea is particularly attractive to men who can't, as yet, give physical birth. As methods of artificial insemination become increasingly part of the popular consciousness the role of the male in reproduction shrinks from its Victorian peak, when every coupling brought possible conception and death in childbirth and male potency was a thing of godhead and terror, to the primitive level where it may not have been known that the male had any part in the process at all, a belief echoed in every childhood before some elementary sex-education can be given.

The dethroned male in compensation invents fantasies of the potency of mind; its ability to create out of nothing. A. E. Van Vogt's *War of Nerves*, part of his novel *The Voyage of the Space Beagle*, embodies this idea. The returning ship is attacked by aliens who by mindpower arouse aggression among the travellers, setting them against each other. The aliens are parthenogenic bird forms; their young budding up from their shoulders like prickly pear shoots. The hero is able to make contact with their minds and divert them from their hostility, which is based on fear of change. When he first sees them they seem to be women. They are all linked in a community of mind by which they are able to use their channelled common power. The humans are all men. Behind the story lies male fear of the linked female cabal, exclusive, rejecting and self-reproducing, causing men to turn on each other and exploiting mythical feminine intuition. Against them is only a man but mercifully, though scientifically, trained in some of their techniques. They are able to create illusory images of themselves; they have no knowledge of technology. To help him the hero has a portable machine which projects a beam of light, uniting male technological knowhow and the penis.

Andre Norton's *Witch World* also attributes mind magic to women although the hero discovers the beginnings of the power in himself. The ability to create, to give birth, is itself magic, the natural magic for which men have developed the technological and artistic magic in compensation. Now the roles are becoming confused. There are still few women writing science fiction and few stories in which they are either sole or equal protagonist. Yet what may seem the thin end of the Women's Lib wedge has been inserted under this predominantly male edifice and interestingly it is to lay claim to the right to secondary rather than primary and physical creation.

S. H. Elgin's short story *For The Sake of Grace*[15] tells of a civilization distant in time and space in which the highest rank is Poet, Seventh Level. The society is male-oriented with the women kept in a form of purdah. The story is told through the angry eyes of a man whose twelve-year-old daughter enters the Poetry Examinations with the alternatives of pass or solitary confinement for life. The girl passes at the highest level. It is an allegory of female suffrage but on a much deeper emotional level than at first appears since the right to compete involves the rejection of physical creation by marriage and of the ties of family affection. The successful candidate is taken away at once to begin her studies and leaves without a qualm, her only message being for her aunt who tried and failed years before and has gone mad alone in her cell.

In case this should be thought a specifically female viewpoint there is Fritz Lieber's *Dr. Adam's Garden of Evil*[16] in which a man who runs a kitten magazine has discovered

[15] *Fantasy and Science Fiction*, Vol. 36, No. 3 (May 1969).
[16] *Strange Fantasy*, No. 8 (Spring 1969).

how to grow girl flowers in his greenhouse which eventually destroy him with the help of a witch queen.

Many stories have an element of homosexual release in them, the love-hate pursuit of one man by another through space to a final reckoning of rayguns measured and spirting against each other in Western last-reel style. Some express it through a convention of the old comrades of the star circuit against overwhelming odds. Father and son relationships often occur; the Hoyles' *Fifth Planet* is an example and the end story in the Aldiss collection *Intangibles Inc.*

I suspect that the founding-of-empire theme which occurs frequently in science fiction, *The Day of the Triffids, Earth Abides*, Asimov's *Foundation* trilogy, is also a related artistic projection from the nine months of gestation. The great emotional success of the popular theory of evolution probably rests on the same basis, backed up by the visual similarities in the growing foetus to the stages in evolutionary development: cell, tadpole, fish, amphibian, reptile, mammal, birth. It provided a replacement mythology of deep appeal for the biblical Adam and Eve parental myth. Science fiction continues the myth-making process by which we break down and assimilate knowledge. In their projection of the possible effects of discoveries before they are made such fictions are therapeutic, enabling us to adapt before the problem arises in the same way that the concept of witchcraft enabled people to deal with misfortunes that knowledge wasn't advanced enough to remedy or interpret: idiot and deformed "changelings," impotence, sexual frustration, barrenness, disease in men and animals, and all the manifestations of "bad luck."

Increasingly however in the present wave of science fiction a different therapy is being offered, no less traditional but in space age dress. This is the journey into the self, recognized by R. D. Laing, whose work is studied by many contemporary writers, as forcibly undertaken by many schizophrenics but undertaken voluntarily by many people in childhood and through the mediation of art. Most of us remember the long bemused days spent wandering and experiencing as children when every sensual apprehension seemed overpowering in its vividness and at any moment we should break through to blinding understanding. All account of time and space was lost, impersonations and fantasy situations were more real than the real. At the end of such a day we wandered home exhausted and unable to explain.

This state is close to the experience, indeed I believe fundamentally the same experience in other emotional trappings, of the mystic and of the lover at the moment of dissolution in orgasm. Psychologically expressed the barriers between the parts of the psyche and between the psyche and the external world are lowered, even perhaps overwhelmed, and there is experienced that same sensation of oneness.

The artistic correlative of this is the journey, often made mythologically specific as a journey to the underworld, since the unconscious knows that time is space and that one may be an image of the other and the underworld is itself the land of the buried and the dead. It is the wandering of Odysseus, of Christian, the pursuit of the Grail, the journeys of the Mabinogion and Robert Sheckley's *Mindswap*.[17]

What is entailed then is:

(i) a voyage from outer to inner
(ii) from life to a kind of death
(iii) from going forward to going back
(iv) from temporal movement to temporal standstill
(v) from mundane time to aeonic time
(vi) from the ego to the self
(vii) from being outside (post-birth) back into the womb of all things (pre-birth)
      and then subsequently a return voyage from.[18]

This is the journey that the artist takes on behalf of other people so that they may take it vicariously and with the guidelines of art which he has strung for them to keep them from whirling away into the abyss of madness. It is a necessary healing and reorienting journey for many people who must live always an object life with no opportunity for

---

[17] Gollancz, 1966.
[18] R. D. Laing, *The Politics of Experience and the Bird of Paradise* (Penguin Books Ltd., 1967).

a life of the imagination. Yet unless the imagination is inhabited from time to time and the parts of the personality allowed to fuse and overflow, life becomes increasingly stale, mechanical, alienated; symptoms which we all recognize.

Everyone has his own appropriate method. Travel in time and space where all things are possible, where the only rules of those of enchantment and we can stop punishing ourselves for even thinking of such things since by the brilliant convention of time travel it hasn't happened yet, is, to some people, to lose so much contact with outer reality that the experience is invalidated and seems merely childish or frightening. For others the white light that is starshine is, as the light that shone from the Grail, the great dissolver from whose effect we awaken weak but refreshed and in our right minds. Marvin, returned to his own body which he has exchanged on a dozen different worlds through innumerable adventures, eventually comes back to earth. The world he returns to is unrecognizable to us as earth yet to Marvin it is home.

> Did not the huge red sun move across the sky, pursued by its dark companion? Did not the triple moons return each month with their new accumulation of comets?
>
> These familiar sights reassured him. Everything seemed to be as it always had been. And so, willingly and with a good grace, Marvin accepted his world at face value, married Marsha Baker, and lived forever after.[19]

This is the enchantment of art itself that for a time it translates us, steeds us on our errantry and finally restores us to our rightful status quo. Love too as enchantment can do the same. Launcelot had no need of the ultimate vision of the Grail.

The new mythology of the space age which doesn't demand belief, only credibility, has already passed the stage of simple legends and is deep in the sophisticated complexities of romance. One wonders where the fairies will go when

---

[19] Robert Sheckley, *Mindswap*, ed. cit.

the last star has been reached, onto whom we shall project our forbidden desires and how we shall embark on our journeys, for I can't believe we shan't need them.

> And you will be a long time upon the road. In Harddlech you will be feasting seven years, and the birds of Rhiannon singing unto you. And the head will be as pleasant company to you as ever it was at best when it was on me. And at Gwales in Penfro you will be fourscore years; and until you open the door towards Aber Henfelen, the side facing Cornwall, you may bide there and the head with you uncorrupted. But from the time you have opened that door, you may not bide there: make for London to bury the head. And do you cross over to the other side.[20]

[20] "Branwen Daughter of Llyr," *The Mabinogion*, ed. cit.

Books Cited and Consulted

(The reference is to the edition used)

Acton, William, *The Functions and Disorders of the Reproductive Organs*, 1857.

Akrigg, G. P. V., *Shakespeare and the Earl of Southampton*, Hamish Hamilton, 1968.

Aladdin and Other Tales from the Thousand and One Nights, trans. N. J. Dawood, Penguin, 1957.

Aldiss, Brian, *Intangibles Inc.*, Corgi, 1969.

Aldiss, Brian, *The Hand-Reared Boy*, Corgi, 1970.

Alford, Violet, *Introduction to English Folklore*, G. Bell & Sons, 1952.

Alford, Violet, *Sword Dance and Drama*, Merlin Press, 1963.

Allingham and Doyle, *In Fairyland*, 1870.

Andersen, Hans, *Danish Fairy Legends and Tales*, trans. Peachey Bohn, 1861.

Antal, F., *Fuseli Studies*, Routledge and Kegan Paul, 1956.

Apuleius, *The Golden Ass*, Heinemann, 1958.

Asimov, Isaac, *Earth is Room Enough*, Doubleday Inc., 1957.

Asimov, Isaac, *Foundation*, Panther, 1971.

Augustine, St., *Confessions*, Heinemann, 1946.

Avery, G., *Nineteenth Century Children*, Hodder and Stoughton, 1965.

Ballard, J. G., "Fictions of Every Kind," *Books and Bookmen*, March 1971.

Ballard, J. G., *The Day of Forever*, Panther, 1967.

Ballard, J. G. *Terminal Beach*, Berkeley, 1964.

Barrie, J. M., *Peter Pan*, Hodder and Stoughton, 1942.

Beardsley, A., *The Letters*, ed. Maas Duncan and Good, Cassell, 1971.

Beckford, William, *Vathek*, Lawrence and Bullen, 1893.

Bede, *A History of the English Church and People*, trans. Leo Sherley-Price, Penguin, 1955.

Beowulf, ed. C. L. Wrenn, Harrap, 1953.

Beowulf and the Finnsburg Fragment, trans. J. Clark Hull, Allen and Unwin, 1950.

Boase, T. S. R., *English Art 1100–1216*, Clarendon Press, 1953.

Blish, James, *They Shall Have Stars*, N.E.L., 1968.

Bradbury, Ray, *Dandelion Wine*, Corgi, 1965.

Bradbury, Ray, *Machineries of Joy*, Corgi, 1969.

Briggs, K. M., *The Anatomy of Puck*, Routledge and Kegan Paul, 1959.

Briggs, K. M., *Dictionary of British Folk Tales*, Routledge and Kegan Paul, 1970.

Briggs, K. M., *The Fairies in Tradition and Literature*, Routledge and Kegan Paul, 1967.

Brophy, Brigid, *Black Ship to Hell*, Secker and Warburg, 1962.

Brophy, Brigid, *Mozart the Dramatist*, Faber and Faber, 1964.

Bullen, A. H., *"The Maydes Metamorphosis" A Collection of Old Plays*, 1882.

Bullough, G., ed., *Narrative and Dramatic Sources of Shakespeare*, Routledge and Kegan Paul, 1957.

Chadwick, N., *The Celts*, Penguin, 1970.

Charlemagne, *Oeuvre, rayonnement et survivances*, Aix-la-Chapelle, 1965.

Chase, R., ed., *American Folk Tales and Songs*, New American Library, Signet Key.

Chatelain, C. de, *Finikin and His Golden Pippins*, Wells, Gardner, Darton and Co.

Chaucer, G., *Poetical Works*, O.U.P., 1947.

Cholmondley-Pennel, *Puck on Pegasus*, 1861.

Clarke, Arthur C., *The Coming of the Space Age*, Panther, 1967.

Clarke, Arthur C., *Expedition to Earth*, Corgi, 1959.

Crane, Walter, *The Fairy Ship*, J. M. Dent, 1869.

Cronise and Ward, *West African Folk Tales*, London Swan; Sonnenschein and Co., 1903.

Davis, R. T., ed., *Medieval English Lyrics*, Faber and Faber, 1963.

Dickins, Bruce & Wilson, R. M., ed., *Early Middle English Texts*, Bowes and Bowes, 1951.

Ekwall, E., *Concise Oxford Dictionary of English Place Names*, 4th edn., O.U.P., 1960.

Ellison, Horlan, *Strange Fantasy* No. 8 (Spring 1969) (*Suicide World*) *Fantasy and Science Fiction* (May 1969).

Finley, M. I., *Aspects of Antiquity*, Chatto and Windus, 1968.

Ford, Boris, ed., *The Penguin Guide to English Literature 1*, 1969.

Forster, E. M., *The Celestial Omnibus and Other Stories*, Sidgwick and Jackson, 1936.

Forster, Leonard, ed., *The Penguin Book of German Verse*, 1957.

Ganz, P. L., *Die Zeichnungen Hans Heinrich Füselis*, Bern, 1947.

Sir Gawain and the Green Knight, ed. J. P. P. Tolkien and E. V. Gordon, O.U.P., 1946.

Geismar, Maxwell, *Henry James and His Cult*, Chatto and Windus, 1964.

Gittings, R., *John Keats*, Heinemann, 1968.

Glob, P. V., *The Bog People*, Faber and Faber, 1969.

Gordon, R. K., tr., *Anglo-Saxon Poetry*, J. M. Dent, 1926.

Gower, *Confessio Amantis*, trans. T. Tiller, Penguin, 1963.

Grahame, K., *The Wind In The Willows*, Methuen & Co., 1956.

Gratton and Singer, *Anglo-Saxon Magic and Medicine*, O.U.P., 1952.

Grimm, Brothers, *Household Tales*, Eyre and Spottiswoode, 1946.

Grimm, J., intro., *Deutsche Mythologie*, trans. Stallybrass, Bell & Sons, 1882.

Halliday, F. E., *A Shakespeare Companion*, Penguin, 1964.

Harington, Sir John, *Nugae Antiquae*, ed. T. Pork, 1804.

Harrison, G. B., *The Elizabethan Journals 1591–1603*, Routledge and Kegan Paul, 1955.

Heinlein, R., *Glory Road*, Avon Books, 1963.

Herrick, R., *Poetical Works*, ed. Martin, Clarendon Press, 1956.

Hough, G., *A Preface to the Faerie Queen*, Duckworth & Co., 1962.

Hoyle, F. and G., *Fifth Planet*, Penguin, 1967.

Hughes, R., *Heaven and Hell in Western Art*, Weidenfeld & Nicolson, 1968.

Huon of Bordeaux, trans. Berners, G. Allen, 1895.

Jacobs, J., *English Fairy Tales*, Puffin, 1970.

James, Henry, *The Turn of the Screw*, J. M. Dent, 1935.

Jonson, Ben, *Complete Plays*, J. M. Dent, 1950.

Keats, John, *The Letters*, O.U.P., 1954.

Keats, John, *The Poems*, Methuen, 1951.

Kingsley, Charles, *The Water Babies*, Headley Bros., 1908.

Kinsley, J., *The Oxford Book of Ballads*, O.U.P., 1969.

Kipling, R., *Kim*, Macmillan, 1958.

Kipling, R., *Puck of Pook's Hill*, Macmillan, 1961.

Kirk, R., *The Secret Commonwealth of Elves, Fauns and Fairies*, 1691.

Laing, R. D., *The Politics of Experience and the Bird of Paradise*, Penguin, 1967.

Latham, M. C., *The Elizabethan Fairies*, Columbia, 1930.

Layamon and Wace, *Arthurian Chronicles*, tr. E. Mason, J. M. Dent, 1962.

Legman, G., *The Horn Book*, Jonathan Cape, 1970.

Levey, Michael, *The Later Italian Pictures in the Collection of Her Majesty the Queen*, Phaidon Press, 1964.

Lewis, C. S., *That Hideous Strength*, Pan, 1968.

Lewis, M. G., "The Castle Spectre," *The London Stage*, Sherwood, Jones & Co.,

Lewis, M. G., *The Monk*.

Longford, E., *Victoria RI*, Pan, 1964.

Loomis, R. S., *Arthurian Tradition and Chretien de Troyes*, Columbia, 1949.

Loomis, R. S., *Arthurian Legends in Mediaeval Art*, O.U.P., 1938.

Lumley Inventory, 1590.

Maas, Jeremy, *Victorian Painters*, Barrie and Rockliff, 1969.

Mabinogion, trans. Gwyn Jones and Thomas Jones, J. M. Dent, 1949.

Macdonald, G., *The Princess and the Goblin*, Blackie.

Maeterlinck, *The Bluebird*, trans. A. Teixeira de Mattos, Methuen, 1927.

Malleus Maleficarum, The Pushkin Press, 1951.

Malory, *Le Morte D'Arthur*, Vinaver's Clarendon Press Ed., 1967.

Map, Walter, *De Nugis Curialium*, trans. Tupper and Ogle, Chatto and Windus, 1924.

Marie de France, *The Lays*, trans. Eugene Mason, J. M. Dent, 1964.

Milton, John, *Areopagitica and other Prose Works*, J. M. Dent, 1946.

Milton, John, *The Poetical Works*, Macmillan, 1896.

Muir, Percy, *English Children's Books*, Batsford, 1954.

Neale, J. E., *Queen Elizabeth*, Jonathan Cape, 1934.

Newman, J., *Apologia Pro Vita Sua*, Longmans Green, 1890.

Nibelungenlied, trans. D. G. Mowatt, J. M. Dent, 1962.

Nichols, J., *The Princely Progresses and Public Appearances of Queen Elizabeth I*, 1823.

Nicoll, A., *Stuart Masques and the Renaissance Stage*, Harrap, 1964.

Norton, Andre, *Witch World*, Ace Books Inc., 1963.

Oakeshott, Walter, *The Queen and the Poet*, Faber and Faber, 1960.

Ovid, *Metamorphoses*, tr. Miller, Heinemann, 1944.

Parker, W. P., *Milton*, O.U.P., 1968.

Partridge, E., *A Dictionary of Slang and Unconventional English*, Routledge and Kegan Paul, 1961.

Pearson, Hesketh, *The Life of Oscar Wilde*, Methuen, 1946.

Perrault, C., *Fairy Tales*, ed. G. Brereton, Penguin.

Pope, A., *Poems, Epistles and Satires*, J. M. Dent, 1949.

Powell, N., *The Drawings of Henry Fuseli*, Faber and Faber, 1951.

Radcliffe, Mrs. Ann, *The Mysteries of Udolpho*, J. M. Dent, 1968.

Rattray Taylor, G., *Sex in History*, Thames and Hudson, 1953.

Read Baskerville, C., *The Elizabethan Jig and Related Song Drama*, Dover Publications Inc., 1965.

Reade, Brian, *Beardsley*, Studio Vista, 1967.

Reeves, James, *The Idiom of the People*, Heinemann, 1958.

Reik, Theodor, *Masochism in Modern Man*, Grove Press, 1941.

Ricket, M., *Painting in Britain in the Middle Ages*, Penguin, 1965.

Rougemont, Denis de, *Passion and Society*, Faber and Faber, 1962.

Rose, H. J., *A Handbook of Greek Mythology*, Methuen, 1958.

Ruskin, J., *The King of the Golden River*, Roycrofters, USA, 1900.

Sayers, D. L., tr., *The Song of Roland*, Penguin, 1957.

Scot, Reginald, *The Discoverie of Witchcraft*, 1584.

Scott, Walter, *The Poetical Works*, Routledge, Warne and Routledge, 1862.

Sheckley, Robert, *Mindswap*, Gollancz, 1966.

Simpson and Bell, Walpole Society, Vol. xii, 1924.

Sisam, K., *Fourteenth Century Verse*, O.U.P., 1946.

Smith, *A Classical Dictionary*, John Murray, 1904.

Sola Pinto, V de and Rodway, A. E., ed., *The Common Muse*, Penguin, 1965.

Spence, Lewis, *British Fairy Origins*, Watts & Co., 1946.

Spenser, Edmund *Complete Works*, Globe edn., Macmillan, 1879.

Stewart, George R., *Earth Abides*, Gollancz, 1950.

Stone, B., tr., *Sir Gawain and the Green Knight*, Penguin, 1959.

Storns, *Anglo-Saxon Magic*, Martinus Nijhoff, The Hague, 1948.

Strachey, L., *Elizabeth and Essex*, Evergreen, 1940.

Strong, R. C., *Portraits of Queen Elizabeth I*, O.U.P., 1963.

Squire, Charles, *Celtic Myth and Legend*, Gresham Pub. Co.

Summerson, J., *Inigo Jones*, Pelican, 1966.

Sweet, H., *Sweet's Anglo-Saxon Reader*, O.U.P., 1950.

Swift, J., *Works*, ed. Hayward, Nonesuch Press, 1944.

Thackeray, W. M., *The Rose and the Ring*, Puffin, 1967.

Theresa, St., *The Life*, trans. J. M. Cohen, Penguin, 1957.

Thomas, Keith, *Religion and the Decline of Magic*, Weidenfeld & Nicolson, 1971.

Thompson, E. P., *The Making of the English Working Class*, Gollancz, 1963.

Thorpe, Lewis, tr., *The History of the Kings of Britain by Geoffrey of Monmouth*, Penguin, 1966.

Treble, H. A., ed., *Narrative Poems of the late 19th Century*, Penguin, 1943.

Trevor-Roper, H. R., *The European Witch-Craze of the Sixteenth and Seventeenth Centuries*, Penguin, 1969.

Troyes, C. de, *Arthurian Romances*, trans. W. W. Comfort, J. M. Dent, 1968.

Vaughan Williams, R., ed., and Lloyd, A. L., *Penguin Book of English Folk Songs*, 1961.

Vidal, Gore, "Reflections Upon A Sinking Ship," *Esquire* (Dec. 1963).

Vogt, A. E. Von, *Monsters*, Corgi, 1970.

Voltaire, F., *Candide and Other Tales*, J. M. Dent, 1937.

Waddell, Helen, *Mediaeval Latin Lyrics*, Constable, 1947.

Waddell, Helen, *The Wandering Scholars*, Constable, 1927.

Walpole, H., *The Castle of Otranto*, ed. Doughty, Scholarti's Press, 1929.

Ward, Sir A. W. and Waller, A. R., *Cambridge History of English Literature*, Vol. 1, Cambridge, 1949.

Ward, A., *John Keats*, Secker and Warburg, 1963.

Warrack, John, *Carl Maria Von Weber*, Hamish Hamilton, 1968.

Waterhouse, E., *Italian Baroque Painting*, Phaidon Press, 1962.

Whitelock, D., *The Beginnings of English Society*, Pelican History of England, 1968.

Wilde, Lady, *Ancient Legends of Ireland*, Ward and Downey, 1888.

Wilde, Oscar, *The Letters*, ed. R. Hart-Davis, Rupert Hart-Davis, 1962.

Wilde, Oscar, *The Works*, Spring Books, 1963.

Wilson, A. E., *Christmas Pantomimes*, Allen and Unwin, 1934.

Wittkower, R., *Art and Architecture in Italy 1600–1750*, Penguin, 1958.

Woledge, Brian, ed., *Penguin Book of French Verse, I*, Penguin, 1968.

Wright, C. E., *The Cultivation of Saga in Anglo-Saxon England*, Oliver and Boyd, 1939.

Index

Cardinal now offers an exciting range of quality fiction and non-fiction by both established and new authors. All of the books in this series are available from good bookshops, or can be ordered from the following address:

Sphere Books
Cash Sales Department
P.O. Box 11
Falmouth
Cornwall, TR10 9EN.

Please send cheque or postal order (no currency), and allow 60p for postage and packing for the first book plus 25p for the second book and 15p for each additional book ordered up to a maximum charge of £1.50 in U.K.

B.F.P.O. customers please allow 60p for the first book, 25p for the second book plus 15p per copy for the next 7 books, thereafter 9p per book.

Overseas customers, including Eire, please allow £1.25 for postage and packing for the first book, 75p for the second book and 28p for each subsequent title ordered.